The Writer's Toolbox

A Comprehensive Guide
for PR and Business Communication

Randy Hines
Susquehanna University

Joseph Basso
Rowan University

Foreword by Fraser P. Seitel

KENDALL/HUNT PUBLISHING COMPANY
4050 Westmark Drive   Dubuque, Iowa 52002

The Writer's Toolbox

A Comprehensive Guide
for PR and Business Communication

Project Coordinator: *Emily Cabbage*
Page Layout and Design: *Claudia Cuddy*
Front Cover Design: *Lisa Baltz*
Toolbox and Blueprint Icons: *Kari Palmieri*
Proofreading: *Stephanie Zultanky*
Permissions Editor: Colleen Zelinsky
Publisher Representatives: *Greg DeRosa and Steve O'Brien*

Foreword

Fraser P. Seitel
Managing Partner, Emerald Partners

Let's face it. Business people are horrible writers. And that includes those business people who write for a living — public relations writers, internal communicators, government relations experts, consumer affairs specialists and so on.

The pity is that in today's business climate, dogged by internal concerns about trust and candor and external credibility problems, persuasive business writing has never been more important.

Managers at every level — and those who aspire to be business managers — need to communicate more straightforwardly, more properly and more effectively. Their own credibility and that of their institutions will depend on it.

But what is a writing-deficient business person to do in order to remedy his or her communications dilemma?

Answer: Consult *The Writer's Toolbox*.

Authors Joe Basso and Randy Hines have provided the context, laid out the framework and enumerated the techniques that make one a better writer. This *Toolbox* contains all the pertinent writing elements — from grammar and style to memos and leads.

What distinguishes the book from others is the unique perspective of its authors.

Dr. Basso is a teacher, but also a lawyer, who understands the corporate kabuki dance between attorneys and communicators that leads to finished copy. Business writing, in particular, must be sensitive to legal nuances and realities. Professor Basso's intimate knowledge of how one writes in a litigious society is not only a unique contribution to the literature, but invaluable to any business writer.

Dr. Hines is a teacher, but also a journalist, who understands the difference between submitting copy for publication and getting that copy published. Dr. Hines' days on "the other side of the desk" make the critical chapters on news releases, features and media kits that much more authentic and valuable.

Both authors also serve as accredited public relations practitioners, and they take time to place the communications challenge within an organizational context and the communicator as an integral part of the management team.

Professors Basso and Hines have, indeed, touched all the right writing bases. The end result, for students and professionals alike, is a "toolbox" that will arm them with all the essentials they require to become competent — even persuasive — writers.

Acknowledgments

We would like to thank the following individuals who assisted in the development of this text with their insightful contributions:

> Garry R. Bolan, Towson University
>
> Dr. Suzanne Sparks FitzGerald, Rowan University
>
> Jack Gillespie, *Communication Briefings* former editor
>
> Dr. David Kaszuba, Susquehanna University
>
> Fraser Seitel, Managing Partner, Emerald Partners
>
> Dr. Doug Starr, Texas A&M University

We would also like to offer appreciation to Dr. Phil West, our doctoral adviser at Texas A&M, who was able to pull us through the classroom and push us outside.

Our heartfelt appreciation goes to Claudia Cuddy of Rowan University who not only produced the page formats of the text, but provided keen proofreading for our final drafts.

We thank Gregory Derosa, Steve O'Brien and the staff at Kendall/Hunt for their support during the entire writing and production process.

On a personal note, we would like to thank our wives Cathy Hines and Lisa Basso for being understanding and patient during the stressful times of writing and editing this book. Victoria, C.J. and Austin Basso undoubtedly have an easier time getting "Daddy" away from his computer these days. Finally, we appreciate the strength and patience we received from God to help us complete this task.

Contents

How to Use This Book

Toolbox Tips

Toolbox Tips offer an assortment of useful ideas to improve writing. They provide readers with an excellent way to stock their writing toolbox.

Blueprints

Blueprints appear throughout the book and offer readers detailed information on a variety of writing topics.

CD-ROM

The CD-ROM developed with Dave Kaszuba provides instructors with an assortment of exercises and projects to complement the book. We developed the CD-ROM for instructors with an eye toward creating exercises, tests and portfolio assignments that neatly and logically correspond to the chapters. We also provide answer keys and explanations to assist with instruction.

To make it thorough, we provide exercises covering an extensive range of topics and writing forms. To make it easy to use, we provide answers and examples for assignments. To make it flexible, we provide a wide range of exercises for beginning PR and business students, upperclassmen, graduate students, and even public relations professionals who simply want to brush up on their writing.

Finally, instructors can tailor the information to their needs. Some may use a sampling of all the assignments while others may select one fictitious company and allow students to create a portfolio of work based on that one company. Whatever your use, we're confident that the instructor's CD-ROM lives up to its promise to be a thorough and valuable resource for your own writer's toolbox.

1.

Strategic Writing and Integrated Communication

In today's highly competitive workplace, business owners and managers seek to hire employees with polished writing skills. Such skills include the ability to quickly organize, construct and communicate information that both informs and persuades. It stands to reason that employers need workers with sophisticated writing skills since success in the information age depends largely on the ability to pen (or keyboard) effective prose. Therefore, clearly written, concise and crisp messages offer the most efficient way to gain success.

Unfortunately, countless studies show that an overwhelming majority of employers find that their employees have difficulty in crafting readable, easy-to-understand messages. Yet, scores of young professionals enter the work force each year graduating from highly respected colleges and universities lacking the most strategic of all business tools — the ability to write.

Author J.D. Pincus, writing in *Communication World*, states that communication and business have become uneasy partners. In fact, Pincus relates findings from his research that reveal that in a study of 215 MBA programs, only half required any type of communication training.[1]

Unfortunately, most people in the workforce forged an understanding of writing by crafting verbose book reports and term papers. While these works were often packed with substance, they usually lacked style and clarity. Furthermore, writers usually cringed at the thought of writing these lengthy documents, and consequently, most forged a negative view of the writing process.

The Writer's Toolbox attempts to help students overcome the fear of writing. In fact, it hopes to empower readers to look at their writing as an opportunity to share their ideas through powerful, thought-provoking sentences. Of course, the process must begin someplace and the most logical place would seem to be looking at writing from a strategic process rather than a creative endeavor.

Organizational communication professionals need to be skilled at the dissemination of information in both a one-way communication model and a two-way communication model. The advent of computer-mediated communication places even greater demands on the need for polished writing skills. Analyzing organizational communication quality underscores the demand for fundamental writing skills crafted for a variety of media and disseminated to diverse and multi-stratified publics.

The emergence of direct links via the Internet places organizations in contact with the consumer or end user at a rate never before envisioned. In fact, the instant dialogue and rapid response of information expand the potential for business success. However, they also increase the likelihood that messages will fail because of sloppy errors and fuzzy language.

Simply put, today anyone working in business must be skilled at planning and crafting a message. To construct effective prose, writers must first master the use of the tools of the trade. These tools include a thorough understanding of the rules of grammar and punctuation, a willingness to plan and organize thoughts and ideas before starting the writing process, and a firm understanding of proper sentence and paragraph construction to avoid miscommunication and shoddy work. Another tool is to follow the mandates or style guidelines dictated by various media.

Why Writing Is So Crucial Today

At the turn of the 20th century, America's economic fortunes turned from a largely agricultural economy to an industrial economy. This era of the Robber Baron, led by railroad tycoon William Vanderbilt, banker J.P. Morgan, oil magnate J.D. Rockefeller and steel impresario Henry Clay Frick, ushered in a time of sweatshop labor and low pay. Workers trolled the factories and work sites with limited flexibility. Business valued a strong back more than it valued a strong mind. However, the industrial revolution made way for a new economic cornerstone in this country — one that required a much stronger intellect.

In the 100 years between the dawn of the Industrial Revolution and the newly coined information economy, businesses began to refine their attitude toward workers. This evolution resulted from a number of political, social and economic changes. Employers recognize that today's information economy requires highly skilled and technical workers. And, the cost of recruiting, training and ultimately retaining these skilled employees places a heavy burden on the organization.

However, business also recognizes that hiring highly skilled and technical workers does not always result in getting someone with polished writing skills. In fact, business reports just the opposite. While economic capital has increased in the areas of computing skills, the fundamental skills of writing have continued to diminish. Unfortunately, such unflattering assessments are also directed at the staff of public relations departments. This creates an enormous burden on companies that rely on written communication skills to advance their business efforts.

Furthermore, the purpose of almost all business writing is to persuade an audience to do something or think a certain way. In business writing, it's necessary to think about the attitudes of the particular public you're trying to influence. You must also know how public opinion is built.

Public opinion doesn't really exist until something affects a number of people who have similar attitudes. The people must be aware of the issue or they will not have any opinion about it. People are much more certain about what they want than they are about how to get it. Public opinion isn't evident unless it can expect to get results.

David Therkelsen, director of marketing for the American Red Cross in St. Paul, Minn., conceptualizes the process of effective communication as follows:

> To be successful, a message must be *received* by the intended individual or audience. It must get the audience's *attention*. It must be *understood*. It must be *believed*. It must be *remembered*. And ultimately, in some fashion, it must be *acted upon*. Failure to accomplish any of these tasks means the entire message fails.

Establishing Cornerstones of Effective Writing

At the heart of the writing process lies the essential tool known as the sentence. In fact, at the core of human thought remains the simple sentence with its clean subject-verb construction.

Blueprint

Philip Lesly, president of Philip Lesly Co., provides the following guidelines for effective, persuasive communication.

1. Approach everything from the viewpoint of the audience's interest. What is on its mind? What is in it for each person?

2. Make the subject matter part of the atmosphere in which audience members live — what they talk about, what they hear from others. That means tailoring the message to their channels of communication.

3. Communicate with people, not at them. Communication that approaches the audience as a target makes people put up defenses against it.

4. Localize — get the message conveyed as close to the individual's own setting as possible.

5. Use a number of communication channels, not just one or two. The impact is far greater when a message reaches people in a number of different forms.

6. Maintain consistency so that the basic content is the same regardless of audience or context. Then tailor that content to the specific audience as much as possible.

7. Don't propagandize, but be sure you make your point. Drawing conclusions in the information itself is more effective than letting the audience draw its own conclusions.

8. Maintain credibility — which is essential for all these points to be effective.

This most basic of all sentences emphasizes one thought and one sentence construction. Noam Chomsky, the linguist known for his transformational grammar, argued that the basic statement — the subject-verb construction at the heart of the sentence — is the core of human thought. Unfortunately, this seemingly easy process often gets clouded when writers construct complex and long-winded prose that confuses, and sometimes alienates, readers.

The most fundamental of all writing problems appears to be the flowery discourse — with its penchant for long introductory passages and the main clause buried somewhere in the middle or end — that pops up in writing at an alarming rate. Simply, it smacks of elitism. And, this elitism tends to alienate readers. Stated another way, many writers try to write to impress rather than to express.

Most writers start off well but lose steam as they get into the middle and ending sections of their documents. In fact, some start off well and end with a great kicker; however, the real substance of most writing — the middle portion — often lacks clarity, focus and style. The biggest culprit behind the problem is disorganization. Here's a rule that should always be incorporated into every writing project:

Every writer should always write a plan for every document.

Now, to keep from scaring writers with the dreaded "O" word (outline), remember that the most successful plans can be short, usually a few words for each section. As elementary as this step sounds, most writers, even seasoned professionals, fail to incorporate this step into the writing process.

Every real story you read has some sort of logic and point to it. Why, then, would business writing be any different? Whether the author is writing a short story about people, or a technical document related to an area of work, many identical aspects exist.

1. Writers can often create a setting for the communication — what's happening and the circumstances surrounding the event.

2. Writers often get a chance to humanize their writing — focus on a major character or some fundamental point that creates interest.

3. Writers often get a chance to deal with a triggering event or occurrence that creates the need to communicate.

4. Writers get the opportunity to present ideas to solve a problem, address a conflict or offer an opportunity.

5. Writers often get an opportunity to draw a conclusion or present an ideal ending.

6. Writers often get an opportunity to peer into the future and set the table for future communication.

Finally, the "6 C's" of business and professional communication help you focus on your reader — the person you need to inform or persuade. This list has transformed over the years to include up to 12 points. We think these six cover the topic thoroughly.

1. **Be Clear**. Use simple words and straightforward sentences with active verbs. Try to keep paragraphs short — in general, six lines or less — and to use topic sentences to help readers follow your points.

2. **Be Concise**. Use the words you need to make your point, but no more. Don't give readers information they don't need.

3. **Be Courteous**. You catch more flies with honey than with vinegar. Write in a friendly, conversational tone. Imagine how you would respond if you were the reader.

4. **Be Correct**. Use a spell checker, and then proofread carefully.

5. **Be Consistent**. If you refer to someone as Susan in one sentence, don't switch to Sue in the next. If you use kilograms in one part of a letter don't switch to pounds in another.

6. **Be Complete**. Be sure to include all the information readers need. You don't want them to have to call or write you for important, but missing, details.[2]

For many writers, the notion of outlining conjures up thoughts of high school English class and constructing very linear outlines that provided greater confusion rather than organization. However, help is on the way in the form of adhesive notepads. These handy devices offer a simple solution to providing organization and structure to writing without the harsh linear construction of the traditional outline. Before starting any assignment, grab a stack of these small slips of paper and follow these steps.

1. **Write an action statement and a purpose statement**. The action statement lets the writer decide the outcome of the communication. You want to concentrate on the receiver of the information. What is it you want him or her to do after reading it? What feeling do you want the reader to walk away with after reading it?

2. **Develop your key writing points**. One-by-one, put your main ideas on a note. Treat these as if they were subheads that should appear in your writing.

3. **Further develop your key points**. Under each key point you develop, come up with a series of points, ideas, information or facts that you want to include in developing this point.

4. **Rank order your key points**. Now put all the points around your action statement and rank order them as you want them to appear in the final work. Remember the purpose behind the inverted pyramid: Put the most important information first, followed by the second, and so on. You now have a completed outline.

The Power of Words

Use words such as *initiative* rather than *proposal* to create a better aura around the idea. Also, use words like *challenge* or *opportunity* rather than the harsh *problem*.

Now that you have given your writing assignment order you can begin the process of crafting the story. Try these ideas:

1. **Develop** your ideas without concern for style and format. Concentrate on packing your story with all the relevant information first. Remember, you can always change the order or delete information when preparing the final draft.

2. **Ask yourself**, does my story answer the questions: who, what, when, where, why and how?

3. **Walk around**, if you can, before editing it. Get some fresh air or a snack. Do another task to give you a mental break. If it's not possible to delay the editing process, get another colleague (or two) to doublecheck your efforts.

Basics of Integrated Communication

Integrated communication (aka Integrated Marketing Communications, IMC or IC) has transformed corporate communication in the information age. The concept simply implies the combining of marketing, public relations and advertising in corporate communication. Such an intentional coordination of a company's communication conveys a consistent and complete message. Most organizational structures previously treated these distinct areas of communication as separate. However, integrated communication has bridged the gap and streamlined corporate communication. Other aspects often included in business IMC packages can be sales promotion, publicity, packaging, trade shows, direct marketing, promotional products and personal selling.

When all departments are on the same page, it's easier for consumers to spot the message coming from that company since they all serve to reinforce one another. For example, the company trucks will bear the same message that's heard on the phone and the radio or that's seen on the Web site when potential customers contact the business. FedEx is a good example of its consistent message being seen everywhere throughout the corporation.

Integrated communication continues to grow as more and more large corporations and outside consulting firms redirect communication efforts to maximize organizational benefits. Integrated communication coordinates and unifies a company's message so that a seamless voice is heard, rather than directing several voices toward the consumer. With an integrated

IMC Defined

The coordination and integration of all communication tools, avenues and sources within a company into a seamless program that maximizes the impact on consumers and other end users at a minimal cost.

Ken Clow & Donald Baack

approach, an organization's entire communication effort achieves greater synergy and clarity.

This synergistic approach creates opportunities for smaller organizations by helping them yield greater results from their communication efforts both internally and externally. Consequently, the *demassification* of the population — the splintering of the mass market into highly specialized groups — becomes a greater challenge for organizational communication specialists in smaller organizations. This splintering of audiences creates a challenge to communicate similar messages through multiple channels often with limited budgets.

Tom Duncan, founder of the University of Colorado IMC graduate program, identified four distinct levels of integration that companies use — unified image, consistent voice, good listener, and at the most integrated, world-class citizen. These levels demonstrate how integrated programs range from narrowly focused corporate monologs to broad, interactive dialogs, resulting in a corporate culture that permeates an organization and drives everything it does, internally and externally.

Duncan further suggests three dimensions to an organization's integration process in order to maximize the synergy benefits.[2] First, Duncan proposes that it should "ensure consistent positioning, then facilitate purposeful interactivity between the company and its customers or other stakeholders, and finally actively incorporate a socially responsible mission into the organization's relationships with its stakeholders." In short, integrated communication offers accountability by maximizing resources and linking communications activities directly to organizational goals and the resulting bottom line.

The dependence on an integrated approach to communication has elevated the need for highly skilled and diverse writing. In today's business climate, writing is no longer reserved only for those employees who specialize in organizational communication. Rather, polished written communication skills are essential for success at all levels. However, communication specialists in an organization have an increased responsibility because they must be skilled at crafting clear and concise messages that satisfy a variety of organizational purposes.

Now that we've established both the need and the general principles of writing we can begin the process of building our toolbox. We begin with the study of grammar. This will provide the foundation for our understanding of written communication.

Beyond the grammar we'll explore how to structure, shape and fine tune our sentences, paragraphs and documents.

Once the foundation has dried we can begin adding the various floors. This will include writing effective leads, adding rhythm and style, and providing transitions from one idea to the next. At the end we'll develop knowledge of specific writing assignments used in corporate and organizational settings. The blueprint has been drawn up. *Let's begin.*

Notes

[1]Pincus, J.D. To get an MBA or an MA in communication? *Communication World*, v 14, n 3, pp. 31-34. 1997.

[2]Arens, William F. *Contemporary Advertising*. New York, NY: McGraw-Hill/Irwin, 2002.

For Further Reading

Kenneth E. Clow and Donald Baack. *Integrated Advertising, Promotion, & Marketing Communications*. Upper Saddle River, NJ: Prentice Hall, 2003.

Tom Duncan, IMC. *Using Advertising & Promotion to Build Brands*. New York, NY: McGraw-Hill Irwin, 2002.

Tom Duncan, IMC. *The New Principles of Advertising and Promotion*. New York, NY: McGraw-Hill Irwin, 2005.

Don E. Schultz. "Four Basic Rules Lay Groundwork for Integration," *Marketing News*. August 1993.

Don E. Schultz, Stanley I. Tannenbaum and Robert F. Lauterborn. *Integrated Marketing Communications*. Lincolnwood, IL: NTC Business Books, 1993.

2.
Foundations of Public Relations Writing

by David Kaszuba

From news releases and speeches, to crisis plans and newsletters, PR professionals write all kinds of different materials. None, however, is as common as the news release. Usually one to two pages in length, a news release tells of some significant event involving the organization or individual whom the PR writer represents. It is distributed to the media — usually by fax or e-mail — with the hope that newspapers and electronic media outlets will share its content with their audiences.

Given the central role of news releases in public relations, they will be discussed extensively in this chapter, as a means of introducing you to the practice of PR writing. In addition, the news release will be revisited time and again throughout several other chapters in this text.

Telling Your Side of the Story

Writing for public relations is a lot like writing for a newspaper or broadcast outlet — with one major exception. Whereas journalists seek to tell all sides of a story, PR writers are primarily interested in telling their own side.

Say, for example, that you are employed as the public relations director at Sweet Tooth Inc., a Chicago-based, candy-manufacturing company that plans to expand and create 250 jobs. A journalist reporting this story would not only highlight the expansion occurring at Sweet Tooth, but would also likely talk to other companies in the area about their expansion plans. As a result, the journalist's story might highlight that your company, Sweet Tooth, is about to add 250 jobs – but that Candy King, your cross-town competitor, is planning to add 500 jobs at its plant.

As a PR professional, you have no interest in calling attention to the expansion plans of your competitor. Instead, your focus is squarely on promoting your organization. Therefore,

David Kaszuba, Ph.D., is an assistant professor of public relations and journalism at Susquehanna University in Selinsgrove, Pa.

when writing a news release, you would concentrate solely on the 250 jobs that your firm, Sweet Tooth, is planning to add. The fact that your rival Candy King will create twice as many jobs is not something you wish to highlight.

Think of it this way: you're a cheerleader for your organization. You're paid to cheer for your organization, not the other team. If you write a news release about the 250 jobs being added at Sweet Tooth, that's the information you want the media to report. Once a journalist receives your news release, it's up to him or her to call around and see if other companies are also planning to expand; that's the journalist's job, not yours. Your job is to promote your company.

Granted, there are times when you may wish to call brief attention to your competitor. Take, for instance, a race between political candidates. Let's say that you're the communication director for Sen. Bob Goodfellow's re-election campaign and that Goodfellow's opponent, Cindy Sampson, has unveiled a plan to increase benefits to senior citizens by $300 million. If Sen. Goodfellow subsequently devises a plan that would boost senior citizen benefits by $500 million, then you, as Goodfellow's communications director, would understandably want to call attention to the difference between the two plans. After all, it's to Goodfellow's advantage to point out that his plan is better than Sampson's. Therefore, if writing a news release trumpeting Goodfellow's plan, your first two paragraphs might read as follows:

> *Sen. Bob Goodfellow today unveiled a plan that would boost senior citizen benefits by $500 million, thus surpassing by $200 million the amount of additional aid that his opponent Cindy Sampson had pledged to seniors.*
> *"My plan goes far and above what my opponent has offered to senior citizens," Goodfellow said at an announcement at his campaign headquarters in Winchester, Va. "I have always been a devoted supporter of our seniors and I will continue to stand and deliver on their behalf."*

After that, your news release would go on to outline the particulars of Goodfellow's plan but probably refrain from calling further attention to his opponent. While it made sense to contrast Goodfellow's plan to Sampson's in the first paragraph of the news release, continuing to mention Sampson throughout the remainder of the release is simply going to give her added publicity. And remember, your job is to promote Goodfellow, not Sampson.

The point again is this: as a PR person, you are to be a cheerleader for your client or company, not for the opposition. So only call attention to the opposition when it is to your client's benefit. And even then, do so minimally. And respectfully. If you write about your competitors with hostility or bitterness, you and your organization/client will be perceived as petty and arrogant. And that, of course, does not create the goodwill you desire among the public.

Striking the Right Tone

While the chapter thus far has compared PR people to cheerleaders, an important distinction must be made. Unlike cheerleaders, who are blatant supporters of their team, PR professionals need to be more subtle in the support for their organizations. In other words, PR practitioners are cheerleaders — but without the pompoms. While PR persons certainly want to promote their organizations, a PR professional does not want to be overly enthusiastic, or "rah-rah," in doing so. It all goes back to what we said at the outset of this chapter — that PR professionals are a lot like journalists.

Read a newspaper story and you'll see that journalists are generally serious and straightforward in their approach. The same is true of most TV reporters and radio newscasters. They don't gush about the news, they simply report it. You, as a PR professional, need to strike the same tone and attitude in the news releases you write.

Return for a moment to consider the earlier scenario involving Sweet Tooth and its plan to add 250 jobs. As a PR person writing a news release about that development, which of the following two opening paragraphs is preferable?

In a candy-licious move that will be an awesome and incredible boost to the local economy, Sweet Tooth Inc. today announced plans to add a whopping 250 jobs at its Chicago plant!

Or...

Sweet Tooth Inc. today announced plans to add 250 jobs at its Chicago plant.

If you wish to write like a journalist — and that should be the goal of all PR writers — then the second paragraph is by far the best choice.

Why the second example and not the first one? Well, what news organization invents words like "candy-licious" or uses adjectives like "awesome" and "whopping" when reporting a business story? And how many times have you seen news stories with exclamation points at the end of the first sentence? Such tactics are rarely used by journalists. So, if you remember what we said earlier — that PR writing is a lot like journalism — you begin to understand that the second paragraph, the one that rejects the "rah-rah" enthusiasm in favor of a more direct and professional approach, is preferable.

Remember, when you write a news release, your hope is this: that newspapers and broadcast outlets will use the release verbatim (that is, word-for-word). And if the media do not use the entire release verbatim, you hope that they at least use a portion of it. But the fact of the matter is this: newsrooms receive dozens, sometimes hundreds, of news releases a day. Not all of the releases can fit into the newspaper or newscast, and so, releases that need extensive editing aren't likely to see the light of day. What editor or reporter, working on a tight deadline, wants to take precious time to rewrite the "candy-licious" version of the Sweet Tooth release in order to get rid of the over-reaching, gushy adjectives and the ill-advised attempts at being clever?

While the PR person who wrote that release may have thought the use of the invented word "candy-licious" was cute, the newspaper editor or television broadcaster receiving the release sees it as useless hype. Therefore, a professionally trained member of the media is likely to toss that release in the recycle bin. After all, there are dozens of releases on his or her desk, all equally newsworthy. So why not simply take and use the ones already written like a news story — ones that don't require a lot of editing and rewriting?

In short, it's imperative that a news release sound like a news story; striking the right tone is essential if you want the media to use your releases.

Structuring the News Release

Not only must a news release sound like a news story, it must also look like one. Just as the tone of a news release must mimic the tone used by professional media outlets, its structure should also follow the format customary of a news story that you would read in the paper or hear on radio. That means news releases must be structured according to inverted pyramid style

Inverted Pyramid

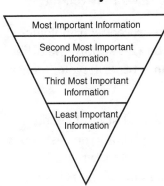

— the style preferred by the majority of media members. If you've taken a journalism class, you probably remember inverted pyramid style involves prioritizing information so the most important facts are placed at or near the top of the story, with less important details coming later and the least important information bringing up the rear.

To better understand inverted pyramid style, let's stop talking about writing for a minute and consider a hypothetical situation.

Let's say you're home visiting your parents for spring break, when a friend fixes you up on a date with someone you've never met. You and your date meet at a restaurant where the two of you immediately hit it off. As you talk, you find that you have much in common, especially your love for hiking and the outdoors. You also find your date to be extremely focused and goal-oriented. Finally, someone with a good outlook on life, you think to yourself. When your meals arrive, both of you find the food to be lacking. "My burger tastes like cardboard," you complain. "Yeah, mine too. It's got to be one of the worst meals ever," your date concurs. Despite the poor quality of the food, the two of you continue to chit-chat enjoyably. Then, without warning, your date stands up, climbs on the table, and proceeds to bark like a dog for 30 seconds. Then, your date sits back down, as if nothing unusual happened. Your date asks if you'd like to order dessert, but you are so embarrassed and confused by what has just occurred, that you simply toss a few dollars on the table, say you must be going, and leave your date at the restaurant while you get in your car and race home.

When you finally arrive back at your parents' house, your mom asks about your evening: "So, how was your date?"

What do you say?

A) *"My date and I really hit it off at first. It turns out that we both like the outdoors. Plus, I was impressed to finally meet someone who had impressive career goals. The food was awful, but we had a really nice time talking. Oh, and get this: toward the end of the meal, my date climbed up on the table and started barking like a dog for no reason. It really threw me for a loop. I was scared and embarrassed, so I came home rather than stick around for dessert."*

Or...

B) *"Oh my gosh, mom. You won't believe it. Part way through dinner, my date — out of the blue — climbs up on the table and starts to bark like a dog. I was so freaked out that I just got up and left."*

Of course, the answer is B. The first words out of your mouth will be about the bizarre barking incident. After all, that's the big news. Why recount the evening in painstaking, chronological order when you can get straight to the point?

The same principle applies in public relations writing. When producing a news release, you take the most important, fascinating piece of news and place it in the lead paragraph. Just as you would have responded to your mom by first telling her about your date's weird behavior, you begin a news release by highlighting the most compelling, interesting news that you have.

In other words, don't feel obligated to proceed chronologically. Get right to the important news. You can supply the other details and background later, even if those other developments actually occurred first.

That's what we mean by inverted pyramid style: pick out the most important information and worry about the rest later. Start with the most important news and work downward, putting the least important details at the end of the release.

To further illustrate our point, imagine you're a publicist for Lola Page, a Hollywood actress who has just signed a $30 million contract to star in three films, including $18 million to play the female lead in a remake of the classic movie *Casablanca*. Even if *Casablanca* is the third of the three films to be shot — and it won't be released for at least two more years — it deserves to be the lead of your news release. For one thing, your client is receiving more money for that role than either of the other two parts she'll play. Also, *Casablanca* is perhaps the most famous movie of all time, again making her involvement in the re-make all the more compelling. Sure, your client is also going to star in two other films, but it's her role in *Casablanca* that will have everyone buzzing. So that's your lead. Details of the other two movies can be incorporated into the release after you deal with the big news: her $18 million role in *Casablanca*.

The reason for using inverted pyramid style is simple: what if a newspaper has a small space that needs to be filled on one of its pages? It decides to plug the spot with one of your news releases. Even though your release might be nine paragraphs in length, the paper only has room for two paragraphs. Not wanting to deal with the hassle of editing the release, the newspaper decides to simply use the first two paragraphs of your release. If you used inverted pyramid style, you can take comfort knowing that the big news — in this case, the news about the *Casablanca* movie — will make it into the paper. If you didn't use inverted pyramid style — and you arranged the news chronologically instead — the paragraphs about your client's role-of-a-lifetime in the *Casablanca* remake will be lost, an unfortunate concession to the space constraints of the newspaper.

So when you write, ask yourself: does my news release meet the cut-off test; that is, if a newspaper editor cut off the bottom portion of the release, leaving just the first couple of paragraphs, would the main point of my release be lost, or would it still survive to find its way into print?

Gathering Essential Facts

Besides using inverted pyramid style, you should also make sure that your news release contains essential information that will interest the media. Like we've said several times already in this chapter, a PR practitioner who writes a news release is a lot like a journalist writing a news story. So when it comes time to put together a news release, think like a journalist. Ask yourself: what types of information would a journalist consider important to a news story — and have I tried to include such information in my release?

For example, journalists routinely measure the economic impact of the news that they cover. If a new skyscraper/luxury hotel is being constructed downtown, a journalist who writes about it will be sure to mention the estimated cost of the construction project. The journalist's story will also incorporate information about the number of jobs that will be created at the new hotel and the kinds of salaries that the hotel expects to offer.

Further, journalists are always interested in size and scope, also known as magnitude. How many stories will the new skyscraper have? Will it be the tallest building downtown? How many square feet will it cover? Plus, journalists are understandably interested in timetables: when will the construction be finished, and has a date been scheduled for the grand opening of the luxury skyscraper/hotel?

Given that journalists are interested in such things, any news release you write should address these same types of questions. Let's return to our earlier example about the planned expansion at Sweet Tooth. In writing a release about this, you should be sure to provide an estimate of the number of jobs that will be created. Simply saying that Sweet Tooth will add "many new jobs" is insufficient; instead, be as specific as possible, saying in this case that "approximately 250 jobs are expected to be added."

You might also mention the salary range, especially if the jobs will pay more than minimum wage and be accompanied by generous benefits. Such news will reflect positively on your company. Also, think about size and scope: How does the size of this expansion project compare to previous expansions at Sweet Tooth? Or is this the first time that the company has expanded at its present location? Will the expansion require that an addition be built on to the existing factory? If so, what's the timetable? Remember, journalists will want to know when the addition will be completed and when the new people will be hired. Perhaps half of the 250 new jobs will be filled next spring, with the other half coming next fall. If that's the case, be sure to mention that information in your news release.

Let's also revisit our earlier example about Bob Goodfellow, the senator who has devised a plan to increase financial aid to senior citizens. If you are writing the news release for Sen. Goodfellow, be sure to address the economic impact: how much will it cost to implement the program, where will the money come from (a tax on cigarettes?), and how many more benefits, on average, will seniors receive? Also, if this is a record increase in benefits for seniors, or the first expansion of senior citizen benefits in several years, be sure to call attention to that fact, since it will surely cast a favorable light on the senator whom you represent. And don't forget about the timeframe: what is the projected timetable for the bill's passage? And if the bill is passed, when would seniors actually start receiving their increased benefits?

These same issues — economic impact, size and scope, and projected timetable — can also be applied to the example involving the star actress who has landed a multi-picture deal. If you were a publicist writing a release about her newly signed contract, you want to address how much she will earn for each picture (economic impact); how many films she will star in, according to the contract (magnitude); and how long it will be until each film is released (timetable).

Getting all of this necessary information will require some legwork on your part. In the case of Sweet Tooth's expansion, however, gathering the facts shouldn't be too difficult. Assuming that you're a member of the public relations department at Sweet Tooth, you're likely to have fairly easy access to the CEO, the plant operations manager, the treasurer and other company officials who will have information you need. After all, you all work on the same team; you are all employed by Sweet Tooth and are similarly committed to the company's best interests. In fact, you as the PR director might be able to call a meeting of key company personnel to gather the information needed for your news release. And if not, you'll likely be able to call or e-mail these individuals for various details you need.

The same is true of the Sen. Goodfellow scenario. If you work as his director of communications, then you're part of the same team as the individuals who have the information you need. Like you, Sen. Goodfellow's campaign manager and policy adviser are working to get the senator re-elected. And so they should be more than happy to cooperate with you to give you the information you require.

Then again, not everything always runs as smoothly as expected in the world of public relations. While Sen. Goodfellow's campaign manager and policy adviser might be more than willing to give you whatever information you need, they might also be distracted with other developments and issues that are suddenly springing up in the course of the campaign. Therefore, your calls or e-mails to them might not be returned as promptly as you hope. In that case, you'll have to be persistent and follow up. But you'll also have to exercise good judgment. If the campaign manager is in meetings all day, is your news release important and urgent enough to warrant interrupting her? Or should you simply wait until later in the day, or even until tomorrow, to talk with her?

That's why it's imperative that you understand not only your responsibilities, but also the responsibilities of others within the organization. Knowing where and how you fit into the organization, and understanding the importance and urgency assigned to a particular news release, will help to determine whether it's necessary to badger colleagues for information or whether you can simply wait.

Meanwhile, an entirely different set of dynamics is at work in the case of Lola Page, the movie star who signed the three-picture deal. As her publicist, you will be able to get comments from her rather easily — and these comments, of course, can be incorporated into your news release. But when it comes to gathering the nitty-gritty details about the movie production schedules and release dates, you'll have to look outside your organization. In all likelihood, you'll have to solicit the cooperation of public relations officials who work for the motion picture company that signed her to the contract.

You might also have to contact the directors and producers of the films for additional information. In light of this, it will be important for you to use your interpersonal skills so that you can form solid working relationships with these individuals. Moreover, you need to bear in mind that these persons do not work for you or with you. They are not employed by Lola Page, as you are. Therefore, working with them may require added patience and flexibility. They might, for example, wish to distribute a joint news release, meaning that both you and the PR department for the motion picture company will need to negotiate the type of language and information that is ultimately included in the release.

Regardless of whether you need to collaborate with outsiders, or whether you have the benefit of accessing all of the necessary information from colleagues within your organization, the overall objective must be the same: gathering essential information that's required to satisfy the media.

Earning Media Respect: Dispelling the Myth of 'Flacks vs. Hacks'

If you produce news releases according to the advice outlined in this chapter — if you gather and provide the essential facts, write in inverted pyramid style, and resist unabashed cheerleading in favor of adopting a journalistic tone — then you're sure to earn the respect of the media.

Too often, public relations professionals get carried away when they write a news release about the organization or client whom they represent. They are so interested in hyping their client, that they allow emotions to get in the way of facts. They color or "spin" the news so that everything always sounds unbelievably rosy for the organization. Granted, you don't want to portray your client in a negative light. But if you swing too far in the other direction — and supply media with releases that drip with shameless enthusiasm or distract from the truth — they will resent it.

Russ Eshleman, former reporter and state capitol bureau chief for *The Philadelphia Inquirer*, recalls a particularly irritating news release issued by a government agency: "The release, which provided an update of statewide employment figures, highlighted the fact that, for so many months in a row, the number of non-farm jobs in the state remained over a certain figure. What the release *did not* say — but what could be gleaned by examining an accompanying chart — was that non-farm employment for that month had actually declined from the previous month. The release was an attempt at hiding the real news...spinning, if you will, the facts that jobs had actually decreased.

"Now, don't get me wrong. Reporters don't expect public relations writers to go out of their way to publicize negative news. But we don't appreciate having our intelligence insulted, either," Eshleman adds.

When PR practitioners deny or gloss over the obvious — when they exaggerate facts or paint shamelessly rosy pictures of their organizations — they often earn reputations as "flacks." To be called a flack is unflattering. It suggests that you, the PR writer, will test the limits of truth or professionalism in order to spin news to your client's advantage. While presenting your client in the most favorable light is clearly your job as a PR practitioner, you must be careful not to patronize the media in the process. Doing so will foster tension and fuel the age-old notion that PR practitioners and media members have a hostile relationship — one where the PR professionals are nothing more than "flacks" who try to pull the wool over the eyes of reporters and where reporters, in turn, are crusty, hard-boiled "hacks" intent on tearing down the organizations represented by the PR industry.

This "flacks vs. hacks" mindset is dangerous because it falsely suggests that the majority of PR practitioners and reporters have unprofessional, adversarial relationships. In fact, the opposite is true. Most PR practitioners and members of the media realize they need each other to succeed. PR writers rely on the media to deliver news about the organizations and clients whom they represent, while reporters depend on PR people to provide them with important news, statistics and other details. In this sense, PR professionals and the media complement each other; they help each other do an effective job.

Sizing Up Opportunities in PR

Given that the media rely on the public relations industry for information, it should come as little surprise that PR practitioners are in greater demand today than ever. After all, there are more media outlets than ever, with traditional newspapers, specialty magazines, all-day cable news networks and Internet sites all seeking to supply their audiences with news. Because these media members regularly turn to PR practitioners for story ideas, news releases and updates on breaking developments, the field of public relations is rich with opportunity.

Just in this chapter, we introduced you to three possible employment avenues: You might work in public relations for a company like our fictitious Sweet Tooth Inc. Or for a government official like Sen. Bob Goodfellow. Or for a movie actress like Lola Page.

But working in corporate communications, government relations or entertainment publicity are just three of the many options available to skilled PR practitioners. Other PR professionals work for nonprofits, including hospitals, universities and charitable organizations. Still others work for professional or college sports teams, or for athletic leagues or associations. Many other PR practitioners are employed by large public relations firms, where the clients change frequently. In these situations, a member of a PR firm might be working to promote an environmental group one week, then trying to diffuse a crisis affecting a restaurant chain the following week.

Despite this variety, there is one constant: no matter where a PR person works, or for whom, the key to success is good writing. Indeed, all facets of PR involve writing. Consider:

- Companies need someone to craft news releases about their latest innovative products.

- The heads of corporations need someone to help write the speeches that they deliver to shareholders.

- Sports teams need someone to draft statements explaining the decision to suspend a player or hire a new coach.

- Labor unions need someone to write letters sent to union members, updating them on the progress of contract negotiations.

- Companies need someone to maintain their Web sites, where corporate histories and mission statements are made available to the public.

- Political candidates need someone to write the scripts for television commercials they wish to air.

- Universities need someone to write stories for the alumni magazines sent to graduates.

- Companies need someone to develop employee newsletters distributed to their workers.

- Corporations need someone to prepare extensive annual reports that summarize earnings and financial prospects for investors.

- Hospitals need someone to write brochures that provide health care advice to patients with high blood pressure and diabetes.

- Charities need someone to write appeal letters that ask community members for donations of time and money.

- Museums need someone to write the brochures that are distributed to people as they enter the latest exhibit.

As you can see, writing isn't restricted to news releases. Nor are opportunities in PR writing limited to companies. Opportunities for good PR writers abound. As we proceed through the remaining chapters, our goal is to impart specific advice so that you may develop and hone writing skills that make you employable and successful in this diverse field of public relations.

3.

Understanding Grammar

Building effective prose requires a firm grasp of the fundamentals of the English language. Writers who fully understand proper word usage, punctuation and syntax have in their literary arsenal the firepower to effectively and efficiently communicate with the written word. Consequently, the writer's toolbox should contain a functional understanding of the parts of speech of the English language.

A phrase often heard in college classrooms comes from students who claim they are poor writers. They bellow this sentiment and project a belief that somehow good writers inherit the ability from the genetic pool rather than developing the skills from a commitment to hard work. These students often fail to view writing from a logical approach and fail to recognize that mastering basic skills of grammar, punctuation and sentence structure provides the tools necessary to complete any writing task. And, mastering these tools enables writers to venture into uncharted waters and explore greater creativity in their writing. Therefore, writers who fail to fully understand the fundamentals of sentence structure and paragraph construction limit themselves and inhibit their creative expression.

Mastery of grammar and proper sentence structure provides the foundation for all good writing. Yet, ask most students to take a basic grammar test and they generally respond with panic-stricken faces and beads of sweat pouring down their foreheads. After all, their minds respond by recalling the trauma of diagramming complex sentences and the fear of defining terms such as dangling gerunds and consonant phonemes. However, the foundation for all good writing, a better understanding of English grammar, often requires only minor amounts of labor.

Before reviewing the basics of grammar, consider these analogies. Any master carpenter knows that the most creative construction ideas can only be achieved if the foundation of the structure is solid and the craftspeople building the project have mastered the basic elements of the trade. This also applies to writing.

For sports enthusiasts, consider that each spring professional baseball players spend weeks preparing for the upcoming baseball season by practicing the fundamentals of the game. They polish their skills by working on rudimentary techniques such as bunting, running the bases, and fielding ground balls and fly balls. Although these athletes performed these same skills since their Little League Baseball days, they recognize the value of continuous attention to the basics. Again, this mirrors effective writing.

Once students establish a solid foundation in grammatical use and sentence construction, they can venture into the world of the grammatical unknown and take greater chances with their written communication. For most students, a look of bewilderment will come over their faces when concepts they feared most are quickly retrieved from the recesses of their memories. The material they disdained for years quickly gets recalled since they now have a greater appreciation for its value. It is therefore vital to underscore the importance of the fundamentals in polishing and broadening writing skills. Mastering the basics prepares us to tackle the more complex writing assignments.

Before beginning our journey we should note that American English often deviates from its established rules and makes occasional exceptions to them. Identifying and studying these exceptions will improve your understanding of grammar. Now, let's get to work in filling our writing toolbox.

Eight Parts of Speech

Grammarians often disagree about the exact makeup of the parts of speech but for our purposes we'll study eight basic parts of speech that comprise the English language. These parts, used in various combinations, form sentences. They provide the bricks we use to construct sentences. The eight parts of speech — nouns, pronouns, verbs, adjectives, adverbs, prepositions, conjunctions and interjections — essentially serve as the raw materials for building effective prose.

For most of us who grew up with television as the dominant medium, recalling these parts of speech sparks a fond memory

Who vs. Whom

The starting point is that *Who* is subject-related and *Whom* is object-related.

Try these simple tips:

1. Use **whom** when it immediately follows a preposition or a verb — unless the pronoun is acting as the subject in another clause.

Examples:
To whom do you wish this directed? (Whom is the object of *to*.)

Whom would you prefer? (Whom is the object of *prefer*.)

2. Use **who** when the pronoun is the subject of another clause.

Examples:
It depends on who is present. (The object of *on* is the entire clause, who is available.)

Please give this to whoever wants it. (The object of *to* is the entire clause, whoever wants it.)

of Saturday morning "School House Rock." Here, clever television writers developed little ditties and animated characters to teach young children about grammar. The simplicity of the programming emphasized the relative ease with which we can gain a basic understanding of grammar. We now begin the task of identifying and learning to use the eight parts of speech and consider innovative ways to build clean and crisp prose. Picture if you will a construction site. The bricks — the eight parts of speech — rest comfortably on the ground waiting for us to assemble them.

The first brick we pick up, a **noun**, operates as the subject in a sentence. Every sentence, in order for it to be complete, must have both a subject and a verb. Simple, right? However, somewhere along the education path many writers lost track of this basic element.

Nouns name particular persons, places, things, ideas or events. In fact, the word *noun* comes from the Latin word *nomen*, meaning *name*. We can recognize nouns, the largest group of words in the English language, in one of three ways:

1. understanding the definition of a noun

2. checking to see if the suspect word can be combined with *the* to form a unit

3. recognizing if the noun has a plural form for referring to two or more items

However, don't get sidetracked with some exceptions to this rule since a few nouns such as *series* take only a singular form. We also recognize nouns by the words that signal them. When we see determiners — words that mark nouns including articles (a, the), possessive nouns and pronouns (Chuck's, his, her), demonstrative pronouns (this, that), quantifiers (many, several), indefinite pronouns (each, every), and numbers — we know that a noun will soon follow. Determiners are simply not used without nouns.

Most nouns take both a singular and a plural form. Collective nouns such as jury, family and audience are often treated as singular nouns. Possessive nouns such as Karen's hat, a day's work and the professor's computer require an apostrophe to show ownership. Occasionally nouns function as adjectives that modify other nouns. Example: You can't make a silk purse out of a sow's ear.

Using the Correct Pronoun

"Between you and I" or "Between you and me"? Answer, "Between you and me." Why? Me is the object of the preposition, *between*, and must be in the objective case.

Beware of a situation where you have more than one subject or object — something grammarians refer to as *compound subjects* or *objects*. You'll find difficulty distinguishing the correct pronoun form by the sound. First, decide the pronoun's case, and then choose the correct form.

Here's a shortcut: Try reading the pronoun alone. You'll pick the correct pronoun form by how it sounds.

The Wordsmith Workshop

The teacher lectured on grammar.

Teacher is the noun; *the* is the article that marks the noun.

Victoria writes exceptionally clear and concise reports.

Victoria serves as a concrete noun.

The *clarity and conciseness* with which Victoria writes reports are exceptional. Here, the sentence deals with abstract qualities of Victoria's reports.

To wrap up our discussion about nouns we should review their uses:

■ First, nouns serve as the subject of a sentence. The subject names the person, place, thing or idea and tells us *who did something or what performs the action suggested by the verb*. In most instances the verb follows the subject. The subject also determines whether the verb should be plural or singular.

■ Next, nouns also serve as direct objects. A direct object follows a verb and tells us *who did something or what receives the action of the verb*. Therefore, a direct object receives the action of the verb.

■ Nouns can serve as indirect objects. An indirect object always follows the verb and precedes the direct object. It answers the question *to whom* or *to what* or *for whom* or *for what* something was done.

The Wordsmith Workshop

The teacher sent a *letter*.

Letter serves as the direct object.

The teacher sent the *student* a *letter*.

Student is the indirect object while letter remains the direct object.

■ The fourth use for nouns is as a predicate noun. Predicate nouns follow linking verbs (be, am, is, are, was, were, seem) and rename the subject. Remember that direct objects name someone or something that is different from the subject. Predicate nouns refer to the same person or thing as the subject of the sentence.

The Wordsmith Workshop

The players are all *superstars*.

Superstars simply renames players.

■ The object of a preposition is a noun that follows a preposition. Prepositions (*from* or *to*, for example) are combined with objects to form prepositional phrases. A prepositional phrase may appear anywhere in a sentence.

The Wordsmith Workshop

For Christmas, the dean *of* our college will take everyone *to* lunch.

Note that the italicized preposition comes before each underlined object of the preposition.

■ Appositives, nouns that immediately follow another noun to identify or explain it, are often used in writing. They serve as a way of adding clarity and deeper meaning to our writing.

The Wordsmith Workshop

Dr. Lucas, my *professor*, counseled the student, *Paula Rich*.

Professor and Paula Rich are both appositives, set off by commas.

■ We often use nouns as direct addresses to personalize our writing. Here, the noun names the reader or listener and seeks to provide a more personal element to our writing.

The Wordsmith Workshop

The suggestion you made, *Mr. Arnold*, proved to be a valuable tool in solving our personnel problem.

The use of the name Mr. Arnold adds warmth and a personal touch.

■ Nouns occasionally are used as adjectives when the noun immediately precedes another noun and modifies the second noun. For example, words such as *finance department* and *pay raise*. The first noun serves as an adjective to modify the second noun.

Compound Adjectives

A compound adjective is formed by joining two or more words as a single modifier expressing a single characteristic. When compound adjectives precede the modified noun, they are hyphenated. When they follow the modified noun, they usually are not hyphenated.

Example:

He is a *well-known* scholar.

That actor is *well known*.

Parenthetical Expressions

The final word on pronoun/antecedent agreement deals with recognizing agreement errors when the antecedent precedes parenthetical expressions. Parenthetical expressions refer to a group of words that are unrelated to the grammatical structure of the sentence. We generally set parenthetical expressions off with commas.

Good writers carefully strip away the parenthetical expressions and identify the subject of the main sentence. Be careful to avoid identifying a noun in the parenthetical expression and treating it as the subject of the sentence.

Example:
Billy White, as well as the other members of the team, feels that he has given his utmost effort this season.

■ Yet another use for nouns is as possessive modifiers. A noun in the possessive case indicates ownership. For example: The *child's parents* told their *neighbor's relatives* that they would be unable to attend the party.

■ Finally, nouns used as an adverb modify a verb. They generally indicate time of the action. Example: The students will compete in the race next *week*. Week is a noun used as an adverb to indicate time.

Now that we've identified the first brick in our foundation, nouns, and added the rules for using them properly to our writing toolbox, it's time to move on to our second part of speech, pronouns. **Pronouns**, used in place of nouns, include personal pronouns, possessive pronouns, intensive pronouns, reflexive pronouns, relative pronouns, interrogative pronouns, demonstrative pronouns and indefinite pronouns. When used properly, pronouns eliminate the unnecessary and often boring repetition of nouns and add needed variety and color to our writing.

Let's begin by first defining the various types of pronouns.

■ **Personal pronouns** refer to specific persons or things. Examples of singular personal pronouns are *I, me, you, he, she, it*. Examples of plural personal pronouns are *we, us, they, them*.

■ **Possessive pronouns** indicate ownership. Examples of singular possessive pronouns are *my, mine, your, yours, its*. Examples of plural personal pronouns are *our, ours, yours, their*.

■ **Intensive pronouns** emphasize a noun or another pronoun. For example: The congresswoman *herself* met us at the door.

■ **Reflexive pronouns** name a receiver of an action identical with the doer of the action. An example is: David cut *himself*.

■ **Relative pronouns** introduce adjective clauses. Examples of relative pronouns are *who, whoever, whom, whomever, whose, which, that*.

Note: Adjective clauses contain subjects and verbs and function within sentences as modifiers of nouns or pronouns. Adjective clauses answer the question Which one? or What kind of? and cannot stand alone as a complete sentence.

Example: Jose's new car, which he purchased yesterday, is parked in the garage.

- **Interrogative pronouns** introduce questions. Examples are *who, whom, whose, which, what*.
- **Demonstrative pronouns** point to nouns. Examples are *this, that, these, those*.
- **Indefinite pronouns** refer to nonspecific persons or things. Examples are *all, anyone, somebody, nothing*.

Now that we've defined various types of pronouns, let's characterize them into their four case forms. Nominative pronouns function as subjects in sentences. They are the "naming" pronouns. Objective pronouns function as objects in sentences or objects of prepositions.

Possessive pronouns show ownership. Unlike other possessive words, possessive pronouns are never formed with an apostrophe. Finally, reflexive pronouns direct the action of the verb back to the subject.

Nominative	I	he	she	we	they	who	you	it
Objective	me	him	her	us	them	whom	you	it
Possessive	my	his	her	our	their	whose	your	its
	mine	his	hers	ours	theirs		yours	its
Reflexive	myself/himself/herself/ourselves/themselves/yourselves/itself							

It's important to remember that antecedents, specific nouns that pronouns replace, agree when they are both singular or both plural. Errors with this relatively simple rule pop up often in writing and severely weaken credibility and clarity of the message.

The Wordsmith Workshop

Singular use – The *doctor* finished *her* rounds.

Doctor and *her* are both singular.

Plural use – The *doctors* finished *their* rounds.

Doctors and *their* are both plural.

We'll explore pronoun-antecedent agreement in greater detail later in the chapter. We reserved a separate section on this topic simply because of the magnitude of errors found in this area.

Verbs, the second essential element of a complete sentence, provide action to sentences. They tell the reader *what is happening* in the sentence. Every verb, without exception, has five forms: the infinitive (base) form, -s form, -ed form (past tense), -en form (past participle), -ing form (present participle).

Imperative Sentences

Imperative sentences give a command or make a request. In imperative sentences, the subject you is understood.

Example:
Turn off the air conditioner when you leave.

Voice

Transitive verbs may be either *active* or *passive*. The verb is in active voice when the subject of the sentence does the action. The verb is in the passive voice when the subject receives the action.

A Tense Situation

Writers who are having difficulty settling on an appropriate point of view sometimes confuse readers by shifting from one tense to another. Tense indicates the time of action. The three simple tenses are present, past and future. The three perfect tenses are present perfect, past perfect and future perfect. Writers should choose a suitable point of view and stick with it.

An easy way to identify a verb is to check whether the word has different forms to indicate present and past action. If it does, it is a verb.

The Wordsmith Workshop

Sample of five forms of a verb.

Base	-s Form	-ed Form	-en Form	-ing Form
read	reads	read	read	reading
pass	passes	passed	passed	passing
fall	falls	fell	fallen	falling

We also classify verbs into three basic forms: transitive, intransitive and linking. Transitive verbs, verbs that have direct objects, express a subject's action that affects someone else or something else.

Intransitive verbs, verbs that do not have objects and do not link modifiers to subjects, express a subject's action that does not affect other persons or things. Finally, linking verbs simply link a predicate noun, pronoun or adjective to the subject.

The Wordsmith Workshop

Bonnie Brown *planned* the party. (transitive verb)

Bob Jackson *snores* loudly. (intransitive verb)

Miguel Daniels *is* my best friend. (linking verb)

Before setting verbs firmly into our foundation and putting the rules for using verbs into our writer's toolbox, let's take the opportunity to emphasize their importance. Verbs provide action to sentences. Action-oriented verbs energize our news releases and invigorate the reader. Two vital areas to effective writing, subject-verb agreement and active and passive voice, will be discussed later in this chapter. These elements will serve as cornerstones in crafting clear and concise writing.

Adjectives, the next part of speech we'll identify and place into our toolbox, modify or describe nouns or pronouns. Adjectives usually answer one of these questions: *Which one? What kind of? How many?* The two kinds of adjectives, limiting and descriptive, perform different functions in describing nouns or pronouns.

Limiting adjectives set limits and indicate precisely how many persons, places, things or ideas we have described. Certain limiting adjectives such as some, any, that and those indicate whether your reference is indefinite and general or definite and specific.

Descriptive adjectives modify nouns and describe the characteristics and qualities of the specific nouns.

We form compound adjectives by combining two or more words as a single modifier. When the compound adjective precedes the modified noun, we hyphenate it. When the compound adjective follows the modified noun, we generally do not hyphenate it. Example: He is a *well-known* professional athlete. The professional athlete is *well known*. Using compound modifiers without hyphens is a common mistake of writers.

The Wordsmith Workshop

The *brave* soldier returned from the battle.

Brave modifies the noun soldier.

Generally adjectives precede the words they modify. However, they may also follow linking verbs, in which case they describe the subject.

The Wordsmith Workshop

The students seem *diligent*.

The adjective diligent follows the linking verb seem and modifies the noun students.

The Wordsmith Workshop

We will read *some* chapters in the book. (indefinite limiting adjective)

We will read *those* chapters in the book. (definite limiting adjective)

The **adverb** is the next part of speech ready for placement into our writer's toolbox. Adverbs modify verbs, adjectives or other adverbs. The mobility of an adverb is its most distinguishing characteristic.

The Wordsmith Workshop

He walked *slowly*.

Slowly he walked.

The adverb slowly works either at the beginning or the end of the sentence to modify the verb walked.

Adverbs usually answer one of these questions: *When? Where? How? Why? Under what conditions? To what degree?*

Comparison in Adverbs

Like descriptive adjectives, many adverbs have three forms:

1. the positive degree (early, regularly)
2. the comparative degree (earlier, more regularly)
3. the superlative degree (earliest, most regularly)

Choose the correct form when comparing how two or more people do something.

Example:

Mitch arrived earlier than Dave for the concert.

Bob attends class most regularly of all the divinity students.

The Wordsmith Workshop

Run *swiftly* at the sound of the gun. (Run how?)

Watch the best players *first*. (Watch when?)

Most words that end in -ly are adverbs although this rule is not etched in stone. Words that end in -ly can also be nouns (bully) or adjectives (lovely). But the majority of adjectives can turn into adverbs by adding -ly.

Prepositions connect nouns or pronouns to other words in sentences. The word preposition, in fact, means placed before. Therefore, prepositions are words **placed before** a noun or a pronoun to form phrases. The noun or pronoun connected by means of a preposition is called the object of the preposition. We refer to the combination of the preposition, its object and any modifiers as prepositional phrases. Prepositional phrases generally function as either adjectives or adverbs.

The Wordsmith Workshop

He climbed *up* the ladder *of* success.

Up and *of* are prepositions, part of two prepositional phrases here.

As we continue to identify the bricks in our foundation and fill our writing toolbox with the basic rules for using and identifying the parts of speech, we find room for the final two parts of speech, conjunctions and interjections.

Conjunctions can best be described as linking logs. They are used to join words, phrases or clauses within sentences. The two types of conjunctions are coordinating and correlative. Coordinating conjunctions are *and, but, or, nor, for, so, yet*. Correlative conjunctions are pairs of conjunctions and include *either/or, neither/nor, but also, not only*.

The Wordsmith Workshop

Chamique *and* Pat remain best friends.

Either set the table *or* clean your room.

The biggest issue when using either coordinating or correlative conjunctions in sentence construction is maintaining parallel form. Parallelism refers to using the same grammatical construction in lists. This includes words to words, phrases to phrases and clauses to clauses. We'll review this again later in the chapter.

Common Prepositions

about	from
above	in
across	into
after	like
against	of
along	off
among	on
around	onto
at	over
before	past
behind	regarding
below	since
beneath	through
beside	throughout
besides	to
between	toward
beyond	under
but (except)	underneath
by	until
concerning	up
down	upon
during	with
except	without
for	

Run-ons

Many run-on sentences result from mistaking a conjunctive adverb for a conjunction. It is easy to prove that these words are not conjunctions. A true conjunction would have to stand between the two word groups that it holds together. It has no mobility. Don't mistake these conjunctive adverbs for conjunctions: then, therefore, besides, however, furthermore, consequently, otherwise, nevertheless.

The misuse of *however* creates a type of run-on sentence. For example, when you have two independent clauses you must have a coordinating conjunction to make it a compound sentence. *However* is not a true conjunction.

Example:

• She enjoyed going to law school, however, she hated studying for the bar examination.

(This is a run-on sentence that needs to be either separated with a semicolon or made into two simple sentences.)

Our final part of speech, **interjections**, shows emotion. Interjections are not related grammatically to other words in the sentence. However, they are single words or short phrases that modify sentences. Interjections generally are punctuated with an exclamation mark or a comma. The exclamation mark indicates strong emotion; the comma indicates lesser emotion.

The Wordsmith Workshop

Wow! That sauce is spicy.

Oh, I have to go to work.

Words that are often recognized as nouns or verbs can also be used as interjections.

Example: Heavens, I wish I could help.

We generally use interjections in personal writing and in advertising to attract attention. Interjections instantly reveal the emotion of the writer. We can compare the use of interjections to the use of tone and pitch in speaking. Certain phrases, when spoken with greater emotion, convey a bolder meaning.

Now that we've identified the eight parts of speech, we can begin the task of forming sentences. We'll start by defining the four sentence structures.

Sentence Structures

The four sentence structures found in the English language are simple, compound, complex and compound-complex. We determine sentence structure by identifying independent and dependent clauses in sentences and counting how many appear in each sentence.

An independent clause contains both a subject and a verb and can stand alone as a complete thought. Dependent clauses, which begin with either subordinating conjunctions or relative pronouns, do not contain both a subject and a verb and cannot stand alone as a complete thought.

In the simple sentence construction, the writer expresses only one independent clause. A compound sentence contains two or more independent clauses but no dependent clauses. We combine the two independent clauses by using a coordinating conjunction, a semicolon, or a semicolon and a conjunctive adverb. Remember that we can separate compound sentences into simple sentences.

Keep This in Mind

Many sentences have only one verb that expresses an action or state of being. We refer to these verbs as main verbs. However, the English language also includes 23 helping verbs. Modals, words that convey probability, possibility or obligation, function only as helping verbs, never as main verbs. Helping verbs indicate when the action will take place and also indicate whether the subject receives the action or performs the action.

A helping verb can also serve as a main verb in a sentence. The 10 modals in the English language are *can, will, shall, should, ought, could, would, may, migh*t and *must*. These 10 helping verbs take only one form and always appear as the first verb in any verb phrase. The other helping verbs — *have, has, so, does, did, am, is, was, were, being, been* — may function either as helping verbs or as main verbs.

Complex sentences contain one independent clause and one or more dependent clauses. Compound-complex sentences contain two or more independent clauses and at least one dependent clause. Writers should always remember that their purpose is to present clear and concise communication. We achieve this by learning to write to *express* rather than to *impress*.

Finally, in order to properly expand our writing toolbox we should develop proficiency in all four sentence structures. This will enable us to develop rhythm in our writing by writing a mixture of short and long sentences. However, our ideal goal is an *average* length of 17 words per sentence.

As we continue to add new tools to our toolbox and solidify our foundation, it is important to pinpoint common writing errors that severely weaken prose and destroy reader confidence.

Our first area of concern deals with subject-verb agreement. A verb must agree with its subject in person (first, second or third person) and in number (singular or plural).

The issue of subject-verb agreement is one that seems simple on the surface but often creates a huge obstacle for writers. This simple rule states: Singular nouns require singular verbs and plural nouns require plural verbs. Easy, right? Well, pitfalls exist on the road to solid writing.

Most writers have few problems when the subject and verb appear side by side in the sentence. But, clauses and phrases placed between the subject and verb often create problems for writers. Adding to the confusion, writers often use subjects as collective nouns that can be either singular or plural depending on the meaning. In addition, some nouns look plural because they end in -s but are actually singular in meaning and therefore take singular verbs.

The best part about studying subject-verb agreement is that specific rules cover virtually every circumstance. The following rules are important to understand:

1. **Singular** subjects get singular verbs.

   Example: "The party *is* under control," the manager said.

   (*Party* is a singular subject; therefore use the singular verb *is* rather than the plural verb *are*.)

2. **Plural** subjects get plural verbs.

   Example: Committee members *are* voting today on the proposal.

(The plural subject *members* uses the plural verb *are* rather than the singular verb *is*.)

3. **If** you join two or more subjects (compound subjects) with the coordinating conjunction *and*, use a plural verb.

   Example: The director and the actor *discuss* the performance after each night.

   (The compound subjects require the third-person plural verb *discuss* rather than *discusses*.)

   Note: An exception to this rule occurs if a compound subject joined by and refers to the same person.

   Example 1: The player and manager *is* considering a lineup change.

   (The same person is both the player and manager in this case; therefore use the singular verb *is* rather than the plural verb *are*.)

   Example 2: His wife and best friend is arriving on the 10 a.m. flight.

   (Again, the same person is both wife and best friend. The omission of *his* before *best friend* points to this.)

   (Keep in mind that this confuses most readers so be selective in writing this way. You can eliminate the confusion in the first case by simply using a compound noun, player-manager. In the second example eliminate the confusion by writing, His wife, who is also his best friend, arrives on the 10 a.m. flight.)

4. **When** using the second-person plural pronoun you always use a plural verb regardless of whether its antecedent is singular or plural.

   Examples: You are a talented athlete.
   You are talented athletes.

   (Even though *you* refers to a singular subject in the first example and a plural subject in the second example always use the plural verb *are* rather than the singular verb *is*.)

5. **When** a compound subject is preceded by *each* or *every*, treat the subject as singular.

   Example: Each chair, table and mirror needs to be cleared.

6. **When** a compound subject is connected by *or* or *nor*, make the verb agree with the part of the subject closest to the verb.

Prepositions at the End of Sentences

Ending a sentence with a preposition is not incorrect. Whether you do so should depend on the emphasis and effect you want to achieve. Also, sometimes ending a sentence with a preposition helps it avoid sounding awkward.

Example:

I wish I knew which house you live in. (informal)

I wish I knew in which house you live. (formal)

Example 1: Neither the coach nor his players *were* on time for the awards banquet.

(The plural subject players is closer to the verb so use the plural form *were* rather than the singular form *was*.)

Example 2: Neither the coaches nor the star player was on time for the awards banquet.

7. **Make** the verb agree with its subject, not a word that comes between them. Writers should strip away the modifiers and isolate the sentence's subject and verb.

Example: The boy, as well as his friends, *was* lost.

(In this example the subject is the singular boy, not the plural friends; therefore, use the singular verb form *was*, not the plural *were*.)

8. **If** the subject has a plural spelling but is singular in meaning use the singular verb form.

Example 1: The news was worse than we expected.

(Since *news* is used as a singular subject, use a singular verb. Don't be confused by the -s at the end of the subject.)

Example 2: The series of lectures is being sponsored by the Student Government Association.

(The subject *series* certainly consists of more than one lecture but it is only one series.)

9. **An** entire prepositional phrase can serve as a subject.

Example 1: After dinner is the best time for friends to gather.

(After dinner in this case is the singular subject requiring a singular verb *is*.)

10. **Treat** collective nouns as singular unless the meaning is clearly plural.

Example 1: Three minutes is a long time to battle an opponent in a wrestling match.

(Although minutes would usually be plural it is treated as one lump sum of time; therefore, use the singular verb *is*.)

Example 2: Fifty million dollars is the lottery jackpot.

(Again, fifty million dollars is treated as one lump sum.)

Example 3: Measles is still a potentially dangerous disease.

Essential and Nonessential Clauses and Phrases

The decision whether to use a comma or not to use a comma sparks many a debate. Here are two simple rules.

We often categorize phases and clauses on how essential they are to the meaning of the sentence. Two rules will help to always get the punctuation correct.

Rule 1. Essential Clauses and Phrases. If the clause or phrase is essential to the meaning of the sentence — as opposed to merely relevant or interesting — introduce it with *that* and omit the comma.

Rule 2. Nonessential Clauses and Phrases. If the clause or phrase adds only incidental information to the main idea introduce it with *which* and include the comma.

(Many people use the plural verb *are* in this sentence because the disease results in multiple spots on the infected person's body. But it is one disease, requiring the singular verb *is*.)

Example 4: Economics is my favorite subject.

(Again, the same rule applies.)

Example 5: The team is coming on the next bus.

(Although team is a collection of two or more players, it's treated as a singular collective noun requiring the singular verb *is*.)

Example 6: The couple were discussing the outcome of the football game.

(This example often gives people problems. Although we consider couple as a singular unit, only individuals can discuss the outcome of a football game. Therefore, we form the sentence using the plural *were*.)

11. **When** the word *number*, *variety* or *majority* is preceded by the definite article *the*, the verb is singular. When *number*, *variety* or *majority* is preceded by the indefinite article *a*, the verb is plural.

    Example 1: The number of students studying public relations is increasing by 20 percent.

    Example 2: A variety of courses are offered for public relations majors.

    (The definite article *the* refers to a group or a collection. Therefore it gets a singular verb. The indefinite article *a* refers to individual members or parts of a group or collection, so it requires a plural verb.)

12. **Predicate** nouns have no influence on the number of the verb. If the subject is singular use a singular verb. If the subject is plural use a plural verb.

    Example 1: Tennis rackets are a great gift.

    (The subject rackets and the predicate noun gift are the same thing. The fact that *gift* is singular has no influence on the verb. The word *rackets* is plural and requires a plural verb *are*.)

    Example 2: My favorite gift is tennis rackets.

    (Here *gift* becomes the subject and is singular requiring the singular verb *is*. The predicate noun rackets has no role in the decision.)

13. **When** one part of the compound subject is used affirmatively and the other is used negatively, the verb agrees with the one used affirmatively. The affirmative subject should most often appear before the negative subject.

Example 1: The manager, never his assistants, appears at the postgame news conference.

(The singular verb *appears* agrees with the singular, affirmative subject *manager*.)

Example 2: His assistants, never the manager, appear at the postgame news conference.

(In this case we use the plural verb *appear* to agree with the plural, affirmative subject *assistants*.)

The Wordsmith Workshop

A police officer is often criticized for always being there when they aren't needed and never being there when they are.

Revised: The noun *police officer* is singular and the pronoun *they* is plural. Change *officer is* to *officers are* to match the plural pronoun *they*.

Pronoun-Antecedent Agreement

A pronoun's job is to take the place of a noun, much like a substitute on a basketball team takes the place of a starter. The noun that a pronoun stands for is called its antecedent.

Errors in pronoun-antecedent agreement seriously weaken prose. In fact, once you master its use and add it to your writing toolbox, you'll find yourself picking up this error in a variety of written materials, including other news releases. Improperly using pronoun-antecedent agreement truly separates the careful writer from the careless writer. And, professional writers can never afford to be characterized as careless.

A pronoun matches its antecedent in person (first, second or third) and in number (singular or plural), even when a group of words separates the pronoun from its antecedent.

The Wordsmith Workshop

Person: All students should bring your books.

(Here the noun and pronoun disagree in person: *students* is third person, but *your* is second person.)

Revised: Students should bring their books.

Number: The board of directors repealed raises they voted on last month.

(Here the noun and pronoun disagree in number. American English, unlike the British, treats collective nouns as singular. Therefore, board of directors is one entity and the pronoun needs to be singular.)

Revised: The board of directors repealed raises it voted on last month.

These tips will help you with pronoun-antecedent agreement.

➤ Most antecedents joined by *and* require a plural pronoun.

Example: Paula and Heather believe they are going to win the election.

➤ Use singular pronouns when two or more singular nouns joined by a coordinating conjunction such as *and* refer to the same person.

Example: My business adviser and finance manager said she would develop the marketing plan.

➤ Use words such as *my* and *the* before each noun that refers to a different person.

Example: My business adviser and my finance manager said they would develop the marketing plan.

➤ A pronoun agrees with the closest part of an antecedent joined by *or* or *nor*. Place the plural antecedent last when you have a mix of singular and plural pronouns.

Example: The manager or the players must confirm that they will attend the banquet.

Example: Neither the account manager nor the members of the creative team said they liked the campaign.

➤ An antecedent that is an indefinite pronoun (does not refer to a specific person, place or thing such as *anybody*, *each*, *either*) takes a singular pronoun.

Example: Anybody who believes that he or she can help the group should attend meetings.

Split Infinitives

Splitting an infinitive occurs when inserting a word or phrase between *to* and the verb. Occasionally splitting an infinitive is acceptable if it makes the expression more accurate or more understandable.

Example:

We need to quickly formulate a plan. (Unnecessary split)

We need to formulate a plan quickly. (Correct)

A meeting to discuss thoroughly the department's proposal to change the curriculum is set for 10 a.m. Wednesday. (Awkward)

A meeting to thoroughly discuss the department's proposal to change the curriculum is set for 10 a.m. Wednesday. (Acceptable split)

➤ A pronoun agrees with its antecedent in gender.

Example: Jane is the leader of the group and she is also its most talented member.

➤ Most collective nouns used as antecedents require singular pronouns. Use singular pronouns when the antecedent is a collective noun representing a group acting as a unit.

Example: The board of directors is meeting today to decide if it wants to pursue the matter further.

Use plural pronouns when the antecedent is a collective noun representing a group acting as individuals.

Example: The Baltimore Ravens played with such fire and passion as if it was their last game ever.

➤ Use both a masculine and feminine pronoun when the antecedent clearly is unknown and use a masculine and femine pronoun when using two singular pronouns of different genders.

Example: A manager should always treat his or her employees with respect.

Example: Each boy and girl should do his or her homework.

(Note: You can avoid the awkward *his* or *her* reference by making singular antecedents plural whenever possible. *Students* should bring *their* projects to class.)

The first layer of our writer's toolbox should be getting quite full at this point. We've detailed the parts of speech and started to present major grammatical errors found in writing. Before we begin stacking the box with more detailed tips and suggestions, we need to cover important information about parallelism, split infinitives and dangling modifiers.

Parallelism, Splint Infinitives and Dangling Modifiers

Concepts such as parallelism, splint infinitives and dangling modifiers are easy to understand and help writers avoid many common errors when constructing their prose. Parallel construction deals with expressing two or more ideas in parallel grammatical form. Single words need to be matched with single words and phrases with phrases. Parallel structure reflects the pattern created by a series emphasizing the similarities or differences among the items, which might be things, qualities, actions or ideas.

Example 1: My favorite foods are hamburgers, hot dogs, roast beef, thick crust pizza and pasta with red sauce.

Example 2: Amanda is caring, bright, intelligent and gifted.

Example 3: Lee likes to lift weights, run and bike.

Example 4: Adam likes sports that challenge him physically and games that challenge him mentally.

Each series is in perfect parallel construction composed of equivalent words: nouns in example 1, adjectives in example 2, verbs in example 3 and adjective clauses in example 4.

Study these tips to understand parallelism and splint infinitives.

➤ In a series linked by a coordinating conjunction, keep all elements in the same grammatical form.

Example: The puppies are tiny, clumsily bumping into each other and cute.

(This sentence is awkward because two elements are parallel one-word adjectives and one is a verb clause.)

Revised: The puppies are tiny, clumsy and cute.

➤ Don't mix verb forms in a series. Avoid, for instance, pairing a gerund (the *-ing* form of a verb used as a noun) and an infinitive (the simple or dictionary form of the verb such as *go* or the simple form preceded by *to* such as *to go*).

Example: Minnesota is a good place to visit in the winter if you like skiing and to skate.

(Here the word *skiing* is used as a gerund and *to skate* is used as an infinitive.)

Revised: Minnesota is a good place to visit in the winter if you like skiing and skating. *or*

Minnesota is a good place to visit in the winter if you like to ski and to skate.

➤ In a series linked by a correlative conjunction, keep all elements in the same grammatical form.

Example: Take my advice: try neither to be first nor last in completing the assignment.

Dangling Construction

When a sentence begins with a participle phrase, an infinitive phrase, a gerund phrase, or an elliptical clause (one in which essential words are missing), make sure that the phrase or clause logically agrees with the subject of the sentence. If it fails to logically agree with the subject of the sentence, the sentence construction dangles.

Misplaced Modifiers

Watch out for misplaced modifiers that create an unintended interpretation.

Example:

One of my students has been referred to a writing tutor with a serious writing problem. (Silly)

One of my students with a serious writing problem has been referred to a tutor. (Clear)

(The error occurs because *to be* follows the first part of the correlative conjunction but not the second.)

Revised: Take my advice: try to be neither first nor last in completing the assignment.

➤ Avoid omitting words that may confuse the reader.

Example: As Jon began to prepare dinner, he discovered the oven wasn't working properly.

(The demonstrative pronoun *that* is needed in the sentence. Jon didn't discover the oven; he discovered that it wasn't working properly.)

Revised: As Jon began to prepare dinner, he discovered that the oven wasn't working properly.

Split infinitives result when modifiers are placed between the parts of infinitives. Infinitives (the word *to* plus a verb) can be split only when the construction is needed to communicate the meaning of the sentence.

Example: We should try to if possible avoid eating too much fatty food on the trip.

(Here the writer splits the infinitive *to avoid* by adding the modifiers *if possible* between them.)

Revised: If possible, we should try to avoid eating too much fatty food on the trip.

Finally, dangling modifiers create problems for many writers. Modifiers are usually introductory word groups that suggest but do not name an actor. When a sentence opens with a modifier, readers expect the subject of the following clause to name the actor. If it doesn't, it results in a dangling modifier.

If we find a modifying phrase midway though a sentence, we assume that it modifies something just before or after it.

Example 1: Feeling a pain in his lower back, an aspirin seemed like a good idea.

(The introductory phrase cannot be said to modify aspirin. In fact, it modifies nothing at all.)

Revised: Feeling a pain in his lower back, he decided to take an aspirin.

Example 2: Upon seeing the barricade, our car screeched to a halt.

(The car cannot see or screech to a halt alone. This modifier is dangling.)

Revised: Upon seeing the barricade, I applied the brakes causing the car to screech to a halt.

By this point we should have mastered the basic elements of English grammar and identified common errors found in poor writing. However, avoid the tendency to rely on your memory for such questions. Good writers always turn to reference sources to double check their work and clarify writing questions. While our writing toolbox continues to fill, we need to remember that occasionally we should refer to the owner's manual for each tool if we question how to use it properly.

Blueprint: Forming Nouns

The following 12 rules from Jack E. Hulbert and Michele Goulet Miller, writing in *Effective English For Colleges*, should help you with forming nouns. Keep these neatly tucked away in your writing toolbox because they will be important in building your foundation.

1. Add -*s* to most nouns to form a plural.
   Example: Student (singular); Students (plural)

2. Add -*es* to nouns that end in -*s*, -*z*, -*ch* or -*sh*.
   Example: Class (singular); Classes (plural)
   Buzz (singular); Buzzes (plural)
   Fox (singular); Foxes (plural)

3. For nouns ending in -*y*, add -*s* if the y is preceded by a vowel. Change the *y* to *i* and add -*es* if the y is preceded by a consonant.
   Example: Journey (singular); Journeys (plural)
   Facility (singular); Facilities (plural)

   We find an exception to this rule when we use proper nouns (names) in the plural. Although most proper nouns are singular, exceptions occur such as in mountain ranges and island groups — the Rockies, the Andres and Falklands — that are plural. For personal names simply add an -*s*.

4. For most nouns ending in -*f* or -*fe*, change the -*f* or -*fe* to -*v* and add -*es*.
   Example: Leaf (singular); Leaves (plural)
   Wife (singular); Wives (plural)

   However, for a few nouns ending in -*f* we simply add -*s* such as belief (singular) and beliefs (plural). Also, several nouns ending in -*f* have two acceptable plural forms such as calf (singular) calves or calfs (plural). The best way to check the proper usage is to consult a current dictionary.

5. For nouns ending in -*o* add -*s* if the -*o* is preceded by a vowel.
   Example: Radio (singular); Radios (plural)

   However, exceptions to this rule exist. Add -*s* or -*es* to other nouns ending in -*o* to form the plural. Again, since a rule does not exist that applies to this usage, you should consult a current dictionary when in doubt.

   Example: Echo (singular); Echoes (plural)
   Piano (singular); Pianos (plural)

6. Some irregular nouns require you to change the spelling to form their plural.
   Example: Child (singular); Children (plural)
   Mouse (singular); Mice (plural)

7. A few nouns require you to use the same form for both the singular and plural.
   Example: Deer (singular); Deer (plural)
   Trout (singular); Trout (plural)

Forming Nouns (continued)

Consider these singular nouns and their plural forms:

Singular	Plural
Courtesy	Courtesies
Ego	Egos
Half	Halves
Inconsistency	Inconsistencies
Rodeo	Rodeos
Series	Series
Survey	Surveys
Valley	Valleys

8. Add *'s* to form the plural of letters, characters and words. (The *AP Stylebook* reminds us to add *s* for combinations of letters, such as ABCs.)
    Example: B (singular); B's
                I (singular); I's (plural, not Is)

    For figures such as 1990 simply add *-s* — 1990s unless clearly possessive.

9. The plural of Mr. is Messrs.; the plural of Mrs. is Mmes. Ms. does not have a plural. For several women listed in a series repeat Ms. before each name.

10. Make no changes in nouns that are already plural in form though singular in meaning.
    Example: Athletics; Ethics; News; Politics

11. The following sample of words retains their foreign plural forms. A few of these words also have acceptable English plural forms. This list is not complete so be sure to consult a dictionary when in doubt.

Singular	Plural
Analysis	Analyses
Appendix	Appendices or Appendixes
Curriculum	Curricula or Curriculums
Phenomenon	Phenomena
Stimulus	Stimuli
Thesis	Theses

12. For compound nouns (nouns composed of more than one word) whose elements are separate or whose elements are joined by hyphens, make the main noun plural.
    Example: Attorney General (singular); Attorneys General (plural)
                Editor in Chief (singular); Editors in Chief (plural)

                Member-At-Large (singular); Members-At-Large (plural)
                President-Elect (singular); Presidents-Elect (plural)

4.
Stylebooks

Is the faculty member who sponsors your local chapter of the Public Relations Student Society of America the advisor or adviser? Is she on first reference Jane Doe; Jane Doe, Ph.D.; Dr. Jane Doe; or Dr. Jane Doe, Ph.D.?

These and sundry other situations prompted writers to gather rules and guidelines to follow. Probably the best reason for the collection — other than the prevention of occasional fisticuffs among veteran newsroom staffers who couldn't agree on a minor point — is consistency of the writing for the readers' benefit.

Unfortunately, we have seen publications that used two or three differently worded versions for the same reference. For example, one newsletter for a large school district used Woodland Elementary School, Woodland School and Woodland elementary school within the same issue. Most readers, of course, probably realize what building is being discussed in such an article, but the professional quality of the writing is suspect with such incongruity.

If you're the public relations intern for that school district, how will you handle references to individual school buildings?

The most frequently used collection of rules is found in *The Associated Press Stylebook and Briefing on Media Law*. But many publications and organizations have their own set of guidelines available for use. Sometimes these larger booklets on writing standards will stand alone. Smaller manuals, on the other hand, usually are used to supplement AP's major stylebook.

Among several guidelines available on our office shelves that thoroughly cover the subject of spelling and style for their own publication staffs are: the *Los Angeles Times Stylebook*, the *Washington Post Deskbook on Style*, and *U.S. News & World Report Stylebook for Writers and Editors*.

Composing on a Computer

If you compose on a computer, be careful when editing your own work. Even experienced writers have a tendency to see what they intended to write rather than what is actually on the page. A neutral editor will help.

Most British newspapers — except for a few large ones that have their own — follow the guidelines of *The Times Style and Usage Guide*. The 2003 hardback version, published by HarperCollins, cost $19 in London in 2004. It's wise to follow British spellings (labour, publicise) for any releases sent to Great Britain or English-language newspapers in Canada. Keep in mind, of course, that many differences exist besides simple spelling. The word *scheme*, for example, has no negative or devious connotations in British parlance, unlike here in North America. And the noun *boot*, in England, has nothing to do with footwear. Always check with media in your intended markets so you can adapt your writing to their unique style when necessary.

Now let's get back to our (properly written) Woodland Elementary School example from above. Many organizations realize that their individual names, local addresses, titles and departments are unique. To provide various company writers with a grasp of specific citations, a business or organization may wish to produce its own handbook of recommended style. All staff members who contribute to various publications, therefore, can use the style manual to produce copy with similar spellings, abbreviations, titles, etc. And interns or new hires won't drive their supervisors crazy constantly asking sundry style questions.

The local manual might, for example, provide the official method to list officers and departments, even though that way violates what are typical style rules. A CEO may demand that his name be followed with a comma before Jr., as one possibility that ignores the Associated Press style. Despite violating two Associated Press rules, another executive might prefer that the name of her firm use the word Company spelled out, with a comma placed before Inc.

In these cases, it's wise for **internal** publication usage to follow what the boss demands, even if you wisely decide to change her preferences to accepted media style for **external** news releases.

As mentioned, almost all major media in North America today adhere to *The Associated Press Stylebook and Briefing on Media Law*. Therefore, it's imperative for public relations and business writers to be familiar with (if not master) contents of the latest version. There are helpful sections in the back on media law, business guidelines, sports guidelines and photo captions. Using correct style will build exceptional credibility with the media gatekeepers who decide the fate of your external public relations writing efforts. In fact, failure to follow media guidelines is one of the major reasons 90 percent of news releases wind up in the recycle bin, whether electronic or actual.

That new dictionary on your desk or in your computer may be a nice tool, but whenever it differs from AP, you'll want to follow the latter. For example, what a computer spellchecker approves could be considered a ghastly error by AP. Consider the following:

A spell Czech can dew a grate job most of the thyme. Butt eye can knot rely on it four all my miss steaks, oar I May bee inn big trouble.[1]

A busy news editor or producer will not take time — even if it were available — to correct style errors scattered throughout your release if you choose to ignore accepted journalism newswriting basics. Careless disregard of such standards may not be the most common reason for dumping media mailings into the office recycling box, but it undoubtedly ranks among the top three.

AP's stylebook (often correctly called "the journalist's bible") has evolved over the decades from the thin first edition in 1953 to the 400+ pages currently being produced. AP and the then-popular United Press International pooled their talents and opted for a common style in 1960. Today's expanded version first came out after two years of work in August 1977, which prompted a special 25th anniversary edition in 2002. Organized alphabetically for ease of use, it has undergone a new edition on average every nine months.

It's wise to pick up one of the latest editions, since new words are added and other terms may change in style usage. An Internet guide was first inserted into the stylebook in 2000. It reminds you to be consistent about the proper capitalization rules for Internet, intranet, World Wide Web and e-mail, among others.

A major change in the 2004 version was using numerals with ages for only humans and animals. So it's no longer an 8-year-old department, but an eight-year-old department. New entries for the 2003 edition included al-Qaida, Amber Alert, bioterrorism, Global Positioning System, ground zero, hillbilly, Saddam, special forces, and Ten Most Wanted Fugitives. Rather major changes from 2002 were using dad and mom in lowercase except for direct address, and spelling freelance and

Electronic Stylebook

"The Stylebook is now available in a variety of electronic formats. It continues to add entries that reflect the language of our fast-changing world. Truly, it is a tool now for wired editors as well as wire editors."

Tom Curley, president and CEO of AP, in the 2004 edition

teenage without a hyphen. So you can see the importance of getting the newest paperback for your external releases. AP also offers online as well as downloadable versions.

Louis Boccardi, AP president and CEO, wrote in the foreword of the 2002 printing:

> "The Stylebook has not only found its way into newsrooms round the world but has also become a fixture in journalism classes, public relations agencies, newsletter production houses, and wherever else people write about daily events, public affairs and other matters of public interest."

Boccardi acknowledges that differences of opinion will continue to be a sore spot for writers choosing — or condemned — to use the popular manual.

One prevalent example, among many, is that some writers often prefer to use the commonly known postal abbreviations for state names instead of the ones advocated by AP. Let's not even mention that eight states are never abbreviated by AP, even with a city. Our feeling is that AP would probably go along with the United States Postal Service decree if only people could remember how to abbreviate all those M states, such as Maine, Massachusetts, Michigan, Minnesota, Mississippi and Missouri. (As all law-abiding citizens know, of course, they are ME, MA, MI, MN, MS and MO.)

Even seasoned public relations practitioners — along with print journalists — still have to sneak a peek at their AP books, especially with yearly changes and new additions. But by having flipped through it so often, they are familiar with its contents and don't waste much precious time. Novices might complain about the difficulty in tracking down certain composition canons.

Let's say you're writing an advance release about a speaker, from whom you've received a biography. She lists her degrees as a B.A. and an M.S. Is that proper style? Where do you look?

- Education? Nothing.
- The initials B.A.? Nothing.
- M.S.? Nothing, but there's something about the courtesy title Ms. if that's ever necessary.
- Degrees? No, but there's a tip to see academic degrees.
- Abbreviations? No, but please notice the suggestion to look up academic degrees nearby.

Quotation Marks

If a quotation consists of more than one sentence without any interrupting elements, use quotation marks only at the beginning and at the end of the quotation. Do not put quotation marks around each sentence within the quotation.

New AP Entries

New entries in 2004 include:
- airfare (one word)
- ATM
- medevac

Other changes are:
- EU is acceptable without periods for the European Union.
- Ages always use numbers but now only for animate objects.
- Lowercase articles in foreign names: de, der, la, von, etc.
- The preferred AP term for Sept. 11 is now the commonly used 9/11 rather than 9-11.

• Academic degrees? Well, why not? Bingo. Here you'll find the correct usage rules detailing if, how, when and where you should write about such diplomas.

Now comes the hard part, however. Will you remember to look up academic degrees the next time the issue comes up (in three or four months) if you don't recall the rule in the first place? Good PR writers don't need to memorize all the stipulations about style, as long as they have ample hunting instincts when they pick up their stylebooks. Much of that will come with experience. Probably the most common investigations into the books are for questions about numbers, addresses, abbreviations and punctuation.

For numbers, AP's general guideline calls for numerals to be spelled out if they are nine or below. One common exception to try to remember is that figures are always used for ages of humans and animals (6-year-old twins), money (5 cents) and address numbers (7 Main St.).

Speaking of addresses, AP rules call for abbreviating Ave., Blvd. and St., but only when used with an actual address (77 Sunset Blvd.). All other such words (Drive, Road, Circle) are never abbreviated, with or without numbers.

AP cautions writers not to use too many abbreviations or acronyms that would confuse readers. Titles before names are usually abbreviated, but AP suggests you check its pages for courtesy titles, legislative titles, military titles and religious titles. Most months (all but March through July) are abbreviated, but only with a date: Nov. 22, 2006.

The best advice is to consider your style manuals your allies rather than your enemies in producing quality copy. The consistency in following the rules will make your prose easier to read, comprehend and even write.

Punctuation Matters

If the eight parts of speech (discussed back in chapter 3) provide the bricks we use to construct sentences, then the marks of punctuation are the mortar that holds the bricks together. Writers who fail to master the rules of punctuation often find that their prose appears as a loose collection of ideas that fails to convey the intended meaning.

Fortunately, the *Associated Press Stylebook* places a valuable punctuation guide near the back of its recent editions. The most frequent punctuation errors made by both student and professional writers in a nonscientific survey seem to be incorrect use of commas and hyphens. In a simple list, for example, AP cautions against using a comma before the "and." (Yes, there are exceptions.) When used, commas — as well as periods — always go **inside** the ending of quotation marks.

The biggest blunder about hyphens is their omission in compound modifiers, two or more words that describe another, such as "Dallas-based agency." (And yes, there are exceptions, such as for the word "very" and for adverbs ending in "ly.")

Commas

➤ Use commas in a sentence where two complete thoughts are separated by *and*, *but*, *or*, *yet*, *so*, *for*, *nor*.

Examples: Mr. Smith did not attend the meeting, nor did he send his report.

We believe you have good ideas, and the planning committee should consider using them.

➤ Set off an introductory dependent clause with commas.

Example: Before we can achieve our goal, we need to train diligently.

➤ Use commas between consecutive adjectives where the comma is really used instead of *and*.

Example: Bruno hated the dark, gloomy office.

➤ When the year follows the month and day use commas to set them off.

Example: On Jan. 30, 2006, I will receive my bonus check.

➤ When addressing someone directly use a comma for emphasis.

Example: Why don't you take some time off, Frank, and get some needed rest?

Semicolons

➤ When you have two independent clauses not separated by a coordinating conjunction use a semicolon.

    Example: The major league club made the playoffs; the minor league club came in last place.

➤ When a series of phrases that already contains commas gets confusing, then use semicolons.

    Example: The faculty came from a variety of schools: J.R. Andrasko, Georgia; Beth Hughes, Texas Tech; Ralph Darrow, Kent State; and Steve Kuhn, Western Michigan.

➤ Semicolons are necessary when using transitions such as *however*, *therefore* and *consequently* to separate two complete thoughts. Place the semicolon in front of the transition word and a comma immediately after the word.

    Example: Donald proved to be an excellent quarterback; however, he struggled with his academics.

Colons

➤ In formal letters use the colon following the salutation. *Note*: Use a comma in personal letters.

    Example: Dear Dr. Sandell:

➤ When a long list is being introduced in a sentence, you should use a colon rather than commas.

    Example: According to the district manager, we have two rules concerning customers: the customer is always right; if the customer is wrong, see the first rule.

➤ Colons are necessary when expressing a ratio.

    Example: 20:1

Apostrophes

➤ Apostrophes are necessary when showing possession. Follow this three-step rule for nouns:

    1. Write the base word. *Boy*

    2. Add the apostrophe. *Boy'*

    3. If no *-s* at the end of the word, add one. *Boy's*

➤ Avoid making errors with contractions.

    It's [Contraction for it is]

    Note: Never write *its'* since the pronoun *its* is already possessive. *It* never gets an apostrophe.

➤ When confusion results from making a single letter plural then an apostrophe is appropriate even though it is not possessive.

    Watch your p's and q's.

    But multiple letters (ABCs) need no apostrophe.

Quotation Marks

➤ When writing a quote from a speaker, use quote marks.

    Example:
    Maria said, "The company will begin production this fall."

➤ Quote marks either go inside or outside the final mark of punctuation.

    Follow these rules:

    1. Periods and commas go inside quotation marks.

    2. Colons and semicolons go outside quotation marks.

    3. Question marks and exclamation marks go either inside or outside, depending on the sentence. Consult your stylebook.

Dashes and Parentheses

➤ Use dashes when showing emphasis, indicating abrupt changes or when setting off information that explains a previous point. Dashes are more emphatic. They shout at you.

    Example:
    We need to build continuity — something we have not had here previously — if we are to build a winning team.

➤ Use parentheses in pairs when setting off nonessential material. They de-emphasize the information. Parentheses whisper at you.

    Example:
    The starting five (all under 24) is the youngest in the league.

Broadcast Guidelines Differ

Those who write for the electronic media must keep in mind that print style differs tremendously from broadcast style. For that reason, broadcast stylebooks are required to keep on track those who produce public service announcements, broadcast news releases or video news releases.

Just as in print, differences of opinion exist when writing copy for the ears. A common motto for broadcasters regarding abbreviations, for example, is "When in doubt, write it out." Public relations writers would be wise to familiarize themselves with their local stations' preferences in such matters.

"It is not considered a crime to break style for good reason," writes R.H. MacDonald in his *A Broadcast News Manual of Style*. "But to break style because of ignorance or carelessness is not easily forgiven. The writer who consistently misspells or ignores the conventions of page format is considered an unreliable coworker and a poor journalist."[3]

Although many styles exist because of the vast number of stations, the most common style followed would be that advocated in The *AP Broadcast News Handbook*, *A Broadcast News Manual of Style* or *Broadcast News Writing Stylebook*.

Fewer abbreviations are used in broadcast copy, for example, to avoid confusion for the broadcaster. But capitalizations are much more frequent so words will stand out easier for narration. Numbers are often written out all the way up to eleven (to avoid confusion with the Roman numeral II). Combinations are frequently used for larger amounts, such as 37-thousand dollars.

The 2001 AP broadcast version is a 476-page softbound issue. Not only does it contain A-to-Z writing and editing tips for electronic journalists, but it provides such advice as using microphones or sending news from the field back to the station.

Scriptwriters, on the other hand, typically follow guidelines adapted by the Writers Guild. Scripts can be informal, as if directed to a smaller audience. "Develop an ear for the simplicity which characterizes spoken conversation. Contractions and simplified word forms, for instance, lend informality to narrative copy."[4]

As in broadcast copy, the best editing process is to read what you have written aloud. If you stumble over your own words, chances are an announcer or a narrator will probably do the same thing on air. Tongue twisters are easier to identify and rectify when spoken, rather than when just written on a computer screen. (See chapter 7 for more tips about electronic news releases.)

Blueprint

Common Misused Phrases and Words

Below are a few writing miscues that frequently appear in print and on air, many of them made by seasoned scribes. Paying attention to these trouble spots now could save some problems in the future.

A While

Writers often misuse awhile and a while. Awhile is an adverb and a while combines an article with a noun.

In general, a while is preceded by for.

Example: Dave worked awhile.

Dave worked for a while.

Affect vs. Effect

As verbs, affect means "to influence" or "stir the emotions of" and effect means "to bring about," "to cause" or "to accomplish." Effect as a noun means "result."

Examples: The test will affect your final grade. (as a verb)

Julio will effect many changes in the program. (as a verb)

He miscalculated the effect of the potion. (as a noun)

All-Time Record

Redundant phrase. If it is a record it must be for all time.

All Together vs. Altogether

All together means "in a group." Altogether means "in all" or "on the whole" or "completely."

Alright

A common spelling error. The proper spelling is *all right*.

Among vs. Between

Between usually expresses a relationship between two people or objects. Among implies more than two.

Amount vs. Number

Avoid interchanging amount and number. If you can count the things being referred to, use *number*. If the reference is to a mass of something, use *amount*. *Example*: The amount of work done in the advertising club is in proportion to the number of students in its membership.

And/Or

Avoid using this slashed term. Often the word *or* will do.

Appraise vs. Apprise

Two words often confused. Appraise means "to set a price for." Apprise means "to inform" or "notify."

As

Avoid this sentence: "Thompson was appointed as chair of the department." Drop the word *as*; it's not necessary. "Thompson was appointed chair of the department."

Beside vs. Besides

Beside means "alongside" or "near." Besides means "in addition to."

Bimonthly

Bimonthly means "every other month" not "twice a month." Semi-monthly means "twice a month." Avoid the confusing bimonthly; instead use every other month.

Bring vs. Take

Both words imply motion and direction. Bring is used for carrying or leading a person or thing to the speaker. Take is used for direction away from the speaker.

Canvas vs. Canvass

Canvas is a closely woven cloth. Canvass is a verb meaning to solicit orders, opinions or votes.

Centers Around

Substandard term. Use centers on or revolves around.

Completely Destroyed

Guard against the redundancy of using completely in such examples.

Convince vs. Persuade

Use convince when you want to cause somebody to believe something and persuade when you want to induce someone to do something.

Disinterested vs. Uninterested

Disinterested means "impartial" or "unbiased." Uninterested means "lacking in interest."

Etc.

Avoid preceding etc. (et cetera) with and. It is redundant. Also, at least two items should precede etc. before using it.

Former

Watch errors such as this: "He was a former football player." Does this mean he is a football player once again? Instead use, "He is a former football player."

Headquarters

This noun takes both a singular and plural form. Therefore, use the appropriate verb to agree with your meaning.

Here's

A common error made by many writers is writing a sentence like this: "Here's several errors writers often make." The true subject in the sentence is errors and it is plural, yet the contraction "here's" indicates a singular verb. The sentence should begin "Here are...."

In Regards To

This is not only grammatically incorrect but also outdated. It should read in regard to, with regard to or as regards. Join modern writers and use regarding or concerning.

Individual

Individual refers to someone distinguished from others in a group because of special circumstances. Avoid writing: "Each individual is responsible for paying his or her cost of admission."

Innumerable vs. Numerous

These words are not synonymous. Innumerable means "too many to be counted." Numerous mean "many" or "very many" but still countable.

Into vs. In To

Into represents motion from outside to inside: "Dave walked into the garage." When the word *in* is used as an adverb, the word *to* should not be joined to it: "Dave went in to make a phone call."

It's vs. Its

Too many college-educated writers still make this fundamental error. It's refers to the contraction for "it is" or "it has." Its is a singular possessive pronoun. "The cat lost its toy mouse."

Irregardless

A substandard word. Use regardless.

Lead vs. Led

Use lead for present and future tenses. Use led for past and past-perfect tenses.

Lectern vs. Podium

Podium refers to the platform on which a speaker stands. The lectern is the stand on which the speaker rests "lecture" notes. The lectern is sometimes on a podium.

Less vs. Fewer

Use less for quantity (money) and fewer for number (dollars).

Lie vs. Lay

Try this tip from the editors of *Communication Briefings*: "When you mean recLIne use lie; when you mean pLAce use lay."

Luxuriant vs. Luxurious

Luxuriant means "growing in great abundance." Luxurious means "marked by luxury."

Masthead vs. Flag

A masthead refers to a box in a publication that contains names of staff, details of ownership, publication address, etc. Flag refers to the name of the publication displayed on the top of the front page. The flag is sometimes called the banner or nameplate.

Meaningful

Replace the substandard "It was a meaningful experience" with "It was a fruitful experience."

Media

Media is the plural of medium. Never use mediums or medias.

More Accurate

Accurate is an absolute; therefore, something cannot be more accurate.

More Preferable

Preferable means "more desirable." Something cannot be more, more desirable.

Myself

Avoid writing, "Bill gave the promotion to Jane and myself." It indicates that you don't know the difference between me and I. Instead, save *myself* for emphasis such as "I myself checked the house." Or use it to refer to another word in the sentence: "I hurt myself."

New Record

Naturally a record just set is new so avoid the obvious redundancy.

None

If it means no single one, it always takes a singular verb. "None of the tech writers was at the meeting." If the meaning is no two or no amount, use a plural verb. "None of the taxes have been paid."

People

According to the *AP Stylebook*, use people rather than persons in all plural uses.

Perspective vs. Prospective

Perspective refers to viewpoint or impression. Prospective means potential.

Phenomenon

Phenomenon is singular. Phenomena is plural.

Prior To

A pretentious, pompous term. Use before.

Proved vs. Proven

Proved is the preferred past participle of prove: "The bike has proved satisfactory." Use proven as an adjective: "He is a proven leader."

Sight vs. Site vs. Cite

Sight refers to vision. Site refers to a place. Cite is a verb meaning "to summon to appear in court" or "to quote."

Simple vs. Simplistic

The two words are not synonymous. Simple means "not complex." Simplistic means "oversimplified."

Than vs. Then

Than is a conjunction used in comparisons. "I enjoy watching football more than I enjoy watching baseball." Then is an adverb that denotes time. "I made breakfast then I went to the gym."

That, Which, Who, Whom

Use who and whom in referring to persons and to animals with a name. Use that and which in referring to inanimate objects and animals without a name.

Their, There, They're

Their is a plural possessive pronoun: "They crashed their new boat."

There is an adverb that indicates direction or place: "We shop there every Saturday." It's also used as a weak pronoun for impersonal communication when the real subject follows the verb: "There is much money to be made in the stock market."

They're is simply the contraction for they are: "They're coming tonight for pizza."

Toward vs. Towards

Both words are prepositions meaning "in the direction of." Towards is the preferred use by the British. Toward is the preferred use in North America, and more important, by AP.

Type

Type is a noun, not an adjective. You must include the word of between type and the noun that follows. "What type of player is the college's new basketball recruit?"

Unbeknownst

Unless you're British or really pompous, use the word "unknown."

Unique

Unique means "the only one of its kind." Don't use most unique, very unique or quite unique.

Who's vs. Whose

Who's, of course, is the contraction for who is. Whose is a possessive pronoun meaning "belonging to whom."

Who vs. Whom

Who is a subjective-case pronoun and used only for subjects and subject-complements. Whom is an objective-case pronoun and can be used only for objects. Who and whom appear primarily in subordinate clauses or in questions.

"The head coach, who is a former professional football player, works his players very hard." (The relative pronoun who refers to the head coach, a person.)

"The counselor whom I was assigned to was very helpful." (Whom is the object of the preposition to.)

Exasperating Style Situations

The following exercises will give you practice on avoiding some of the common errors that creep onto the pages of many writers. If you're confident about your grasp of AP style, try to make corrections the first time without using your style manual. There could be several errors per sentence. Then go back over the sentences — checking everything thoroughly with your stylebook — to see how well you did.

1. The six year old girl was born at 7:00 a.m. on the morning of June 8 in Houston, Tex.

2. Teen-agers can earn eight dollars an hour selling t-shirts on Monday.

3. The four women congratulated each other when the National Organization of Women voted 325-90 to okay the change.

4. The accident occured one half mile past the bridge when the car rolled onto it's side.

5. Erin said the company verbally insured the accuracy of their rain gage.

6. The 75 degree heat Mar. 6 set a new record for that day.

7. The university chapter hosted their first annual internet conference.

8. Reverend Al Jones will canoe down the Rio Grande River this Aug.

9. World-wide sales should be worth five to six million dollars.

10. She Xeroxed five copies of the Okla. zip codes before 12 noon.

Notes

[1] Randall W. Hines. "Writing for Public Relations," in Bruce J. Evensen, ed., *The Responsible Reporter*. Northport, AL: Vision Press, 1997.

[2] Norm Goldstein, ed. *The Associated Press Stylebook 2002 and Briefing on Media Law: With Internet Guide and Glossary*. New York, NY: The Associated Press, 2002.

[3] R.H. MacDonald. *A Broadcast News Manual of Style*. White Plains, NY: Longman, 1994.

[4] William J. Van Nostran. *The Scriptwriter's Handbook: Corporate and Educational Media Writing*. Newton, MA: Focal Press, 1996.

For Further Reading

Norm Goldstein, ed. *The Associated Press Stylebook 2004 and Briefing on Media Law*, New York, NY: The Associated Press, 2004.

Keith Leslie, ed. *Broadcast News Style Guide,* Broadcast News, 1997. [Broadcast News is a unit of the Canadian Press.]

R.H. MacDonald. *A Broadcast News Manual of Style*, Boston, MA: Addison-Wesley, 2002.

Robert A. Papper, ed. *Broadcast News Writing Stylebook*, Needham Heights, MA: Allyn & Bacon, 2001.

5.
Two Views of Leads

by Jack Gillespie

The hardest part of writing a news release is the lead — that first sentence that must grab readers' attention or you'll lose them. According to some experts, you have eight to 10 seconds to do the grabbing. And keep this in mind: as a public relations professional writing releases, you have a much more demanding audience whose attention you want — the editors and station managers who receive your releases. So the carefully crafted lead is vital.

You may already know that every lead must contain one or more of the traditional five W's and the H (Who, What, When, Where, Why and How). To that rule, add this: To be effective, a lead must be accurate, honest, brief, informative, clear, energetic and conversational. And here's another idea for you to ponder: All leads are either **direct** or **delayed**.

Look at any newspaper and you'll see mostly direct leads — those that hit you with the basics of the story up front. *Example*:

ALABASTER – The Alabaster University College of Medicine said yesterday it has hired a consulting firm to investigate the possibility of taking over financially troubled Clairvaux Hospital.

A delayed lead on the same article might read like this:

ALABASTER– People in the Lafayette neighborhood who depend on the emergency room at Clairvaux Hospital got some good news yesterday from the board of directors at Alabaster University College of Medicine.

For weeks, those living near the hospital have been concerned that the hospital might close its doors after 78 years.

But yesterday, the medical school's directors said they have hired a consulting firm to investigate the possibility of taking over the hospital.

Jack Gillespie, popular author and speaker, is former editor of Communication Briefings Ideas that Work. *He is Professor Emeritus at Rowan University.*

Two Views on Leads reprinted by permission of Jack Gillespie

Here's an example of a direct lead that starts with *who*:

PLUMVILLE, S.D. – Edward B. Carver, vice president and dean of the College of Plumville at Appleyard University, has resigned his administrative post to resume teaching at the Plumville campus.

The same article, with a delayed lead, might start:

PLUMVILLE, S.D. – When students at the College of Plumville at Appleyard University return to school in September, they won't find the dean in his office.

As you can see, the lead delays telling readers exactly what the article deals with. Its purpose: to intrigue readers and force them to continue reading. Here's another who lead from a standard, promotion release:

TARNISH – Russtea Copper Co.'s President Barney Burgundy has announced the promotion of James Shinn to supervisor of the firm's Salvage and Reclamation Division.

Besides being dull, the lead features the president rather than the person who got promoted. If you must write such a lead, at least feature the person promoted, not the one who announced it. However, you'll see lots of these backward leads on the pages of business publications. Chances are that editors switch some of them so all the leads won't look alike.

Some CEOs and other executives insist on having their name or the company's name featured and those writing the releases have little choice except to follow orders. If you find yourself in that situation, you'll have to decide if it will be possible to tactfully educate your boss or if you, too, will have to follow orders. Here's what a direct lead featuring the person promoted might say:

TARNISH – James Shinn has been promoted to supervisor of Russtea Copper Co.'s Salvage and Reclamation Division, President Barney Burgundy has announced.

At least the emphasis is where it belongs, but the lead still contains a problem. It uses the has announced trick. When you use the present perfect verb, formed with has or have, readers get no clue to the freshness of the news. To avoid that, use the past tense plus a time word. Say, for example, announced last week or announced today. It's more honest and readers know how fresh the news is. That aside, let's see what happens if we write a delayed lead that emphasizes the person who got promoted:

TARNISH – Jim Shinn remembers waiting with other salvage gang members each morning for the foreman to return from the supervisor's office with the day's work orders. He remembers it well because he did it for eight years.

Seven years ago, Shinn, as foreman, became the one who made the trip upstairs each morning.

But starting June 1, the foreman will come to see Shinn, who was promoted two weeks ago to supervisor of the (Russtea Copper Co.'s) Salvage and Reclamation Division.

(The firm's president,) Barney Burgundy, who announced the promotion yesterday, praised Shinn for his 15 years of service, saying …

(For an in-house publication, you could drop the company name and change "The firm's president" to "President.")

This version puts the emphasis on Shinn. In a few words, it shows him as someone who worked his way through the ranks. The emphasis is on the person, not the one who announced it. Burgundy doesn't show up until later. Although he decided on the promotion and announced it, he didn't do the work that brought the promotion. So feature the one who did do the work. Don't overlook the fact that you can load the release with Shinn's quotes and relate them to how he plans to operate as supervisor.

Let's look next at a release that starts with a *what* lead. The what in this lead is some new software. This is a version that might appear in an in-house publication, although with some minor changes, you could make it into a news release. But keep in mind that most editors won't care if your new software speeds billing. But they will likely be interested in how the new software will improve service to or cut costs for customers.

PLATEVILLE – New software recently installed in the billing department will speed up the monthly invoice process.

The Puppet 210X system purchased from the Abrakadabra Corp. in Meeshaw, Mich., has cut average billing time from two weeks to two days.

Jim Leeds, office manager, said the Puppet 210X allows sales offices to get their orders to the billing department more promptly.

"The old system," said Leeds, "was somewhat slow and hard to use. As a result, sales offices put off sending their orders in as long as they could, and we always got a big rush of orders during the last week of the month.

"That meant we had lulls in work in the first part of the month and then a lot of pressure on the staff near the end of the month.

"Now the work is spread out," he said, "and all that last-minute pressure has been eliminated."

Sentence Length

Strive for an average sentence length of about 17 words per sentence and an average paragraph length of 4–5 typed lines. However, a combination of short and long sentences and short and long paragraphs gives writing rhythm.

The release typically would go on to talk about savings, speedier service, etc., but you get the idea. But look what you might write — with a delayed lead — if you talk to the people who were under all that pressure. And keep in mind, if you were writing this for an in-house publication, your readers will certainly prefer to read about people rather than software.

PLATEVILLE – Laura Henders always dreaded the big rush during the last two weeks of the month.

Henders, who works in the billing department, described the huge rush of orders that typically arrived every day during those two weeks as a "mountainous headache."

"We literally typed until we dropped, trying to make the end-of-the-month deadline," said Henders.

Henders' colleague, Curt Evanston, said the worst part was the monthly eyestrain he suffered from looking at so many orders in a short time period. "I even gave up watching my favorite TV shows during that period," Evanston said.

But thanks to the department's new computer billing software, the mountainous headache looks more like a molehill and Evanston's eyes are no longer strained.

Jim Leeds, office manager, said the new system, unlike the old, is easy to use and allows all sales offices to send orders more promptly to the office at the time they are placed.

He said the Puppet 210X software, purchased from the Abrakadabra Corp. in Meeshaw, Mich., has cut average billing time from two weeks to two days.

(After quoting Leeds, go back to Henders and Evanston for more quotes. Result: The emphasis would be on people, not a machine.)

Even leads that feature *why* can be written as delayed leads. Here's one written in direct style:

MUGWUMP – Reduced enrollments will cut the staff of Mugwump High School next year, Superintendent Lawrence Bookthrower said yesterday.

The delayed version might say:

MUGWUMP – When Harvey History reports to school in September, a lot of student seats will be empty, and he won't have any trouble finding a spot for his car in the faculty parking lot.

The reason: Reduced enrollments will cut the staff of Mugwump High School next year.

Superintendent Lawrence Bookthrower said yesterday that he expects …

You might also try the delayed approach with a *how* lead. The direct version might say:

> WASHINGTON, D.C. – Using skills polished riding his father's farm tractor, a Texas boy yesterday won the National Spelling Bee.

The delayed version:

> WASHINGTON, D.C. – Entym Ology found plowing his father's Texas cornfields boring. To help pass the time, he memorized the correct spelling of 50 words each day.
>
> Yesterday, his scheme to relieve the monotony paid off when he won the National Spelling Bee.

Where and *when* leads, used less often than other types, may prove tougher to write in delayed style. In fact you usually won't want to write them as delayed leads. But it can be done. Here's a *when* lead in direct style.

> BOGOTA – Friday is the deadline for Mugwump Scholarship applications.

The delayed version:

> BOGOTA – If you expect to apply for a Mugwump Scholarship, you better do it in the next three days.

A *where* lead written direct:

> MAXWELL – Cooper and Vine streets will be the site of the new elementary school, the school board announced last night.

A delayed version of the school site lead:

> MAXWELL – The makeshift ballfield at Cooper and Vine will soon become an official playground, and everyone who goes to elementary school will have to play there.

Delayed lead caveats: Delayed leads won't work on every release. In fact, you should realize that when it comes to the kinds of releases you'll be sending, most editors prefer direct leads. Also, delayed leads can repel as well as attract. Some readers, conditioned by years of reading inverted-pyramid stories, still want the facts up front. They lose patience if they have to read all that "cute" stuff to get to the "news." Despite that, you should know how to write both kinds because you may often prefer to use delayed leads on articles in your in-house print and electronic publications.

Person (First, Second and Third)

Subjects and verbs must agree in both number (singular or plural) and in person (first person, second person and third person). *First person* refers to the person communicating the message. *Second person* refers to the person receiving the message. *Third person* refers to the person, place or thing being written about.

Next we'll look at several "standard" news stories, the kind you'll probably have to write either for the media or for an in-house publication. As we do, we'll examine ways to write them with either a direct or delayed lead.

Appointment/Hiring, Election, Promotion, Retirement

Here's a practical fact to keep in mind: The larger the news organization, the more likely the editors will prefer a direct lead and will use just the bare facts. In many cases, that will be the lead and perhaps the second paragraph. The reason: They just don't have the space to run lengthy stories about every person who gets appointed, elected, promoted or who retires.

What you'll usually see is one large section made up of one or two sentences about each appointment, election or promotion. The section will carry few stories about retirements unless the person is a key manager of a large organization. Smaller media outlets may want the longer version. So it's basic public relations: Get to know the media you deal with and what they want and don't want — and tailor your releases to match their wants.

That said, the four kinds of stories listed above remain standard fare for news releases or in-house publications. When you write one — with either a direct or delayed lead — it should answer some or all of these questions.

1. Who was elected, appointed, or promoted or who retired?
2. To what position was the person elected, promoted or appointed?
3. Who (or what group) elected, appointed or promoted the person?
4. When's the election, appointment, promotion or retirement effective?
5. If the person is retiring, will someone replace him or her? If so, who?
6. If applicable, what will the salary be?
7. Why was the person appointed, elected or promoted (new position, replacing someone, etc.)? A retirement release might also say why the person is retiring (age, by choice, sick of it all, etc.).

One-sentence graph

An occasional one-sentence paragraph works great as a transition or to create emphasis when surrounded by multi-sentence paragraphs.

8. What will the person do in the new post or in retirement? This is the place to use quotes from the person who will take the post or retire. In a promotion, appointment or retirement story, get quotes from the person's supervisor or other superior. In an election story, you might get quotes from the past president or the executive director of an organization or a board of directors.

9. What is the person's relevant background? This data should always go in reverse chronological order. Start with what the person has done lately and work your way back to the ancient stuff. This is done to make it easier to cut the story because of space limits.

Here's an example of an appointment/hiring story with a direct lead. Note that the story uses what is called an indefinite who or blind lead — meaning the lead doesn't name the person. You can use that lead when the person is not well known.

SMITHVILLE – A plant guard at the Smithville Manufacturing Co. has been appointed as the first full-time security coordinator for city schools, Superintendent Claude Quackenbush announced yesterday.

Alfred T. Kelly, 38, of Lincoln Avenue will take the $46,750-a-year post July 1.

Quackenbush said the school board has been concerned for some time about vandalism, thefts and break-ins at the various school buildings. He said damage and repairs cost the school system $96,000 last year.

The superintendent said he got the idea for the security post from the Brookdale City school system, which has a security force of several persons working in cooperation with police.

Quackenbush said Smithville can't afford a security force, but he suggested several months ago that the board hire one full-time person. He said the board studied the matter and recently authorized him to hire Kelly.

Kelly said he will contact people living near the schools and ask them to call him if they see suspicious activity around the school buildings. He said he will work closely with police.

Although Kelly is scheduled to work regular daytime hours, he said he will be on call during off-duty hours. He said he will check on the schools on a staggered time schedule.

Kelly has worked at Smithville Manufacturing for five years. Before taking that job, he was a city policeman for 10 years. He graduated from the State Police Training School and the Adams County Police Academy.

Before he joined the city police force, Kelly worked as a plant guard at Great Lakes Utilities. He has a law enforcement degree from Adams County College.

###

Bad news

A useful way to communicate bad news is to place it in an opening, weaker dependent clause followed by good news in a stronger independent clause.

Example: "Although profits are down, morale remains high."

You'll find a possible delayed lead in the third paragraph. It might read like this:

> SMITHVILLE – Thefts and damage repairs cost the city school system $96,000 last year, and the school board has decided to do something about it.
> Starting July 1, Alfred T. Kelly, a plant guard at the Smithville Manufacturing Co., will become the school district's first full-time security coordinator.

Award

The award story, with either a direct or delayed lead, should answer these questions:

1. Who or what got the award? You must consider what because awards sometimes go to organizations, corporations, buildings, etc.
2. What is the award called?
3. What was the award given for? Early in the release the reasons should be general. Specific actions that brought the award should appear later.
4. Who gave the award (sponsor)?
5. When was it given or when will it be given?
6. Who presented the award?
7. Where was it presented?
8. What is the person or group's relevant background (reverse chronological order)?
9. Who or what received the award before (optional)?

> CONTENTMENT, Maine – Woodcutter Inc. last night received the Corporate Stewardship Award from the Maine Society for Corporate Citizenship at the society's headquarters in Contentment.
> The newly established award recognizes one small, one medium and one large company that exemplify the highest ideals of corporate stewardship. Woodcutter received the award in the "Small Company" category.
> In presenting the award to Robert Right, Woodcutter's founder and president, George Noble, the society's executive director, cited Right and his firm for their total performance and contribution to economic, community and social progress.
> Noble also commended the firm for the proper use of the state's natural resources and for its commitment to uniting its ethical values and economic mission in lumber production.

"It's a great honor for me to accept this award on behalf of Woodcutter's employees and all of the partners that we work with every day," said Right.

"Woodcutter, along with all the award winners and nominees, represents the best of a business making a difference in its community," said Noble. "Woodcutter's leadership serves as an inspiration for others to follow."

The release covers almost all the basics outlined in the guidelines: who got the award, what it's called, reasons it was given, who gave it, when it was given, who presented it and where it was presented. You could add a bit more background about the company, but it's not absolutely necessary. Of course, the release says nothing about previous recipients because this was the first time it was given. Here's a possible delayed lead:

CONTENTMENT, Maine – When Robert Right first started working in Maine's timber industry 17 years ago, he vowed that he would he would always be a good steward of one of the state's most valuable resources.

The Maine Society for Corporate Citizenship last night recognized that commitment when it presented Right's Firm, Woodcutter Inc., with the society's first Corporate Stewardship Award.

The newly established award recognizes one small, one medium and one large company that exemplify the highest ideals of corporate stewardship. Woodcutter received the award in the "Small Company" category. The award ceremony was held at the society's headquarters in Contentment.

In presenting the award to Right, founder and president of Woodcutter, George Noble, the society's executive director, cited Right and his firm for their total performance and contribution to economic, community and social progress.

(From here, pick up the original at paragraph four.)

Coming Event

The main thing to remember about the coming event release is this: If you want people to attend something, you must tell them what it is, where it will take place, when it will be, who can attend and how much it will cost, if anything. Also, if the event is free, you should feature that point early in the release.

If the event has an admission charge, you can put the price in the release, but some editors will chop it because they may feel you should buy an ad. If you know from experience that an editor will cut the ticket price, you could instead include a phone number for people to call about ticket information. Most editors can live with that. If you're not sure what to do, put the ticket price near the end of the release. Then, without too much revision, editors can cut that information if they want to. Note: Most publications will leave the price in if the group is a non-profit or the event is for a worthy cause.

A coming event release needs to stress some benefit to readers. It must somehow entice them to attend the event. Granted, some people will be inclined to attend even before they read the release, but it's the others you must try to reach. Whatever event you're writing about, look for the hook. It's always there somewhere. Here's a short example that uses *free* as the hook.

HUMBART – A free multimedia show titled "Scotland" will be shown at the Osage County College Langdon Center Wednesday, Sept. 28, at 8 p.m.
Sponsored by the college and the Humbart Photographic Society, the show will use slides, film and sound to feature the pageantry, people and places of Scotland.

The "free" aspect might work to entice some to attend, or you could stress the show's content:

HUMBART – If you want to learn about Scotland's pageantry, people and places, you should attend a free multimedia show at the Osage County College Langdon Center Wednesday, Sept. 28, at 8 p.m.
The show, titled "Scotland," is sponsored by the college and the Humbart Photographic Society.

Note that both versions contain essential information you must include in any coming event release: the kind of event and the cost, place, day, date and time. Here's a somewhat longer example that uses a direct lead.

DELIRIOUS, N.C. – A conference to explore the future of public affairs reporting will be held Oct. 4-5 at the Lumbago University School of Journalism in Delirious.
The conference, "Reporting Public Affairs in the Year 2025," will bring together public affairs reporters and media analysts to discuss ways in which traditional and new media will report public affairs, what resources public affairs reporters can expect to have, what readers and viewers will be like in 2025 and freedom of the press in the next part of the 21st century.
A grant from the Cropwell Foundation will underwrite the conference.
"It should be a skull session that addresses how public affairs reporters will be doing their jobs in 2025 and beyond," said Harry Hyphen, a Lumbago journalism professor.

The symposium will be held at LU's Gutenberg Center and will be open to the public.

Assistant Professor Thomas Dash will coordinate the program. His address: School of Journalism, 242 W. 18th St., Lumbago, NC 28555. Phone: 910-555-6281.

The release contains some problems. "Open to the public" should appear earlier. Of course, even though the program is open to the public, not that many average citizens are thirsting to find out the future of public affairs reporting. So from the outset, you're dealing with a topic that likely has a limited audience of academics, editors and reporters who will trudge to LU to get the latest scoop. That fact alone should determine what publications — print or electronic — it goes to. This may well be a release that you don't send to the general media but to those that you know will reach the intended audience. Note: That should be true of all releases.

The writer also tried to squeeze too much into the second paragraph. That you could forgive, but not the hard-to-follow 62-word sentence. Those problems aside, here's a delayed lead that might prove more enticing.

DELIRIOUS, N.C. – Will readers and viewers in 2025 and beyond be the same as today? Will we still have the same freedom of the press 20 years from now?

You'll hear some expert opinions on these questions if you attend "Reporting Public Affairs in the Year 2025," a conference that's open to the public Oct. 4-5 at the Lumbago University School of Journalism in Delirious.

In addition to tackling those questions, reporters and media analysts will talk about the future of public affairs reporting.

A Cropwell Foundation grant will pay for the program

"It should be a skull session that addresses how public affairs reporters will be doing their jobs in 2025 and beyond," said Harry Hyphen, a Lumbago journalism professor.

To register, contact Assistant Professor Thomas Dash. His address: School of Journalism, 242 W. 18th St., Lumbago, NC 28555. Phone: 910-555-6281.

Some who read the questions in the lead just might say, "Yes, I would like the answers to those questions. And it is open to the public, and it says the Cropwell Foundation is paying for it, so it won't cost me anything to attend." Of course, you can't be sure of that, but the enticement factor is about as good as it can be given the limited appeal of the topic.

Also note that "open to the public" appears early in the

release. And the second version doesn't say "a grant will underwrite." It's clearer to say they'll pay for it. It also uses the phrase
"to register" instead of the fuzzy "will coordinate the program."

Report, Survey, Poll or Study

You may have to write articles based on the results of a report,
survey, poll or study. Such stories demand that you carefully
examine the results and digest them into clear terms. No matter what kind of lead you use, include these elements:

1. Title of the report, survey, poll or study.
2. Author or authors of the report, survey, poll or study.
3. Sponsoring agency, group, etc., if any.
4. Reason or reasons for the report, survey, poll or study.
   You may not need this in every article.
5. Main points of the report, survey, poll or study. Use a mix
   of direct quotes and paraphrased material. And keep in
   mind that research shows direct quotes make articles
   more readable.
6. The accuracy of a poll, usually stated as plus or minus a
   certain percentage.
7. If copies are available, explain how readers can get them
   and list the cost, if any.

Whether you choose a direct or delayed lead, you must base
the lead on some dramatic or interesting point from the document. The sponsor or publisher, the report, survey, poll or study
title and the author or authors should appear early in the story.

Another important element of this kind of article is attribution. You must attribute every statement to either the document
or the author or authors. Some lazy writers don't always do
this, but you should. You should vary the location of the attribution. You can place it at the beginning, middle or end of a statement, but don't put it in the same place all the time. Move it
around to avoid monotony.

One other point: You can use either past or present tense for
the statements you attribute. For example, use said or says,
maintained or maintains. Whichever you choose, use the same
tense throughout the article. Here's an example:

ATLANTA – In the next 10 years, shortages of engineers
and other high technology graduates are likely to persist in

Short course on transitions

Note how the release uses transitions, those words and phrases that help tie paragraphs together and move readers through a story. Note, for example, mathematics in paragraphs 3, 4, 5 and 7 and trigonometry and calculus in paragraph 6. Engineer, engineers and engineering help connect other paragraphs. Other transitional words and phrases — *but, in addition, in, indeed, another* and *in short* — also help move readers smoothly from one paragraph to the next.

the nation, according to a report from the National Education Board.

The report, "Engineering and High Tech Worker Shortages: The Mathematics Connection," was prepared by NEB economist Ludwig Trig.

Trig says the present low level of participation in high school math courses represents "a fundamental constraint" on rapid expansion of high technology workers.

"To a considerable extent," the report maintains, "the production of engineers, mathematicians, physical scientists and computer programmers depends on a strong background in mathematics."

But, the report continues, women and minorities, who helped create the boom in higher education enrollments, have not been inclined to study mathematics in either high school or college.

The report also notes that several states estimate that only one out of 10 of their recent high school graduates has taken trigonometry, the essential pre-calculus course.

In addition, many school districts are plagued by shortages of mathematics teachers, in part because of the many better-paying opportunities for mathematics graduates elsewhere in the job market, the report says.

"In the engineering field," Trig says, "where supply and demand tended to roller coaster over the years, enrollments are surging again."

Many public engineering schools, he says, are already at peak capacity, and it is difficult to shift faculty and other resources to high-demand programs.

"Indeed," Trig says, "faculty shortages in engineering are already reported, and the starting salaries commanded by engineers divert many students from graduate study."

In short, notes Trig, without deliberate action at all educational levels, if present trends are allowed to continue, then a serious shortage of high-technology workers may occur.

Review copies of the report are available from NEB information officer Elizabeth Sanderson at 407-876-9244. The general public may purchase the report by sending $2 to NEB, 185 Seventh St., N.W., Atlanta, Ga. 30313.

The lead on that story would likely work well. It follows the guideline that suggests you pick some dramatic or interesting point from the document and use it as a lead. A different approach might work this way:

ATLANTA – Over the next 10 years, U.S. firms won't find it any easier than they do now to find engineers and other high technology graduates.

It's not that much different, but it could makes readers ask,

"Why?" That just might entice more people to continue reading to get the answer.

Taking a Stand on an Issue

Another standard news release deals with a stand taken by a firm or organization on an issue. Typically, this kind of article gets written in response to some action by a government agency, but other situations may also generate such a release. For example, a company or a union might issue a statement about a position on contract negotiations or a pending strike. Some guidelines:

1. Identify the firm, group or agency taking the stand early in the release.

2. Summarize the organization position early in the release, usually with one word, such as opposes, supports, criticized, defended, favors, backs, praised, etc.

3. Use statements from an official of the firm or organization to list objections or approvals. If a statement has been issued, quote from the statement.

4. Attribute all statements.

5. Vary the attribution location.

6. If the firm or organization has acted on the issue or plans to, tell readers about it.

Here's an example describing a stand taken by an organization:

MINNEAPOLIS – The Minnesota Business and Industry Association opposes the proposed Bottle Bill that would make most glass containers in the state the deposit-return type, the group's executive director said today.

"According to our surveys," said the director, Sandy Greenglass, "passage of this bill would, in the long run, cut at least 4,500 jobs in the glass industry alone."

She said the association also has discovered that statewide recycling efforts have already created a used-glass glut.

"In Minneapolis," she said, "the city has stockpiled 680 tons of crushed glass and can't find a taker because glass plants already have more than they can use."

The bill, A-391, got Assembly approval two weeks ago. A Senate committee changed the bill just a bit last week, and the measure faces a vote by the full Senate Friday.

Greenglass also said her group feels the legislators have failed to properly consider what the lost jobs will mean to the state.

"The Legislature should realize that putting 4,500 people out of work could affect property tax payments, reduce sales tax revenue and boost the cost for unemployment benefits," she said.

Greenglass stressed that the association agrees the bill could do much to reduce the amount of waste sent to landfills and thus allow them to stay open longer.

"But," she noted, "we have yet to see any exact figures to show the effect on landfills. Before any vote is taken, we think the bill's sponsors should consider funding a study to provide those numbers."

Greenglass said the association's legislative liaisons have buttonholed dozens of legislators and called or e-mailed many others in the past two weeks.

"Over the next few days," she said, "we'll redouble our efforts to convince the Senate to postpone the vote."

She stressed that the association seeks to postpone the vote rather than trying to defeat the measure because the group agrees with many of the basic environmental concerns the bill addresses.

"All we're asking," said Greenglass, "is that the Legislature give this bill more thought and seek more facts before they vote."

Note: If you write a release such as this and send it to the media, don't be surprised if the outlet that uses it includes the other side of the story. In this case, that would be reactions from legislators. That's just good journalism — presenting both sides of an issue. Even if they do that, you've still done what you set out to do: You got the media to tell your side of the story. Of course, if you've established the kind of media contacts you should have, you may not have to write the release. Instead, you may be able to call a reporter and get the reporter to listen to your story. Here's a possible delayed lead for the same story:

MINNEAPOLIS – Would you pay 10 cents more for a bottle of beer if it meant you could get part of your dime back when you returned the bottle? And would you pay the extra dime if it also meant your local landfill could operate longer?

Maybe you would, but would you do it if it meant your neighbor might lose his job?

According to the Minnesota Business and Industry Association, 4,500 of your neighbors could be out of work if the state Senate approves the Bottle Bill this Friday.

The association's director, Sandy Greenglass, said today the possible job losses are only one reason the group opposes the bill that would make most glass-containers in the state the deposit return type.

You could continue this version by picking up the original at the third paragraph. Note that all paragraphs in the original except paragraph five include attribution. That paragraph needs no attribution because it's not an opinion. It's merely a statement of fact — background information to help readers understand the story. It bears repeating that research shows that direct quotes make a story more readable. The story also makes clear what action the group has taken or will take.

Program or Project

You also may have to write a release about a company or organization program or project. It could be about one that's already in place or one that will soon start. An interview works well for this kind of article. Just talk to those involved and let them describe the activity. As with any interview, you must ask the right questions. Some guidelines:

1. **Before** the interview, read all the background material you can find.

2. **List** at least 20 questions you want to ask. Mark those you consider most vital with an asterisk or other symbol and ask them first. That way, if the interview is cut short, you'll have the important information.

3. **Don't** ask questions that an interviewee can answer with "Yes" or "No." If you do, it will be a short and uninformative interview. Some basic questions you might ask:

   A. When did the program or project start or when will it start?

   B. Why did the program or project start or why will it start? (The purpose.)

   C. How long will the program or project last?

   D. Who's involved in the program, both those running it and those taking part?

   E. How much will the project cost and where is the money coming from? (Usually when taxpayer or donor dollars are involved.)

   F. Do you use or will you use any special or unusual equipment in the program?

   G. What do you expect to accomplish with this program or project?

   H. What problems have you encountered and how have you dealt with them?

   I. How will you evaluate the program?

4. **When** you write the release, use a mix of paraphrased material and direct quotes.

5. **Attribute** all statements you get from those you interview and vary the location of the attribution.

6. **Use** background information — statements you can add from your knowledge or that you have researched — to help readers understand. Such statements must be matters of fact, not opinion. As such, they may not require attribution unless they come from a source that you cite as an authority or expert on the subject.

Here's an example about a project:

SUTURE – "Our goal has always been to offer the best and most technologically advanced health-care treatment to the patients in our communities."

And to that end, said James X. Ray, Painlys Hospital's president and CEO, the hospital has invested $8.2 million in its latest project, the Cardiovascular Center.

"The center," he said, "at Lancet Drive and Gauze Lane, will open June 15 and will integrate highly skilled nurses, technicians and cardiovascular specialists with the most advanced technology."

Ray said cardiologists from Hale Cardiac Care at Hearty University Medical Center will provide low-risk catheterization services at the center. That means, he said, that patients will no longer have to travel 30 miles to the university to get the care they need.

"Along with the low-risk catheterization lab," Ray said, "the new facility includes a state-of-the-art, $1.4 million MRI, an angiography suite, a digital ultrasound, a vascular lab and cardiac noninvasive testing services."

The MRI price tag may seem high, but the hospital will also use it for emergency patients, inpatients and outpatients, Ray said.

According to Ray, the top floor of the 28,000-square-foot building will house the backup for the hospital's main computer system.

"About $6 million of the cost for the center will come from the hospital's building fund, money donated over the last five years by area residents," Ray noted, "and the rest will come from a federal/state grant program."

Painlys now offers more than 40 medical and surgical specialties, over 300 of the region's finest doctors, an outstanding nursing staff and more than 1,500 employees who are dedicated to serving our area residents, he added.

"Last year," Ray said, "Painlys provided care for more than 100,000 patients, delivered more than 1,600 babies, and admitted over 33,000 patients through its emergency department."

Note the "commercial" for the hospital in the last two paragraphs. It's perfectly acceptable to add something about your organization at the end of a news release. Some editors will welcome it and some will cut it. That's why you should always put it at the end. Here's a possible delayed lead:

SUTURE – Starting June 15, if you or a family member needs the latest in care for a heart problem, you won't have to drive 30 miles to Hearty University.

That's because starting on that date, cardiologists from Hale Cardiac Care at Hearty's medical center will provide the services you need at Painlys Hospital's new $8.2 million Cardiovascular Center at Lancet Drive and Gauze Lane.

"The center," said James X. Ray, Painlys Hospital's president and CEO, "will integrate highly skilled nurses, technicians and cardiovascular specialists with the most advanced technology."

Along with a low-risk catheterization lab, Ray said the new facility includes a state-of-the-art, $1.4 million MRI, an angiography suite, a digital ultrasound, a vascular lab and cardiac noninvasive testing services.

(From there, you could pick up the rest of the release starting with paragraph six.) Here's another example about a school district program:

WEIGHOUT TWP. – "Weighout Township families are aware of the importance of preschool learning."

That's the opinion of Loretta Markham, communication/language arts coordinator for the township's public schools.

She said she bases her statement on data gathered from tests conducted in each of the district's five elementary schools last May. The tests will be given again this May to incoming kindergarten pupils.

"Last May was the first time we tested incoming kindergarten pupils," said Markham. "The tests were in addition to regular registration procedures."

The district uses the nationally validated test "Let's Get Ready for Kindergarten."

"Naturally, we found the expected individual differences between children," she said. "However, when we looked at the districtwide results from over 400 pupils, we found that achievement reflects a positive learning environment in their homes."

According to Markham, most members of the current kindergarten class gave correct responses when they counted objects, named the primary colors, identified single-digit numbers, printed their first name, recited the alphabet and numbers sequentially, and recognized letters of the alphabet.

"Surprisingly, many children had difficulty with home information which relates directly to their safety," said

Markham. "Pupils had trouble with their own first name; their parents' full names, and their phone numbers and addresses."

Markham said parents should not be concerned about children who have not yet mastered the skills in which many youngsters showed success.

"At this age," she said, "youngsters show very uneven skill development. We expect this, and our program is planned to handle individual differences."

She said some children will be learning these skills well into the first grade.

"At the same time," Markham pointed out, "if I were a parent, I would be asking myself some important questions, such as: Do I read to my child daily? Do I answer my child's questions about numbers, letters and words? Do I talk and listen to my child?"

As you can see, the story allows Markham to do all the talking and her comments accurately describe the program. The story uses proper attribution and varies the location of "Markham said," "she said," etc. The last sentence of paragraph three and all of paragraph five qualify as background and need no attribution, but you could attribute them to Markham if you wanted to.

Note the direct quote lead. It works because it's short. In fact, you should never use a long, involved direct quote as a lead. It tends to confuse readers and may make them decide the article will be too much trouble to read. Remember, you have only eight to 10 seconds to grab their attention.

For a more delayed lead, you also could start this story in reverse by using some of the quote in the last paragraph:

WEIGHOUT TWP. – Do you read to your child daily? Do you answer your child's questions about numbers, letters and words?

If you said "No" to these questions, it could mean your child will have trouble with the test the school district will give to all incoming kindergarten pupils in May.

But Loretta Markham, communication/language arts coordinator for the township's public schools, says parents should not be concerned about children who have not yet mastered the skills in which many youngsters showed success.

"At this age," she said, "youngsters show very uneven skill development. We expect this, and our program is planned to handle individual differences."

She said some children will be learning these skills well into the first grade.

Markham also said data gathered from the same test given last year in the district's five elementary schools convinced her that Weighout Township families are aware of the importance of preschool learning.

You could finish the story by adding paragraphs five through eight of the original. Note that the second version starts on what might be seen as a negative view. That's why it's important to come in fast in the third paragraph with the soothing statement that tells parents not to be overly concerned. The word but provides the needed transition from the negative to the positive. Also note that the soothing continues in paragraphs four through six.

Announcing/Selling a Product or Service

Whether you're merely announcing — or trying to sell — a product or service in a news release, follow three principles: complete, interesting, brief. Some guidelines on what to include:

1. Name and description.

2. Who makes it or offers it?

3. What's it for? What does it do and how does it do it?

4. What's the benefit? You must clearly state the benefits in terms of how its specific features work.

5. How does it rate against a competing product or service? Is it improved, better, faster, etc? Don't say this unless you're absolutely sure that your product or service is improved or better or faster than the competition. In short, follow this two-word guideline: no hype. Go easy on the adjectives and keep this thought in mind: How many times each year have you seen or heard "The best movie of the year"? Only one can be the best. And in any case, the constant use of the expression renders it meaningless.

6. What does it cost and how do I get it if I want it? A few editors and station mangers still view releases with this information as ads in disguise and may refuse to use them. But including the information is a must for publications that you know review new products or services. Again, as noted earlier, it's Public Relations 101. You have to know what they want or will accept. Just blanketing the media with a one-size-fits-all release and hoping for a hit is not the way to get the coverage you want.

In most cases, you'll probably find that newspapers and electronic media are probably the least likely to run these kinds of releases, except for those that regularly review new products, usually in their business sections. Your best bet for these releases are trade newsletters and magazines — print and electronic — whose editors will welcome the releases because it's something their readers want to know about. Many of these publications regularly run such reviews.

To attribute or not to attribute? Many releases of this kind include no attribution, and that's fine. Of course, some do carry attribution. It usually depends on the product or service. In some cases, attribution helps because it adds credibility to what's being said about the product or service. So the answer to the question is do what you think is best in each situation. Here's a release about a new air purifier that includes attribution but could work just as well without it:

> KLEEN, Neb. – A new electronic air purifier from the Breeze Corp., the Humdinger 404, will reach stores and on-line sites early next month.
>
> The Humdinger is made especially for cleaning a larger area than any model now on the market, according to Frank Furter, Breeze Corp. marketing director.
>
> "All the purifiers now available," Furter said, "will clean no more than 500 square feet, but the Humdinger will handle 1,000."
>
> Furter noted that despite cleaning a larger area, the Humdinger uses the same amount of electricity as a 40-watt light bulb, while every other machine on the market uses the equivalent of a 60-watt bulb.
>
> Among the many other features, Furter said, are a super quiet fan that cleans the air twice as fast as other leading purifiers and an ultraviolet light that kills bacteria, mold and other pollutants.
>
> Like the firm's earlier models, the Humdinger has a permanent filter that can be wiped clean with a special cloth that comes with the machine, Furter added.
>
> The Humdinger will sell for about $300, Furter said, and will soon be available in all major stores and at their online sites.
>
> Breeze Corp. was established 37 years ago and is a leading manufacturer of heating, cooling and air purification systems. For more information about the Humdinger and the firm's other products, visit its Web site at breezecorp.com or call (888) 777-8777.

A check of the guidelines shows that the writer names and describes the product and answers all the questions listed in 2

There is…There are

Avoid beginning sentences with the phrases *There is…*, *There are…*, or *There was*. It signals weak construction. Recast the sentence and make it more active.

through 6. Moreover, the release contains no hype. It would be easy to describe the purifier as "revolutionary," "state-of-the-art" or even "incredible." Instead, the writer makes the point about how good the machine is by saying that it cleans a larger area, uses less electricity and cleans the air faster than other purifiers. The release lists the cost and tells where it will be available. Note the last paragraph. That's typical for this kind of release and it's where it belongs — at the end. Here's a possible delayed lead or the same release, but keep in mind that you'll need to know which media outlets will accept delayed-lead versions.

> KLEEN, Neb. – You've put off buying an electronic air purifier because you need one that will clean a larger area. You also want one that works faster and uses less electricity than current models.
>
> Well, your wait will be over early next month when the Breeze Corp.'s new Humdinger 404 will become available in stores and at online sites.
>
> "All the purifiers now available," said Frank Furter, Breeze Corp. marketing director, "will clean no more than 500 square feet, but the Humdinger will handle 1,000."

(From this point, just add the original release starting with the fourth paragraph.) Here's an example of a release announcing a service:

> HELPFUL, Iowa – "If you're caught short by unexpected staffing needs or the loss of a key employee," says Arturo Antidolorifico, CEO of FlexiSource, "you need help fast."
>
> FlexiSource, a small firm that specializes in both outsourcing and insourcing of jobs, can give you what you need, Antidolorifico said, because it can move faster than a big company and maintains closer personal relationships with the organizations it serves.
>
> One service the firm offers is finding people to work for a company or organization on a contract basis. These self-employed workers may work inside or outside of a customer's location, at a number of locations where assignments need to be done or in their own facilities.
>
> These contract employees can work on a long- or short-term basis. Some examples: service technicians, interim executives, project managers and programmers.
>
> FlexiSource's insourcing supplies employees who work inside an organization's workplace but are actually employees of an outside company.
>
> The workers perform in what some call a "seamless" or "transparent" environment. If you don't realize they actually work for another company, you would believe they are

Use Strong Nouns and Verbs

Avoid using too many adjectives and adverbs. Good writers get the job done with strong nouns and verbs.

employees of the host organization.

This insourcing service works well for human resource services, staffing, training and development, information technology, logistics, and maintenance services. Companies that have used the service have been able to reduce their payroll, increase accountability and still keep the functions together in one work area.

FlexiSource also provides the typical service that supplies temporary workers to an employer when they are needed.

The company has a top reputation in the industry for how fast it can provide a flexible workforce to meet changing needs. For more information about its services, visit flexisource.com or call (888) 234-5678.

The release follows the guidelines reasonably well. It describes the various services. It explains what the services can do for you, although it doesn't say how the company does what it does. But that's not really necessary. Benefits, rather than being spelled out, are implied in the lead and the second paragraph. But that also works.

It doesn't say a lot about how the service rates against competitors except to note that because it's small, it can move faster than a big company and maintains closer relationships with those it serves. That's fine because it certainly avoids any hyping of the services. Note that the release mentions no cost figures, and that's appropriate in this case. Cost will depend on how many people a firm needs and for how long so they'll differ for each one. Here's a possible delayed approach to the same story:

HELPFUL, Iowa – Do staffing headaches plague you? Are you frustrated by the pain of losing key employees just as you need every staff member you've got?

If so, you'll find the relief you need with FlexiSource, a small firm that specializes in both the outsourcing and insourcing of jobs.

FlexiSource can ease your pain, said Arturo Antidolorifico, FlexiSource CEO, because it can move faster than a big company and maintains closer personal relationships with the organizations it serves.

(From here, pick up the original at paragraph three.)

Here's a related but slightly different release — one that announces publication of a book, pamphlet, etc. The release should include these basics:

1. Publication title.

2. Author or authors.

3. Publisher.

4. Contents (general and specific).

5. Number of pages.

6. Hardcover, paperback and tape or CD versions, if any.

7. Cost (not for every publication).

8. Where to get it.

Too many of these releases start this way:

> WASHINGTON, D.C. – The Commission of School Attorneys, a component of the National School Association, has announced publication of its revised and expanded edition of "School Law for Beginners."

> WASHINGTON, D.C. – The Council for Education today announced its latest book, "How History Was Made," by James Olden and George Past.

Both leads force readers to wade through a lot of *who* before they finally get to *what*, and it's the *what* that the lead should feature, not the *who*. In the first lead, we again see the "has announced" trick making it impossible to know how fresh this news is. The second at least uses "today." Both examples offer some basic data but do nothing to excite interest in the publication.

Here's a better example:

> OTTAWA – Roberta Trouncer can put you on the right track to overcome writer's block, the obstacle that often frustrates writers of any age or profession.
>
> Trouncer knows that this frustrating feeling can dampen or even halt the efforts of a freelance writer struggling against a deadline or the business executive writing a major report.
>
> In her latest book, "Right-Brain Writing," Trouncer offers practical tips to beat the block by relying more on the right side of your brain.
>
> She explains — and proves with some strong evidence — how increasing right-brain activity can boost your creativity, innovation and productivity.
>
> Specific techniques and easy-to-follow directions in the 242-page book will show you how to refocus your right brain to jump-start your creativity.
>
> The book, published by Power Publishers in Ottawa, also features advice from famous writers, including Barbara Blank, Hubert Harried and Alexander Anxious.
>
> "Right-Brain Writing" will be available in November on amazon.com and in major bookstores.

Points to note: The lead speaks directly to you, and the rest of the release maintains the second-person approach. The appeal is to more than one audience — "writers of any age or profession" and "the freelance writer" or "the business executive." The writer subtly lists the number of pages in paragraph five, and the publisher appears in paragraph six.

This is one of those times when it doesn't pay to list the cost because the release is not trying to sell the publication directly — just letting people know it's coming. Also, book prices vary widely at online sites and in U.S. and Canadian bookstores. But if you were trying to get people to order, for example, "School Law for Beginners" directly from your organization, you would note costs and ordering information.

One other note: You could add a blurb about the author at the end of the release. It would most likely say what other books the author has written along with any relevant background. In Trouncer's case you could list any reporting or editing positions she held. By putting this information at the end, you leave it up to editors to include it or cut it.

Here's a possible delayed lead for the book announcement:

OTTAWA – Late on Wednesday afternoon, your boss told you to have your sales report on her desk by 9 a.m.

Now it's 2 p.m. on Thursday. You have over half the report written and you've hit that brick wall known as writer's block.

According to Roberta Trouncer, you — and writers of any age or profession — can break the block by boosting your right-brain activity.

(From here, pick up the original at paragraph three.)

Note: Some firms don't send out releases on products and services. Instead, they supply editors with a fact sheet that offers all the essential data and lets editors decide what to use. Software firms do this quite often. That's certainly a lot easier to do, but again, as the song from "The Music Man" says, "You've gotta know the territory." In short, you need to know what the media you deal with prefer. Some may want fact sheets and others may dislike them because it's more work for them and their staff. Find out.

Business Announcement

As the name suggests, these releases announce something — a merger, an acquisition, a production change, a switch in sales or marketing procedures, information about earnings or dividends, stockholder meetings. These releases also might try to boost a company or an organization's image by telling the world about some innovation, discovery or technological breakthrough.

You'll find it difficult to write delayed leads for business announcements. That doesn't mean you can't do it, but it may not prove easy or even desirable. The reason: You'll write most of these kinds of releases for a specific audience — those who read business publications or read the business pages of a newspaper every day. So this is one time when you can be fairly certain that editors — and busy readers — will prefer a direct lead. Here are two typical business announcements:

RADNOR, Pa. – Airgas Inc. today announced that it has agreed to acquire the assets of Interstate Welding Sales Corp., a leading Wisconsin-based distributor of welding equipment supplies; industrial, specialty and medical gases; and fire protection systems. The acquisition is expected to close March 31.

The operations, which generated about $35 million in annual sales in 2004, would significantly enhance Airgas' presence in Northeastern Wisconsin and Michigan's Upper Peninsula. The acquisition would include a main office and cylinder fill plant in Marinette, Wis., and branches in Appleton, Fond du Lac, Green Bay, Manitowoc, Milwaukee, and Schofield, Wis.; and Escanaba, Iron Mountain, and Marquette, Mich., on the Upper Peninsula.

Airgas plans to run these locations as part of Airgas North Central, one of 12 regional companies within Airgas, the nation's largest distributor of gases, welding supplies and related products. It plans to offer employment to Interstate's 160 employees.

"We are very excited about welcoming the Interstate associates to our company," said Ron Stark, president of Airgas North Central. "Interstate will give us great presence in geographical markets and businesses where we have very little presence today. The combination of our services and locations will help us offer even better service to Interstate and Airgas customers."

WHITEHOUSE STATION, N.J. – Merck & Co. Inc. today announced it has successfully completed the spin-off of 100 percent of the outstanding shares of Medco Health Solutions

Inc. common stock to Merck stockholders.

Shares of Medco Health common stock have been distributed to Merck stockholders on the basis of 0.1206 Medco Health common shares for each Merck common share.

As previously announced, the spin-off is structured as a tax-free distribution to Merck stockholders for U.S. federal tax purposes, except to the extent cash is received in lieu of fractional shares.

"Together, Merck and Medco Health have enjoyed 10 years of growth and success. By all measures, the acquisition of Medco Health by Merck has been highly successful," said Raymond V. Gilmartin, Merck chairman, president and chief executive officer.

In their original form, both releases were much longer. The first included details about the history of the two companies and said which executives would be doing what under the new arrangement. The second also added details about the history of the companies and added detailed information on how they made lots of profit. You can put that in — and as a public relations person, your employer will want you to. But bear in mind that most publications will strip your release to its basics. Still, some may use it all. Again, it's up to you to learn who wants what.

Note: This chapter deals with leads on only eight standard releases, the ones you'll likely have to write most of the time. No doubt you'll get other assignments that don't involve specific types covered here. But you'll have some notion about what kind of lead will work best and what the release should contain.

6.
Writing the Print News Release

Now that you understand a little more about leads, there's another important thing to keep in mind before you even reach the computer keyboard. Please be sure to use the proper terms for your releases. The ones you send should not be called publicity or press releases. Even though we're talking about items sent to the print media, it's best to use the neutral phrase of news release. If you get in the habit of saying press release, the broadcast media are offended since they don't own or use presses. When you call it a publicity release, red flags go up in the newsrooms of most publications and broadcast outlets.

Reporters and editors are **not** looking for publicity. They're looking for real news that will be of interest to their readers or listeners. Publicity is a poor substitute for news. The ongoing rift between journalists and public relations writers is linked to the publicity-shoveling practice that was so prevalent 100 years ago. The father of public relations, Ivy Lee, in an attempt to halt the practice, issued his Declaration of Principles. He sent his revolutionary document to city editors in newspapers across the country:

> *"This is not a secret press bureau. All our work is done in the open. We aim to supply news. This is not an advertising agency; if you think any of our matter ought properly to go to your business office, do not use it."*

Supplying news and objective information is the opposite of what most editors were receiving from the fledging public relations profession at the beginning of the 20th century. Lee encouraged other colleagues to follow his avant-garde example. PR people have been trying to live down the derogatory term "flack" that was given to them by newspaper staffs for the publicity drivel that has been sent to newsrooms for over a century.

We've talked about the importance of writing style, grammar essentials, writing traps and the Associated Press dogma. So are we ready to write releases yet? Not quite.

The next statement may frustrate or anger you. At least 90 percent of news releases sent to daily newspapers in North America are immediately discarded. We know because we've worked in newsrooms (and surveys have backed up such alarming statistics). Some releases are even tossed in the recycle bin without the envelope being opened. We know because we've fished a few out, read them and then used them as wonderfully bad examples for our public relations writing classes.

So why do you spend so much time futilely forwarding releases at a fast and regular pace? Although they loathe to admit it, print media depend on the news submissions for their survival. Various estimates show that the daily newspaper relies on releases for up to three-fourths of its contents. These releases come from a variety of sources: government, corporations, nonprofits, entertainment industry, associations, PR firms and even individuals.

Two reasons exist for the high rejection rate. The first is simple but serious. A crisis exists within the public relations profession. It's being addressed by the Public Relations Society of America and the International Association of Business Communicators at every one of their conferences. It's discussed and analyzed in *PR Tactics*, PRSA's monthly periodical for members. That crisis is poor writing ability among practitioners. When asked what skill is essential for success in the field of public relations, writing ability almost always tops the list.

The second reason for the inflated failure quotient is that so many releases are sent to newsrooms by people who have no clue what editors are looking for. If you can write well, determine what editors want, and then deliver that to them, your placement rate will soar well above the pathetic average. You literally have to think and write as a journalist would.

Avoid Editors' Wrath

Surveys have been conducted to gather editors' complaints about news releases that bombard their offices on a regular basis. Near the top of every list of complaints is the lack of news value. What is news to one paper may not always be the same definition at another. Yet, journalism textbooks remind students that there are some common determinants of news value. No universal list exists, but most of them in no particular order include the following: magnitude, localization, timeliness, length and objectivity.

1. Magnitude

Does the event or news affect many readers? Will emergency road construction inconvenience rush-hour traffic in the morning or slightly delay only two people living in a dead-end alley? Recall the front-page news in January 2004 about one bovine with mad cow disease infecting cattle in eight states. (The American Meat Institute quickly entered a crisis mode that January with $60,000 per month in PR spending.)

The impact about past, present or future news can be enormous or it can be minimal, depending upon how many people are affected. A federal gasoline tax increase will hit everyone who drives a gas-powered vehicle. An ice fishing license hike for one Wexford County lake in Michigan will have many local winter fishing fans in an uproar. The promotion of an individual from assistant professor to associate professor at Texas A&M University will make one person (and perhaps a few relatives) happy. However, the latter example does not affect the country, northwest Michigan, or even College Station, Texas.

2. Localization

Some dim-witted public relations pretenders will send an identical mailing to a nationwide list of publications in hopes that at least a few of them will use the release. That wastes a lot of money and time, not to mention opportunities to impress newsrooms with your skill in understanding media needs. Lack of localization is near the top of editor complaints about the PR industry. If an event happens in the circulation area of the paper, you've increased your chances of it running. A new swimming pool liner that doesn't fade may be a great news release for papers across the Sun Belt. But it would be foolish to send it to Sault Ste. Marie, Ontario, unless the designer hailed from there or the company that made the liner is located there.

One of our pulled-from-the-trash examples actually could have been a good release from the John Deere Co. In one page it described a new (at the time) system to recover and recycle Freon from industrial and agricultural equipment. A nice but lengthy quote even appeared from a Deere manager. Unfortunately, the quotee originated in the Moline, Ill., company headquarters. The last sentence after the quote said the process is available to dealerships worldwide. Why not, instead, use words that emanate from the mouth of an area manager? Sure, that would take a little extra time to get the name (and address of the community dealer), but I'm sure the success rate of the revised, localized release would more than offset the additional effort.

3. Timeliness

Editors are not thrilled when they receive a news item for an event that's taking place that very day. You have given no lead time to run the article or to plan coverage if it's deemed worthy. What's worse is when they receive releases about "future" events that have already occurred. Perhaps the public relations person was preoccupied with other details and didn't think about media exposure. Not only do you get zero coverage, you (and your organization or client) get a poor reputation in the newsroom. Yesterday's news is history. Journalists always want fresh information.

It's always best to send items to daily and nondaily papers — if possible — at least two weeks ahead of when you would like to see it printed. That gives editors plenty of time to obtain their own quotes or doublecheck details they may have questions about. It also meets advance deadlines that many outsiders aren't even aware of. For example, many papers have religion sections that appear Friday or Saturday. The cut-off day for submissions to that section may be as early as noon on Wednesday.

4. Length

One of the fallacies that many beginning writing students have is that news releases can only be one page long. I'm not sure if that was an admonition from early professors — who wanted fewer pages to correct in the evenings — or from harried editors — who were sick of the lengthy tomes being delivered to their newsrooms. In any case, news releases can easily continue beyond the first sheet. Many times, they need to explain more particulars so readers get the whole story.

What bothers editors more than brevity, however, is the release that acts like the Energizer bunny. If it just seems too long, that may be reason enough to toss it in the recycle bin. Rarely is a news release so earth-shattering that it has to go beyond two or three double-spaced pages.

Again, let's go to the newsroom trash can for an actual release example. A Houston-based anti-terrorism course is described in great detail. In fact, it has three, full, single-spaced pages examining the types of training, the costs, the

Ideas Per Sentence

Writers often pack writing with multiple points that confuse the reader. Present one, or at the most two, ideas per sentence. Too many ideas per sentence makes the reader have to work too hard to get the meaning.

instructors and about 10 favorably exciting quotes, all by the same entrepreneur, who stands to make a nice profit if enough nervous candidates apply for his 21-day adventure.

5. Objectivity

Advertising puffery, subjective claims about goods or services, is legally protected commercial speech. (Canada, by the way, is much stricter than the United States in that regard.) Claims about appearance, smell or taste can be dropped into advertising without proof of such phrases. But those terms don't belong in any news releases. When they show up, astute journalists and their editors know the writer is looking for free publicity, rather than sharing actual news with their subscribers. Fox commentator Bill O'Reilly said releases should be "puffery-free zones."

So how can you as a PR practitioner attempt to give a product or an idea some exclusiveness? How might you describe it so you satisfy your superiors without ticking off the media gatekeepers? If you need to use subjective expressions, stick them into a direct quote that has some meat on it. They may survive an editor's delete key that way. But never overdo it.

Some ineffectual corporate communicators feel it's in their contract to use the company name and trademark at least twice in every sentence. "The XYZ Co. announced Monday that it is proudly sponsoring the XYZ Walkathon as part of its XYZ community involvement program." We have numerous actual examples, but would hate to offend the guilty parties. A similar weakness in releases is inserting too many times the CEO's name — usually with a quote — even if the story isn't about her. "Harriet Hodgepodge, CEO of the XYZ Co., announced Friday the appointment of Bill Bradley as the Ontario plant's recycling director. Hodgepodge said, "Bill Bradley will coordinate…."

Prepare It Correctly

Another important consideration before starting on that release is its appearance. Now you know what to do within the release to avoid the wrath of editors. Sometimes the format alone can likewise make journalists reject its use. Because of budget and environmental interests, the standard paper release is now often printed on both sides of the page, some-

Gray Copy

Copy that is gray and dense with text is often pushed aside because it appears too difficult to read. Always double space and use short paragraphs to make a news release more appealing.

thing almost unheard of 20 years ago. Such ecological activity by itself will not get your message tossed aside.

Since you want the release to be as newspaper-looking as possible — by adhering to AP, for example — you'll want to follow similar customs:

- Use at least a one-inch margin all around the paper.
- Use organizational letterhead, either the regular style or one designed just for releases.
- Place today's date near the top of the page.
- Provide a contact's name and phone numbers (especially for after-hours calling).
- Don't hyphenate words at the end of lines.
- Don't break from one page to the next unless it's between paragraphs.
- Put "more" at the bottom of page one and "end" or "###" or "30" on the last page

These may seem like common-sense rules that no one would ignore. Yet, without a date, as some releases do arrive dateless, the journalist doesn't know if the word "tomorrow" in the copy refers to the next day or yesterday, depending on when it was written.

Similarly, many reporters have wanted to obtain more particulars about a release, but no one is in the office when they get around to calling at 5:15 p.m. Sports department staffs at most morning newspapers, for example, work up until deadline in many cases, so they don't even get to the office until late afternoon. If you as the PR person cannot be contacted after 5, it may doom your wonderfully written release. That's one reason why two names are often listed at the top as contacts. A journalist's decision to delay the use of a story because of the inability to confirm a couple details usually spells disaster on time-sensitive copy.

Datelines — that immediately tell readers where the story originated — are not difficult to write. Yet their constant misuse brands the writers as incompetents. Look at several newspapers. Is the dateline indented? Then indent yours. As the journalists' (as well as PR writers') bible instructs, the dateline city should be typed in all-capital letters. The state name — if needed — should follow in normal style. Canadian datelines call for the all-caps city followed by the province spelled out (with four metropolitan exceptions). Again, AP lets you know what cities stand alone, both in the dateline and within the text of your copy, and what states to abbreviate. Too many datelines we see in our writing classes are not indented. The state name is often abbreviated incorrectly using the postal ZIP code style rather than AP.

Another format issue is open to occasional debate. We encourage the use of a one-line, boldfaced headline just before you type the dateline. When you think about the reasons for newspaper headlines on stories — summary of main point, getting audience's attention — you can see their need for releases as well. After all, you want to help the media gatekeeper by summarizing your copy. Your newsroom audience is usually just one person, but it's the key individual you have to fully inform (entice, entertain or persuade) for your organization's

Blueprint

Regarding the preparation of news releases and background there are some basic guidelines:

1. Write simply and factually. Forget the hype. Facts and figures attract journalists' attention. "The world's leading," "largest," "pioneering," "leading-edge," "turn-key solution," and similar data sheet marketingese seldom excite a journalist unless they are backed by facts. Make certain that you tell the complete story as quickly as possible.

2. When the story dictates, prepare background with customer and industry expert inputs/contacts as well as biographical information that gives facts, not personal "puff." This kind of information should inform editors, not flatter management.

3. Photographs should be available that are real with sharp contrasts, not retouched ad shots. Increasingly these should be electronic photos that can be sent as an attachment (when requested) or put on a CD and mailed. Make certain that the caption is attached to the photo, explains the photo and ties into the release.

4. The release should contain the name and e-mail address as well as day, night and cellular telephone numbers of the person who should be contacted for additional information.

5. Write the release with the specific publication's readers in mind. Don't take the easy way out by doing a one-size-fits-all announcement. When a product has a number of applications, it pays to prepare a release for each class of publication/reader. It's a simple matter to modify the lead and body copy, but it can produce greater results because editors can quickly see how the product would be of interest to his or her readers.

(from G.A. "Andy" Marken, "Following Fundamentals Builds Journalist Relationships," *Public Relations Quarterly*, Spring 2003) contribution to proceed throughout the chain, from newsroom desk, to pressroom, to consumer delivery. Some would argue that headlines are the task of the copydesk, but you're not writing a final version for the publication. You just want to capture the gatekeeper's attention.

Again, it's best to emulate the journalism style for headline writing. Not all of these classic standards are being followed by today's newspaper copy desks. However, it's wise for you to mimic them anyway to help your headline have impact in just a half-dozen or so words. That means to use:

- short, simple words
- no articles
- few adverbs or adjectives
- a comma rather than the word "and"
- present or future tense verb instead of past tense
- active voice verb instead of passive voice
- a single quote mark (apostrophe) rather than double

Pretend You're a Journalist

After reading everything in the text so far, you're now skilled in public relations techniques, grammar rules, leads and Associated Press maxims. One more advantage to possess as you write your organization's news releases is the reminder to write as if you were a journalist. You already know what a newsperson considers to be determinants of news. So make them part of your outbound writing style.

Pretend you're a journalist writing about your company. Of course, that doesn't mean you have to write such a balanced story that it involves getting quotations from your competitors. But it does mean you will avoid overloading your story with hyperbole, sickeningly syrupy quotations by a CEO, and legal but nevertheless obnoxious puffery about your product or service. If your boss dreadfully insists on including such waste in narratives, try a split-run experiment. Write one the old way and write one the journalism way about an event and send them to various media. Find out the success rate for each. Contact journalists to whom your experiment was sent — but not while they are on their deadlines — to obtain their comments about the reasons for running or rejecting your submission.

Be positive
Limit the number of times you use the negative. Using words such as *not* and *no* add to reading time. When sentences are written in a positive way, they require the reader to do less work.

Voice
(Active and Passive)

All transitive verbs have voice. When the subject is the "doer" of the action, the sentence is in the **active voice**. When the subject receives the action, it is in the **passive voice**.

Example:
The selection committee presented the author its Writing Excellence Award. (Active Voice)

The author was given the Writing Excellence Award by the selection committee. (Passive Voice)

Occasional Passive

Occasionally using passive voice verbs softens the tone of your writing. However, writers should try to use the active voice in 85-90 percent of their writing. Reserve use of the passive voice for only about 10-15 percent.

One of the major advantages of having news about your organization in the media is that it automatically obtains third-party credibility. Media gatekeepers have given their seal of approval to your copy (or, you hope, a close resemblance to your original work). It now appears in the print or electronic media as if it was legitimate news, which it should be, of course. Readers assume that the information was gathered by the news crews at the media outlets. If the media you're using are considered reliable by their constituents, then your item is also deemed trustworthy.

You could get your news out to your publics by buying advertisements or broadcast commercials. You would have much more control of your message then. Since you're paying for the space or air time, you manage the total content of what needs to be said. You also have some say in when it appears, although that can be quite expensive. Your half-page ad could be in Sunday's business section or you could sing your message during 60 seconds of morning drive time.

But North American consumers have been especially wary of advertising since it expanded its influence through television commercials more than 50 years ago. Some scholars say the typical North American consumer is exposed to 2,000 paid-for messages per day. So many messages will get lost in the clutter of media bombardment. Readers realize that an advertisement contains a lot of subjective claims about a product or service. It's the company's showplace to brag and to brainwash — according to the accusations of many ad critics. Not so with the news article. It comes with the unpaid endorsement of the objective print media.

Since we've already suggested that you get to know the media — whether that's the local paper or trade publications — you now should have an understanding of the types of materials they are interested in. In fact, you can easily impress your media contacts if you can provide them with tips, resources or story ideas that don't even involve your organization. Many of them are probably getting low on creative ideas and energy. Even more stressful to journalists, at some papers the writers have a quota. They need to write a certain number of publishable stories for their annual performance evaluation. The more valuable you can be as a source, the more they will trust you for reliable information in the future, even when it does concern your own organization.

Reporters at smaller publications and nondaily papers may not have to worry about a quota. Their immediate concern is filling 16 pages by Tuesday with a staff of three persons, which includes the ad rep. They too need assistance and will often run your worthy contributions without much editing or deleting.

As a communicator, your job now is to produce unique stories about your company — products, services, employees, history, future plans. It's something you should also know intimately. New and improved products and services are typical fare for many releases. Hiring and personnel changes are usually positive mentions by the media as well. For nonprofits, stories about clients who have been helped by your services are always winners.

Keep in mind that journalists are not trying to impress a CEO. In fact, most writing styles at North American papers are geared for about a ninth-grade education. So continue making your words short, your sentences short and your paragraphs short, as mentioned elsewhere in this book. Jargon is a major turnoff for both readers and journalists. Your job is to translate client gobbledygook into understandable prose. Readership studies over the years have concluded that the ideal average sentence length is 17 words. (That one was 16.)

Unlike what your English teacher said in ninth grade, paragraphs do not have to contain an entire theme. In fact, they can be only one sentence long. Many times copy desks and layout personnel will break paragraphs into convenient lengths just to create some white space in a document. A long column of gray type looks uninviting. And, keep in mind, six lines of copy for one paragraph in a news release format will become at least twice that many in narrow news columns.

One popular journalism text, *News Reporting and Writing*, suggests reporters follow eight simple guidelines for writing their stories. Remember, if you're thinking like a journalist you also need to be writing like one.

Eight Steps to the Organized Story

1. Identify the focus or main idea of the story from notes.
2. Write a brief summary of the main idea.
3. Using the summary, separate in notes the material relating to the main idea from secondary matter.
4. Organize the secondary matter in order of importance.

5. Begin to write, making sure that the separate parts are linked with transitions.

6. Read the completed story for accuracy, brevity, clarity.

7. Read the completed story for grammar, style, word usage.

8. Rewrite if necessary — and it usually is.[1]

Of course, seasoned public relations writers may do the first four stages in their heads. They know they have to focus on one issue or their story will ramble forever. They sit down at their laptops and crank out the release, double checking a few notes and then making sure the direct quotes are OK with the sources. (Yes, it's true. Sometimes in public relations work, with permission, we have to provide quotations for our busy colleagues and supervisors. If we know them and their responsibilities, however, we usually can come up with an appropriate quote that makes them seem intelligent. If you must do this at times, make sure you run the quotes by the supposed speakers for approval, even under deadline pressure. They don't like surprises in print. And don't breathe a word about this to others outside the profession.)

Consider Sidebars

A sidebar is one other journalism technique you can try occasionally to get additional information from your organization or client into the print media. Readers have a fascination with sidebars, those smaller collections of facts related to a main story. Why not periodically produce a short sidebar to send along with a release?

As the name implies, they traditionally appear beside the main story. They are often boxed or have other typographical devices to set them apart from normal copy. And they use clever headlines to attract attention.

Because they're short, readers find them more inviting and editors find room for them. You should follow the style of the ones you read, since they have passed the media gatekeeper's seal of approval. Typically they include practical information that will help the publication's readers. Often written in an informal feature style, sidebars need to be referenced to the main article without repeating identical information. Although they're fun to write, moderation is the key for external media use.

Blueprint

Top 10 Typical Sidebars

Sidebars can come in several flavors. There's no clear-cut description or category, since many of them can blend into other types. But these may be among the most common.

1. Localization – This might interpret new developments from Ottawa or Washington, D.C., into local significance.

2. Resources – Your readers may want more information about a product or service. Give them appropriate Web sites, addresses, phone numbers in the sidebar.

3. Lists – Even before David Letterman popularized the Top 10s, lists have been favorite reading material.

4. Background – Many readers want more details than one story can tell them. Provide those eager learners with a timeline, history of an issue, or particulars about how a product or service developed.

5. Informative – Provide instructions on how to obtain flood insurance or make arrangements for a wedding.

6. Quiz – These short tests get high reader marks, whether serious or whimsical. Of course, remember to include the answer key.

7. Quotes – Often there's not enough space to include enough good quotations in the main release. The sidebar can be the perfect place for their placement.

8. Personality – Rather than detract from the major article, the sidebar can include tons of biographical information about a key individual.

9. Related Event – Give readers a look at what happened during a similar situation in the past.

10. Details – For those readers who must know every exact fine point on an issue or product, you can satisfy them with sidebars without slowing down others.

Ask About Preferences

Now that you're ready to distribute your news release, you'll want to find out to whom it should be sent. Nothing makes a release wind up in a trash can faster than the anonymous addressee of "newsroom." Send it to a staff member by name. Equally important is to find out how the media professionals prefer to receive their releases. The best way to do that is to ask, especially local reporters. Many may prefer the old-fashioned mail delivery. Others like e-mail or faxes (now that the latter machines no longer use wax paper for printouts).

Blueprint

Fake Releases Frustrate Reporters

Another reason for the rift between journalists and public relations writers is the occasional faux news release. One that surfaced a little over 10 years ago following the O.J. Simpson episode supposedly was from Ford, where the lead proudly announced: "The Ford Bronco has officially been selected as the vehicle of choice for all felons in the United States." It went on to boast of such features as a cell phone with speed dialing for 911 calls and a famous football star blow-up doll. It also was equipped, according to the release, with a "high-powered, well-qualified lawyer who will greet you when you arrive home" after eluding police vehicles.

For out-of-town and national outlets, you can consult one of the major media directories — such as Bacon's or Burrelle's — to get names. These yearly editions, available in bulky print or electronic versions, list news personnel by their specialties, along with contact information. Magazine staffers, for example, often suggest tips on what they're looking for, when is the best time to contact them, and how to do it.

The handy directories, although pricey, come in specialized editions for daily newspapers; non-daily newspapers; magazines and newsletters; and television and cable. It's wise to always consult the latest version because of the amount of turnover in the industry.

As magazine editors often lecture to freelance writers, study the periodical before submitting articles. You also need to know what kinds of stories the publication typically prints. Don't embarrass yourself and your organization, for example, by sending English-language news items to many of the newspapers in Quebec that are published in French.

Notes

[1] Mencher, Melvin. *News Reporting and Writing*. New York, NY: McGraw-Hill, 2003. p. 139.

Blueprint

Anatomy of a News Release

➤ Place the date the release was written at the top

➤ Indicate on the release either For Immediate Release or an embargo date. The rarely used embargo date is when information is sent early to a media outlet but the actual release date of the information is for a later date.

➤ Always place a contact name at the top of the release along with phone numbers so media members can easily contact you with questions.

➤ Write a short headline for the release just like a newspaper would.

➤ Indicate the city where the release is sent from on a city line.

➤ Indent paragraphs. Research shows that readers like indented paragraphs.

➤ Double space copy. Editors like white space.

➤ Always end each page of a release at the end of a paragraph and begin the new page at the beginning of a paragraph. Avoid the tendency to jump pages in the middle of a sentence or the middle of a paragraph.

➤ Write (more) at the end of a page to indicate that additional information follows.

➤ Add a boilerplate at the end of the release. A boilerplate is a standardized statement about the company or organization that journalists often find useful as background or filler information.

➤ Place a page number at the top of releases longer than one page along with a portion of the headline to help keep order with multiple page releases.

➤ To indicate the end of the release, use one of these:

end

-30-

###

Sandell College
Sandell, Indiana 47100
www.sandell.edu
800-SANDELL

DATE   Contact: Beth Gividen
For Immediate Release   PR Director
                                              (812)555-5555

Sandell Sponsors High School Workshops

SANDELL—High school journalism students and their advisers can pick up skills at Sandell College Media Workshops this June.

Running June 12 to 16, the all-day sessions will provide training in writing, editing, advertising, graphic design and photography. Yearbook and newspaper advisers will attend seminars and help their staffs plan for next year's publications. College or continuing education credit is available for advisers.

Student highlights of the week will be a news conference with quarterback Peyton Manning of the Indianapolis Colts and a concert by Kenny Chesney.

"This is the ninth year of offering these sessions for regional high school students," said Dr. Steve Kuhn, associate professor of journalism and workshop director.

"We had 200 students here last year from five states, as well as 23 advisers," Kuhn added.

(more)

Page 2
Sandell College Workshops

Students will live in air-conditioned dormitories, dine on campus and use Sandell's athletic facilities during the week.

Instructors for the workshops will be Sandell College mass communication faculty and experienced high school advisers whose publications have won awards over the years.

Students will produce a 24-page, full-color tabloid paper as part of their training.

Other guest speakers include Sen. Juanita Garcia, Sandell College President James Swanson and book publishing giant Preston Scott, a 1959 Sandell graduate.

"We're excited about the week already," Kuhn said. "Having Peyton and Kenny will add to the excitement for the high schoolers."

Applications are available from the Department of Mass Communication, PO Box 210, Sandell, IN 47100. The cost is $110 for commuters and $240 for resident students.

Sandell College is a Christian liberal arts school founded in 1915 by Gustav Sandell, a Swedish minister who immigrated to the United States in 1910. The campus is located on 160 acres in southern Indiana, about one hour south of Indianapolis.

-30-

7.

Writing Electronic Releases

"We'll have dispatches from Hell before breakfast," said Gen. William Tecumseh Sherman when he learned that three Civil War correspondents were missing.[1] That cantankerous quip on the battlefield of Vicksburg almost 150 years ago still echoes the sentiment that exists today. News reporters and newsmakers often share a tumultuous relationship. However, their dependence on each other to get information out to the masses is indisputable.

One of the most common errors committed by organizational communication professionals is considering that all media will be equally satisfied by the print news release. Failing to disseminate information in a style and manner that meets the needs of the electronic media often dooms messages or results in them being off target when reported. Strategic planning requires communication professionals to produce information with a keen eye toward clarity and a willingness to construct messages in a variety of formats.

Today's communication experts must be schooled in writing for a variety of media outlets. Writing for the electronic media requires a firm understanding of how modern audiences process information. That being said, PR staffs must be well versed at writing for television and radio as well as online media. Television, with its unique blend of video and audio, must grab viewer attention and persuade and inform in a seamless message that combines strong visuals with powerful prose. Radio combines a delicate blend of the right level of language, an easy-to-remember format, and interspersed with memorable phrases.

Video news releases or VNRs are prepackaged video and audio that broadcast stations incorporate into their news programming. They are particularly attractive for small stations with limited crews to cover events or for stories that broadcast outlets cannot duplicate. In short, they are television's version of the print news release. They translate the company's printed word into the sound and pictures that television needs.

Today, much of what we see on the nightly news, even on major networks such as CNN, ABC, NBC, CBS and FOX, features VNRs produced by organizations using in-house

Blueprint

Writing Copy for Online Media

Public relations practitioners live in a hybrid world. A practitioner must be ready to respond both to users who want information in their hands and those who need access to information online.

As with any public relations writing, knowing the requirements of the media and their audiences are essential first steps. Here are tips to maximize your writing in reaching several online media:

Online news releases: Corporate pressrooms and information portals are essential tools for journalists. Take a look at **http://www.prnewswire.com** and **http://www.businesswire.com** for examples of online repositories of information about companies. Online, it is useful to provide photos, brief video clips or useful links to supplement information in your story. The most effective news releases contain multiple subheads, frequent paragraphs and numerous quotes. Readers should find information as quickly as possible. Journalists are particularly interested in relevant numbers — numbers such as quarterly sales figures, when a company was founded and how many employees are employed. These should be prominently featured.

E-newsletters: Cut, cut and cut is the best advice to follow for online newsletters. Look to write in small chunks. For paragraphs, look at the 1-2-3-4-5 formula of Jon Ziomek, a professor at the Medill School of Journalism at Northwestern University — and then shorten further! In print, he advised using one main thought, taking up two to three short sentences and lasting four to five lines on a page. Many online newsletters feature paragraphs of two to three lines. Write so easy scanning is possible. Use creative headlines that grab information. Keep your content fresh and frequently use links that take readers to supplemental material. Look to establish an informal style of writing that creates a feel of community. In e-mailing, keep the subject line brief and highly relevant so readers do not delete before reading. Most e-newsletters should be read on one screen.

Blogs: This area is burgeoning with growth, as evidenced at the 2004 political conventions. Freelance journalists and public relations practitioners use blogs to communicate directly with the public. Blog writing is personal and filled with opinion. Contractions and slang are widely accepted. Best advice — keep focused on the target audience. Write in a first-person diary style. Vary sentence length. Follow long sentences with short ones like "I'm serious." As with e-newsletters and online press releases, generously mix in links; use up-to-date references; and grab the reader with short exciting headlines.

(By Garry R. Bolan, lecturer in Strategic Public Relations and Integrated Communication at Towson University, Towson, Md.)

production facilities or by public relations firms hired by these organizations to get publicity or information out in a timely manner. Produced in broadcast style, VNRs enable organizations to get word of a product launch, corporate merger, timely event or feature story out to television stations with the ease once reserved only for the print news release. Simply, every major television network and local affiliate use VNRs on a regular basis.

Surprising? No. The proliferation of television and the insatiable appetite of the public for news created a need for organizations to provide broadcast quality information to stations. Now, network or local news crews no longer exclusively dig for, report on and produce electronic news. Rather, the nightly newscasts have turned into a combination of network- or station-originated stories and corporate- or political-sponsored footage. In fact, according to Medialink, research shows that about 75 percent of all television station newsrooms regularly use VNRs.[2]

The United States Congress for more than 10 years has had its own fully equipped, taxpayer-supported production facility to send out VNRs.[3]

Learning how to use broadcast contexts for increasing outreach is essential for operating in an increasingly multimedia world. In fact, use of audio and video techniques to maximize message retention increases dramatically the possibility of persuading a potentially willing public.

Formats and Structures for VNRs

Brevity is critical in writing for the electronic media. The typical news VNR seldom runs longer than a minute to two minutes. The information contains "sound bites" or "actualities" (in radio lingo) showing the source in direct speech. Of course, at the heart of any VNR rests the essential basic rule that reporters report news impartially and do not serve as advocates for the organization. Closely aligned with this basic rule is the credo of all good reporting — good writing is clear writing and the more complicated the story, the more important the need for clear writing.

According to Sara Calabro, writing in *PRWeek*, most television producers receive a pile of video news releases weekly, and at least twice as many pitches and follow-ups. Calabro said she believes that grabbing the attention of these newsroom gate-keepers requires being honest but subtle, persistent but not bothersome, and helpful but not presumptuous.[4]

Often in their zeal to get publicity, writers for companies and clients forget the single most important component of any media release, newsworthiness. Remember that journalists use research, legwork, and telephone and source copy from the wires or from newspapers to build a story. They rely on facts and news value in determining whether a story should appear on a legitimate news program or discarded because it lacks newsworthiness. VNRs that offer legitimate news get favorable treatment in a newsroom. VNRs that offer fluff get cast aside.

Upfront honesty is imperative, but that doesn't mean producers will be receptive to blatant commercial messages. Be honest. If a VNR references products or services tell the producer. Then, reference the newsworthy elements to the story. Too much surprise will destroy the professional relationship.

For example, Medialink, a global leader in corporate communications services, produced a VNR to promote Jennifer Lopez's perfume, Glow. The VNR focused primarily on J Lo as a Hispanic role model and one of *People Magazine*'s recently rated most beautiful people. The story aired on E!, Good Day Live, Extra, VH1, and even some Hispanic stations in Canada (Calabro). The story had newsworthy value because it focused on the newsworthiness of J Lo's role in the Hispanic community rather than her hawking perfume.

Even pitching a VNR requires an eye toward newsworthiness. An elaborate and long-winded pitch usually sends up a red flag that the story lacks essential newsworthy elements. Keep it basic. Keep it focused. And, send it to the appropriate reporter.

Calabro offers these technique tips:

- **Do** always tie your pitch to something newsworthy
- **Do** learn how to convey a story's relevance to the station's audience without overstepping boundaries with the producer.
- **Do** familiarize yourself with a station's producers and their schedules prior to pitching to ensure your story reaches the right person at the right time.
- **Don't** pitch a story that clearly only has local relevance to a national news program.

Avoid Redundant Phrases

Omit repeating expressions. They bloat writing and delay getting to the point.

- **Don't** assume that a VNR is useless just because it does not initially get picked up in the form you originally envisioned.

- **Don't** try to fool producers by acting as though your VNR is not being pitched for promotional purposes.

Putting it Together

By now, communicators should be clear that the fundamental purpose of any information released by an organization must be its newsworthiness. Many small, regional television stations that have limited budgets for news production are understaffed. Consequently, these stations rely heavily on the use of VNRs to offer journalistically sound information to pass along to viewers. This offers an opportunity for organizations to get their message out with high quality VNRs. However, the need of smaller stations creates a heightened ethical responsibility to produce news, not advertisements.

Here's a formula for writing a VNR offered by the Associated Press.

Write simply, yet intelligently. News stories tend to be complicated, and the writer's task is to unravel them and present them in an understandable form. The stories should be simply structured, one fact leading into another. And there's no need to use a big word — or several — when one will do. For example, why say "utilize" when you can say "use"?

Use the simple declarative sentence. The best way to say something is to simply come out with it.

Always keep the listener's ear in mind. Some words sound better together than others. Sentences, paragraphs and entire stories, much like music, have textures and rhythms. A series of short and long sentences, and short and long paragraphs give writing rhythm.

Build your story logically. Once you've chosen a lead, think of the next obvious question it raises. Lay the groundwork. Then build the story with a progression of facts that cover all the major questions the listener could ask.

Always use appropriate attribution. The requirement for strong and clear attribution is a basic tenet of journalism; report the facts — only what you know to be true. Don't guess; don't draw conclusions.

Important Words or Phrases

Avoid placing important words or phrases in the middle. Remember the importance of the soundbite.

Know the laws in your state. When dealing with stories where there is a legal issue, make sure you know just what that issue is — and make sure your story reflects it. Also, be careful with attributions. This is especially true when reporting any statistics and public polling data. Remember that surveys and polls merely suggest, predict or estimate opinions.

Be informal. Be careful of falling into what AP refers to as wire-ese — the awful habit of falling into stodgy, stilted sentences that state the facts but put the listener to sleep. Use images, familiar phrases and sometimes colloquialisms to get the point across.

Don't put stumbling blocks in your copy. As a story progresses, the copy must gain momentum. If a long and difficult phrase suddenly appears, that momentum will come to a crashing halt — and the story will lose direction and the listeners will lose interest.

Use contractions. Contractions work fine in broadcast writing. In fact, people speak using contractions all the time.

Be grammatical. English is a complicated, seemingly irrational language. However, many rules are basic and understood by most people. Avoid grammatical errors that diminish credibility.

Avoid slang. The line between what's appropriate and what is not appropriate constantly shifts. Don't step over it.

Use words properly. It's your job to know the language. Know the meaning of the words you choose to avoid losing credibility.

Typically, organizations provide video news packages that are transmitted via satellite to news organizations, along with a fax or e-mail of the script. Some VNRs are distributed via mail or at news conferences in the form of a videocassette and script. Normally, the video material contains several packages of about 90 seconds each. The package contains both completed stories and stories that allow a station to add its own voice-over. Typically the package also contains B-roll video (background video) that allows a station to produce its own story by editing together video clips. The script, along with other support materials, gives the station relevant information to develop the story.

A VNR script should contain relevant information at the top such as contact information and a description of the visual materials being sent. In addition, it should contain a suggested introduction. The copy needs to be tightly edited and offer an objective, newsworthy account of the situation.

Figure 1

Sample Video News Release for the fictitious American Farmers Association

---

American Farmers Association
112 County Lane. Sioux Falls, SD 57106. (800) 333-FARM
Contact: Victoria Marie Parker, Director of Public Relations (605) 289-1975.

EDITED STORY + B-ROLL AND EXTRA BITES
TRACK 1—VOICE-OVER ONLY TRACK 2—NATURAL SOUND ONLY**

JAPAN TRADE IMBALANCE AFFECTING AMERICAN RICE FARMERS

(SUGGESTED INTRODUCTION)
In a free market economy, quality and price should rule. However, Japan's government seems to be playing a game of protectionist trading by placing higher tariffs on imported agricultural products such as rice. This policy has hurt American farmers. But, for the American Farmers Association, the buck, or in this case the rice, stops here.

(SCENE)	(SUGGESTED VOICE OVER)
LOUISIANA RICE FIELD HARVESTING RICE CROP OUTDOOR MARKETS IN JAPAN (20 SECONDS)	Every day, Louisiana rice farmer C.J. Kaplan tends to his fields. C.J. and other American rice farmers grow a grain of rice that is preferred by people the world over including in Japan where it costs about half the price as Japanese grown rice.
B-ROLL U.S. SENATOR AUSTIN MARTIN SPEAKING ON SENATE FLOOR (20 SECONDS)	(SOUND-ON, AUSTIN MARTIN) "The American people embrace the notion of a free and open market in a global economy but Japan continues to play protectionist politics. It's time that America fights back and demands that trade be free and balanced. Open trade must be a two-way street."
RICE BEING PROCESSED IN PLANT (25 SECONDS)	The United States Senate continues to debate a proposal on the senate floor concerning trade imbalance. At the heart of the debate are restrictions imposed on American products that prohibit many businesses from competing on a level playing field in foreign nations. The debate has raised many questions about America's trade practices.
LONG SHOT OF UNITED STATES CAPITOL BUILDING (25 SECONDS)	Agricultural trade imbalance has triggered a heated debate pitting senators from America's heartland states, against those from largely industrialized states. The debate focuses on whether Senator Austin Martin's (R-Louisiana) proposal calling for stiff tariffs on imported products would help reduce the trade imbalance or damage the delicate relationship between America and its foreign trade partners.

Radio Releases

An audio news release is generally a 60-second packaged news story that includes a 15- to 20-second sound bite from a designated spokesperson. The story is pitched and fed to interested stations and networks. Often these audio news releases are also produced in 30-second and 15-second formats to increase their chances of getting aired.

Just as you would do with a VNR for a television station, you should supply radio stations with a script to complement the audio. The script should be set in triple space to make it easy to read. The general rule of thumb is that for each second of airtime the average person can speak approximately 2 words. Don't forget to leave time for music or sound effects in calculating your word count. The lead-in gets the reader ready for the story. The lead itself should be about 16 to 20 words for ease of reading. Finally, difficult-to-read words should be spelled out phonetically to help the station's news presenter.

Sometimes organizations distribute interviews to radio stations for publicity purposes. These interviews, distributed either by phone or by audiocassette, are called actualities or audio feeds. They provide a wealth of information and news programming for radio stations, particularly those in small

Figure 2
Fictitious Sample of Radio Script for the American Lung Association

---

American Lung Association

Philadelphia, PA 19145
(215) 888-4398
(215) 888-3323
Nicholas Jonathan Hunter
Director of Public Relations

January 5, 2005 05:1

Slug Line: American Lung Association set to kick off Annual Bike-Trek

(Time :30 seconds)

Cyclists the world-over converge in Seattle, Washington, on Saturday, March 12 to begin a cross-country journey to Atlantic City, New Jersey. The purpose of their trip is to raise money for the American Lung Association's Annual Bike-Trek. The Lung Association sponsors the annual event to raise money for research and treatment of lung diseases including emphysema and lung cancer.

###

---

markets. A cataloging number appears after the date of the release to help the organization keep track of the number of radio releases it sends each year. Following the last two digits of the calendar year include the sequential number for that release. For example, 05:3 would indicate that the particular radio release is the third release produced in 2005.

Public Service Announcements

Public service announcements (PSAs) provide advertising time, free of charge, to organizations that wish to promote messages for the public interest. Prior to the deregulation of broadcasting, television stations and radio stations were required to provide a percentage of their time to nonprofit organizations to air public service announcements.

Now, the Federal Communication Commission only requires that radio and television stations operate in the public interest. They no longer must devote a percentage of their broadcasting time to PSAs. This has led to dwindling opportunities overall, particularly on radio. However, well-written news items that connect with a station's local listening audience will still get air time. It's your job to create PSAs that are exciting enough to break through the clutter.

Television PSAs range from low-cost, announcer-read scripts to high-quality productions created by international advertising agencies. Today, most radio PSAs offer only short, announc-

Figure 3
Fictitious Radio PSA from New Jersey Department of Motor Vehicles

New Jersey Department of Motor Vehicles
Radio Public Service Announcement
(30 Seconds)

DRUNK DRIVING KILLS Hundreds Each Memorial Day Weekend in New Jersey

Do you know the single deadliest weapon in New Jersey? If you guessed automobiles operated by drunk drivers you're correct. Each holiday weekend, State Troopers respond to hundreds of fatal accidents caused by drunk drivers. Stop a friend from driving drunk. You'll save a friend's life — and possibly the life of an innocent motorist. A public service announcement from New Jersey Motor Vehicles and this station.

###

er-read spots. Radio PSAs often provide an opportunity for local nonprofit organizations to air their messages. The same writing techniques apply for PSAs as mentioned above. The focus remains on newsworthiness and clean, concise prose. Most radio PSAs run 10, 20, 30 or occasionally 60 seconds. The variety of your spot lengths can increase the chances of your announcements fitting seamlessly into a station's broadcast schedule. Television PSAs should be 10 and 30 seconds in length. Longer PSAs generally appear in overnight broadcasts when stations have difficulty selling advertising time to a smaller viewing audience.

Edit in Stages

When it comes to written communication — even when it's seen in a broadcast format — faster doesn't always mean better. Relying on computer spelling and grammar checks exclusively also invites error. And, making blanket edits, looking to correct all errors in your writing with one pass of the pen, often results in mistake-filled releases.

The quality of the information produced reflects on the communicator's professionalism and the client. Therefore, taking extra time to edit lessens the chance that writing contains muddled language and errors in grammar and punctuation.

The idea of editing in stages increases the likelihood that you'll catch all your errors. Although the method requires additional time, it adds an additional safeguard against releasing information riddled with passive voice, problems with pronoun/antecedent agreement, poor transition from one idea to another and other writing mishaps.

General Preparation Tips

- Create a list of key ideas you wish to include in your work, whether it's a PSA or a brochure. Check these items off the list as you write.

- Develop your ideas without concern for style and format. Concentrate on packing your story with all the relevant information first. Remember, you can always change the order or delete information when preparing the final draft.

- Ask yourself, does my story answer the questions: who, what, when, where, why and how.

Get to the Point

Get to the point and stop using vague, third-degree terms. Avoid using phrases such as "a situation occurred today at work." Instead, be specific and write, "an argument concerning our billing practice took place today."

- Set your work aside before editing it. Try to avoid the trap of editing without giving yourself time to walk away from the story for a few hours. If time constraints prohibit you from putting work aside consider having one or more members of your office read your work for clarity and style.

Editing stage 1: Check for passive voice

Passive voice robs writing of vigor and saps the energy from your prose. Simply, passive verbs fail to assign responsibility. But some passive construction may add variety to your writing. Therefore, you should strive for active voice to comprise about 80 percent of your total verb use. To check for passive voice you should edit your document one time looking only for passive voice. Do this by:

➤ identifying the subject and verb in each sentence.

➤ determining if the verb is a form of the verb to be (note: an active verb does something to someone or something).

➤ recasting the sentence (without changing the meaning) using active voice as often as possible.

Editing stage 2: Check for pronoun/antecedent agreement

Writers often make the mistake of renaming a subject using the wrong tense of the pronoun.

For example: *The school board voted on the budget. They [sic] will meet again next week.* "School board" indicates only one board; therefore, it is singular. Yet, many writers often rename the subject with the plural pronoun *they*.

To check for proper pronoun/antecedent agreement simply:

➤ Find the subject(s) described in your work.

➤ Determine if the subject(s) is singular or plural.

➤ Circle each pronoun (antecedent).

➤ Draw a line from the pronoun to the subject it renames to check for agreement.

Editing stage 3: Check for transition

Transition words and phrases lend order to your writing and signal a relationship between and among sentences. Essentially they serve as guides and help move the reader from one idea to another smoothly and efficiently. For a list of transition words, see Blueprint.

By reading through your work and focusing on proper use of transition words and phrases you can identify if you guide the reader clearly from one idea to another. Do this by:

➤ identifying when you introduce a new idea or subject.

➤ testing to see if transition words would make it easier for the reader to understand the order of ideas.

➤ rewriting sentences to include transition words and phrases when appropriate.

Editing stage 4: Check for proper punctuation

Even the most experienced writers and editors occasionally encounter problems with the use of proper marks of punctuation. Commas and apostrophes seem to cause writers the most problems.

First, let's focus on commas. Some of the distinct functions of commas include:

➤ separating items in a series.

➤ setting off introductory clauses and phrases.

➤ separating two independent clauses connected by a coordinating conjunction (examples: and, but, or, nor).

Without commas, sentence parts would collide into one another. You can identify problems with commas by:

➤ circling the commas used in your first draft.

➤ identifying if commas are used to separate items in a series or clause or if they are used with a coordinating conjunction.

➤ determining if the sentence flows better and sounds clearer with the use of commas.

Now let's tackle apostrophes. Apostrophes indicate possession. Properly used, apostrophes:

➤ show ownership such as Dan's hat.

➤ make broadcast-friendly contractions such as it's (it is).

Two areas to focus on when editing include:

➤ using -'s if the noun does not end in -s or if the noun is singular and ends in -s (boy's hat, Louis's car).

➤ using -s' if you want to show ownership for a plural noun that ends in -s (writers' tools).

Editing stage 5: Check for clarity, sound and accuracy

You've dissected your work and focused on key elements in the writing process. You've made all the necessary changes. The editing process appears over, right? Well, you're almost there.

If possible, set your work aside for 24 hours. Now you're ready for the final edit. You should:

➤ Check all numbers and facts in the work to make sure they are accurate.

➤ Make sure that the final draft contains all changes included from the other editing stages.

➤ Become the reader and read the work out loud to ensure that it sounds good and is pleasing to the ear. This is always essential for broadcast material.

➤ Proofread it at least two more times before sending it out.

Although these stages may add time to the writing process, they may help eliminate errors. Your time is worth the effort.

Blueprint

Transition Words and Phrases

Source: Jack Gillespie

Transition – Words, phrases, sentences and even paragraphs that help the reader follow the writer's line of thought from one idea to the next.

Transitions assure the reader that the writer has a sense of direction. They give the reader a context and suggest what to expect from the onset of the article. (note the use of they, a pronoun, as a transition — a word that refers the reader to what was just said.)

In fact (another transition), writers commonly use pronouns to refer to words or ideas in preceding sentences. *Examples*: he, she, they, this, these, those, them, it. Some of the same words, this, those, these, often appear as adjectives. When they do, they do the same job.

You also can use connectives — words or phrases that connect what has preceded with what follows. The connective you use depends on what you want to express. You may want to add to, illustrate or extend a point. Or you may want to establish time, link cause and effect, summarize, restrict, qualify, argue, infer, refute, compare, etc.

Here's a list of some transitions by category (see next page):

Transitions by Category

To add to, illustrate or extend a point: and, furthermore, also, or, nor, moreover, along with, similarly, for instance, for example, for one thing, for another thing, especially, altogether, undoubtedly, happily, glumly, sadly, earnestly, in addition.

To argue: nevertheless, even so, except, unfortunately, however, but, notwithstanding, yet, doubtless, in spite of, even if, certainly, conversely, although, whereas.

To cite: for instance, for example, to illustrate, another case, first, incidentally, in fact, specifically.

To conclude: finally, lastly, to conclude, in conclusion.

To compare: parallel with, allied to, comparable to, in like manner, in the same way, similarly, likewise, more important, of less importance, next in importance, in contrast with, conversely.

To demonstrate: thereof, thereby, thereto, therein, therefrom, in this case, in such a case, at such times, just as, here again, here.

To emphasize: indeed, moreover, furthermore, besides, further, even without this, in addition, even, more, especially, in particular, yet again, above all, most of all, again, to repeat, to explain, once more, in other words, in short, equally important.

To establish time: already, that day, that evening, the next morning, the next week, the next month, years later, now, then, usually, until, not until, afterward, later, eventually, meanwhile, finally, immediately, soon, no sooner, at once, frequently, infrequently, occasionally, never, rarely, always, sometimes, at last, thereafter, previously, formerly, in the meantime, after this, at length, henceforth.

To except: with this exception, except for, excluded, without exception, excepted, excluding this point, unless, all but, everything except.

To infer: so, therefore, consequently, accordingly, hence, thus, then, as a result, because, for this reason, under these circumstances, in this way.

To link cause and effect: as a result, because, that caused, that resulted in, the outcome was that, inevitably, that brought about, that produced, this is bound to produce, naturally, as a consequence, consequently, therefore, that let to, that will lead to, the reason is that, the explanation is.

To mark a change in tone or point of view: at least, seriously, to speak frankly, for my part, in another sense, in fact, to come to the point, of course, you see, as things are, but.

To mark a reference: with respect to, concerning, as for, on that point, about that.

To refer: this, that, they, those, these, most, he, she, it, them, none, nobody, each, all, few, some, who, whom, many, not a one, everything, everybody.

To refute: otherwise, else, were this not so, on the contrary, never, hardly.

To restrict or qualify: provided, in case, in some cases, unless, last, if, when, not unless, occasionally, rarely, only if, even though, in no case, sometimes, perhaps.

To show correlation: on the one hand, on the other hand, in the first place, in the second place, whereas, therefore, as long as, so long, if, while, though, yet, wherever, there, just as, so, but...and, either...or, neither...nor, not only...but also, since, then, also, the more.

To summarize: at last, so, finally, hence, and so, therefore, consequently, in short, that meant that, in sum, to sum up, briefly, in brief.

Most words and phrases listed above appear at the beginning of sentences and paragraphs. But words, usually nouns, repeated within sentences and paragraphs also provide transition.

For example, a feature about stonecutters would no doubt use key words like stonecutter, craftsman and artisan to provide transitions between sentences and paragraphs. In this case, the writer may repeat stonecutters several times or use craftsmen and artisans as synonyms. So you can also use synonyms to provide transition.

Example:

In 1978, Benny Lopardo, a stonecutter from Milan, Italy, came here to do a job that was to last three months. He liked it here so much that he decided to stay.

Now, this skilled craftsman is in demand by companies all over the country.

Last week, along with four other artisans from Italy, Lopardo started work on the new Bevridge building on 14th Street.

Words of caution

Transitions will help you write a story that glides from start to finish. But they cannot create coherence if none exists. So don't just throw transitions in here and there and think you've done your job.

You must make sure that the transitions you use make clear to readers the exact relations within and between sentences and paragraphs. Don't use anything that will sidetrack readers. Make every word and phrase flow naturally from what has gone before.

Transition Words and Phrases reprinted
by permission of Jack Gillespie

Notes

[1]Brad Kalbfeld. *Associated Press Broadcast News Handbook: A Manual of Techniques & Practices*. New York, NY: McGraw-Hill, 2000.

[2]Medialink. *The Video News Release Handbook*. New York: Video Broadcasting Corp., 1990.

[3]Robert P. Charles. "Video Newsrelease: News or Advertising." *Media in Review*, September 1994, vol. 9. www.worldandi.com.

[4]Sara Calabro. "PR Technique: Winning Over Television's Gatekeepers." *PRWeek*. January 19, 2004.

For Further Reading

Mervin Block. *Writing Broadcast News: Shorter, Sharper, Stronger*. Chicago, IL: Bonus Books, 1997.

C.A. Tuggle, Forrest Carr and Suzanne Huffman. *Broadcast News Handbook: Writing, Reporting & Producing in a Converging Media World*. New York, NY: McGraw-Hill, 2004.

8.
Media Kits

An updated media kit is an indispensable tool for public relations success, whether it's for an individual, a nonprofit organization or a major corporation. It's one more item in the toolbox that can help create positive media relations for your client. In its simplest format, the media kit is a folder with inside pockets containing key information about your company. Usually the folder is printed with a logo or design so a journalist can tell at a glance for whom it was produced. Fancier ones may come in three-ring binders or with special covers. *Rolling Stone* magazine in the early '90s produced a media kit with front and back spiral-bound covers made of thick rubber. In addition to supplying paper copies of media kits, many organizations today produce CD-ROM or Macintosh- and PC-compatible computer disks containing information for journalists.

Items found in media kits vary greatly, depending on the size of the client and the reasons for their production. Some — produced from a sales perspective — anger members of the media. They are full of puffery and hyped-up claims about the superiority of a product or service. Journalists, on the other hand, want facts related to their occupation of gathering news about your client or the industry. Therefore, save the sales collateral and ad slicks for the marketing department staff. Although publicists like to get their clients noticed by the media, public relations professionals should know better than alienating journalists with trickery and gimmicks. Putting a pound of confetti in a mailed media kit so it gets noticed in the newsroom will only get your client notoriety, not fame.

And make sure the appropriate media representative receives your media kit. It will probably be discarded if sent to the wrong individual. That doesn't result in any positive media play. Nor does a media kit that's woefully outdated. A common assignment for college interns is to have them update media kits so they serve a useful function. Probably the best argument for updating the kits is their invaluable use during a crisis, when all the journalists in the state want one yesterday.

For the past 10 years or so, most organizations have realized that having a Web media kit is productive. It provides access to whatever you choose to make available to the media or the public 24 hours a day. Often called an online media center, this site is one you need to publicize among the journalists who deal with your industry or product/service line. It will help them produce a quick and accurate article. One of the major advantages is that you can create links to tons of other materials — such as streaming videos, prior annual reports and PowerPoint presentations — that couldn't possibly fit inside a normal media kit. You can also provide a variety of formats and lengths so you don't need to individualize your kit for each medium, of course, as you do for the traditional folder variety.

Before analyzing contents of typical media kits, you should understand their background. Historically, their primary use was for distribution to the media who showed up for a news conference. Back then they were called press kits and press conferences. Now, to be more considerate of our electronic colleagues, obviously, they are media kits and news conferences.

News Conferences

Journalists, however, grew weary of coming to press conferences during the late 20th century where little legitimate news was actually provided to the news media. This became especially frustrating for television stations who assigned camera crews to trek across town, find a place to legally park their van (usually), lug heavy equipment into a conference room, set it up, and then tear it down after some minor, five-minute pronouncement about an insignificant change in company policy.

As a reaction to such non-news conferences, many journalists stopped showing up, at least in the droves they usually did so they wouldn't be scooped by their competitors about some major news announcement.

News conferences are still valid outlets for media kits, but only when organizations need to share significant news to as many local media as possible in a short time period. One of the main advantages of calling for the infrequent news conference is that the company can't be charged with playing favorites regarding its news dissemination. It's a come-one, come-all

Online Media Kits

According to a 2004 Vocus survey of more than 1,000 journalists, online media kits are rated highly by journalists, much more so than PR professionals realized. While 93 percent of reporters rated media kits valuable, only 71 percent of practitioners thought they were.

Executive bios were given a high value by 91 percent of journalists but by only 58 percent of those who wrote them.

invitation to get the latest and most significant news that you'll be sharing publicly. You're not favoring the metropolitan morning paper over the small nondaily that's mailed to all homes in the county every Thursday. You're not providing more information to the local television network-affiliate than the local radio station that's all-talk all day and all-sports all night.

Following the brief statement by your media-savvy spokesperson, the legitimate news conference quickly becomes a two-way communication process. Public relations professionals who choose to distribute media kits before the actual presentation of information often lose their audience. It's advisable, therefore, to present media kits after important information is presented by the speaker.

Reporters will ask probing questions. It's the PR staff function to make sure the answers to those tough questions have been rehearsed. Reporters genuinely feel they have the right to ask questions on behalf of their customers after the news proclamation. So make sure your spokesperson is prepared to welcome such inquiries from the media. (See chapter 11 for other tips when responding to reporters.)

To maximize the impact of your news conference, selecting the best time and place is second only to inviting the appropriate journalists to attend. Doe River Gorge, a Christian camp and conference center in northeast Tennessee, decided to hold a late-morning news conference to kick off a major expansion and fund-raising campaign. Located in a rural setting with inadequate parking (at the time), the camp's staff decided that a centrally located facility was needed for the announcement. The nearby Tri-City Airport, located in the middle of Kingsport, Johnson City and Bristol, became the ideal setting for all the major media in the region. A large conference room was available, along with adequate parking, restrooms, electrical outlets and smaller rooms for follow-up interviews.

The late morning selected for the conference allowed videographers enough time to edit the package for their stations' local newscasts at 5:30 and 6 p.m. It gave print journalists enough time to write and edit their stories as well as select photographs of the camp for the next morning editions. Fridays, holidays and weekends are not ideal times for news conferences. Weekend news crews in most markets are downsized and often less experienced than the regular journalists. Many of the large Sunday paper's inside sections often have been run off by Friday night.

Journalist invitees who do not take the time to show up for your organized conference shouldn't be off the hook. Since Doe River Gorge had wisely personalized each media kit for the local outlets, it had representatives personally deliver the ones not picked up to the absent stations and newspapers immediately after the conference. This resulted in additional promotion of the soon-to-be successful fund-raising campaign.

One more tip for the success of your news conference. Feed the media — not just legitimate information — real food. Print journalists won't feel you're trying to bribe them into writing a positive story if you provide a light spread for them. In almost every case, their newspapers' ethics codes even allow such indulgence. Assignment editors at TV stations keep their crews busy jumping from one location to another. So videographers also would appreciate a quick bite and a soft drink before hauling heavy equipment back to the van for another trip across town.

Media distribution services such as Business Wire or PR Newswire will help coordinate a news conference when it's more convenient to conduct one by audio or video tele-conferencing. That may occur because of widespread offices of the sponsoring organization or of participants being in distant cities or countries. Materials, including kits, are dispatched to the interested journalists, previously contacted by a media advisory.

News conferences — in whatever format — are still frequent allocation sites for media kits. Other common venues are special events (such as grand openings and groundbreaking ceremonies), new product launches, and those inevitable crises that make the media your most frequent visitors.

Contents of Media Kits

Visual/Audio Inserts

Knowing what each medium needs dictates what to enclose in your various media kits. For newspapers and other print outlets, for example, sharp black-and-white photographs are essential. A color picture is also valuable in case your story lands on a section front page. Provide full identification of the people or places in the photo for the publication. It's better to have a couple faces that are identifiable than too many that become mere tiny dots when reproduced. Good photos can give your client's story an advantage over those without.

Radio, of course, has no visual impact for its listeners. But an audio tape of the entire news conference, or of key portions, can be played and replayed by local radio stations in your market. In fact, a few clever news directors will cooperate with an organization to interject their own voiced questions into the delayed airing of a news conference Q-and-A session. It gives their listeners the impression that the news crew is busy at work covering important news events throughout the community. In actuality, except for large markets, the local radio news team is so understaffed and budget-restrained that it rarely can cover minor or major events with on-the-scene reporting.

Television needs both verbal and visual images for its audience. Doe River, in this example, provided stations with two video packages along with whatever footage they took with them from the news conference. One showed the enthusiastic camp director talking about the expansion plans. He pointed out where a "miracle mountain" literally was added to the site for free by highway construction crews through their need to dump loads of earth from a nearby widening project. Another video, called the B-roll, showed the camp setting with natural sounds, but no narration. It could then be used as a visual while the local station announcer shared with viewers the news from that morning's conference.

Other visuals found in most media kits, besides product or building photographs, are recent head and shoulder shots of an organization's executives. These are especially helpful for one-column newspaper photos. Television stations, on the other hand, prefer color slides of key management personnel that can be shown on the screen behind the news presenter.

News Releases

If your media kits are being distributed at a news conference, there needs to be a legitimate newsworthy reason for conducting such an event. That becomes the rationale for enclosing at least one news story with that day's date in your packet. And remember to write the release in the style for the particular medium, keeping in mind the specific style requirements for broadcast. Quite often other recent, related releases are also included to give journalists an update regarding the current situation. That's especially useful if these reporters did not receive the earlier dispatches or discarded them at the time because of the usual deluge of news items pouring upon their desks from sundry organizations. With all the other materials in your media kit, they will have plenty of information for writing their stories, even under deadline pressure.

Even if your release is not used directly, it may be used by the media to spark a related story. Estimates say the content in most American dailies — from one-half to three-fourths — originates to some degree from news releases. However, don't use such figures around journalists. They wouldn't want to admit they rely on PR practitioners, just as public relations pros must rely on print and electronic journalists. Remember to follow the typical guidelines for your releases, with a contact name, e-mail and phone numbers.

Be careful, however, of putting all your releases from the previous six months in a media kit. It's a waste of paper for one thing. Second, it's overwhelming to almost all journalists. For the one lone individual who wants do to an entire investigation of your written output, let her access them from the previously discussed Web site. That way she can pick and choose what's relevant for her audience and her own interests.

Fact Sheets

As the name suggests, these are pieces of paper full of facts. They're the media kit's equivalent of *Cliff's Notes*. Almost always one-page long, a fact sheet will list tidbits of information on a company, an event or a product that can prove useful to a journalist. Organized often in single-space outline or bullet form, the fact sheet may tell about the chronological history of an event, list participants, or give details about the host site. Sometimes a question-and-answer format is used. Media kits may contain one such fact sheet or a few. Again, be careful about overloading the journalists.

A national high school band competition media kit, for one example, contained two fact sheets. One told about the number of schools participating and what states they were from. The other highlighted the host university, with specifics about the indoor stadium (age, seating capacity, structural size) where the event occurred.

"Black Diamonds: The Story of Negro League Baseball" produced a media kit with a two-page fact sheet describing the exhibit, listing some highlights (Jackie Robinson's Brooklyn Dodgers cap from his rookie season in the major leagues), and giving particulars, such as location, times, admission and sponsors.

A fact sheet on "The Passion of the Christ" listed affirmative comments from individuals about the movie when it first opened. Excerpts from noted people included Christian evangelist Billy Graham, author Dr. James Dobson, journalist Matt Drudge and Jewish movie critic Michael Medved.

When several related topics need to be covered, it's usually best to write separate, isolated fact sheets. Developing a series of specific one-page fact sheets works because people are more inclined to read shorter documents. It also facilitates adding or updating details without having to change other content.

The popularity of fact sheets may be that they are so practical for the reporters working on their stories, both now and in the future. Various particulars are used to fill out the prose, which gives readers the impression that the journalist worked hard to "dig out" all such details. Anytime that you can make a reporter look good, you have done your job and won points with that journalist.

Biographies

Bios, as they are universally called, are also helpful inserts in media kits. Typically used for the chief executive officer and other key personnel, the article will provide detailed highlights about the company leader and other key positions leading to the current appointment. It can be a rather in-depth personality profile — going back to college activities and all subsequent achievements — or a briefer biographical sketch.

No matter which version you choose, make sure it's regularly updated. You want the public to think highly of your leaders so be sure to include all of their latest accomplishments in your media packet bio. The media rely on these bios a great deal when an administrator receives a major award, gets into legal hot water or dies.

Backgrounder

A major writing task, the backgrounder is often placed in media kits when appropriate to the subject. Essentially a lengthy report, a backgrounder provides indispensable details about a topic, event or organization. Not only valuable to the media, backgrounders can be useful for internal staff writers working on speeches, releases, reports, newsletters or other publications.

Backgrounders generally supply a complete historical overview of a situation in detailed fashion that's heavy on facts and light on opinion. They serve as a proactive tool so public relations professionals can best address the demands of media members who need detailed information immediately.

Similar in function to their smaller cousins — the fact sheets — backgrounders provide in-depth examination rather than skimming the highlights. Good backgrounders are organized in such a way so that media professionals can extract relevant information quickly and effortlessly. They too make the journalists look as if they are seasoned investigative reporters with their comprehensive coverage. So anticipate their questions by putting such extensive information into the backgrounder in the first place. Good public relations writers constantly update background information and record a date on each piece noting when it was last revised. Once again, interns are often asked to perform this task.

Because of the expanded context needed to fully explore an issue, backgrounders are often three to five pages long. An introduction explores the topic, then points are developed in a logical and factual manner. Remember, this is not the document for subjective claims. Format options for the backgrounder include graphs, tables, photographs and plenty of subheads to smoothly guide the readers. It frequently is printed on both sides of an 11 x 17 piece of paper, folded once, so it becomes a convenient four-page document.

Position Paper

Similar to the backgrounder in length and format, the position paper is also written to inform but it attempts to influence at the same time. Its research findings and facts are objective, but it draws conclusions and attempts to persuade the readers about a particular viewpoint.

To give recipients an understanding of where your company or organization stands on an issue, it's common to include a position paper in your media kit. This is especially relevant when a hot topic is brewing on the horizon that affects your client, whether it happens to be rezoning laws, legalized gambling or offshore drilling. (Please see chapter 10 for a more thorough discussion of position papers.)

Blueprint

Ontario Science Centre Media Kit

Agents of Change Backgrounder

June 15, 2004
Backgrounders

WHY INNOVATION

There is a growing national consensus that a collective commitment to innovation is essential to secure Canada's future in the new century. But the skills and attitudes that lead to innovation must be developed at an early age. A sustainable culture of innovation in Ontario and Canada will depend on more young people interested in and excited about futures in science and technology.

As a leader in informal education, the Ontario Science Centre is reinforcing its unique role in the cultivation of creative citizens interested in science and technology by embarking on a major transformation — one that will address a changing world and build on a prominent history.

Agents of Change is a $40-million initiative that will transform more than 30% of the Ontario Science Centre's public spaces by the spring of 2006. This involves renewing key exhibit spaces, creating new approaches to visitor experiences, deepening and extending partnerships province-wide, and making significant architectural improvements to the building.

Major new areas will feature content that explores the theme "Solving 21st Century Problems." Through the compelling experiences offered in these new spaces, young people will be exposed to the attitudes, skills, networks and tools that will enable them to become the drivers of a sustainable culture of innovation.

The core of Agents of Change is the Weston Family Innovation Centre which will consist of five distinct experiences: Hot Zone, Challenge Zone, Citizen Science, Media Studios and Material World. The Agents of Change initiative also includes four other areas: Grand Central; KidSpark; Exploration Plaza; and Youth Exchange.

WESTON FAMILY INNOVATION CENTRE

The Weston Family Innovation Centre is the engine that will propel Agents of Change — a series of five linked experience areas that will both spark and enable innovation in our visitors.

Hot Zone: Would you eat genetically modified food? Would you wear a microchip identifier? Visitors' opinions count in the Hot Zone's "Question of the Day" interactive poll. Visitors will encounter real-time field diaries from scientists on location across the globe, catch up on current science headlines and breaking stories, and enjoy live updates on topical issues by Science Centre staff and guest experts.

A scientific Times Square, the Hot Zone will be a dynamic hub for exploring and understanding current science and emerging technology, presented in unique and unexpected ways. Thought-provoking multimedia projections and engaging interfaces will highlight new developments and perspectives. On-site and Web site presentations will tackle today's "hot" science and technology through illuminating context and relevant, real-world connections. The Hot Zone will also house a nexus for youth to express and share their news and views on science.

Challenge Zone: During the Apollo 13 crisis, ground engineers managed to solve a critical problem for the astronauts using only the bits and pieces on board the space craft. A Challenge Zone experience will pose similar real-world challenges, offering participants the opportunity to become part of a collaborative, risk-taking team of problem-solvers.

Presented with a "Challenge of the Day," participant teams in the Challenge Zone are encouraged to design and build practical solutions using a variety of common and unusual materials within an allotted time. Sometimes someone directly affected outlines the challenge: a young Brazilian woman, whose village is suffering drought, asks the teams to find a way to carry river water to crops without electrical power or manual labour. Other times, current events spark the challenge: how would you adapt the Mars rover to cope with unexpected situations arising on the red planet? Challenge Zone facilitators will always be on hand to guide participants toward innovative solutions and ensure that everyone has a chance to exercise their ingenuity in a fun, creative atmosphere.

Citizen Science: Citizen Science will engage visitors in research projects, asking them to: build a sensor to monitor sulphur dioxide levels in their home and send the results to a central server; measure their daily mood and use a cell phone to add data to a real-time city-wide mood map; help track sunspots to create an animation of the Sun's activity level over time; check the health of the Science Centre wetland through on-site and on-line observations.

Citizen Science will be the place to get involved with professional scientists working on real research projects. Visitors' sulphur dioxide results will help scientists understand local air quality patterns. Their mood data will help scientists investigating the variables – such as seasons – that affect people's moods. Sunspot monitoring will help scientists correlate the Sun's activity with possible environmental impacts on Earth. Wetland observations will help scientists monitor the effects of climate change on a marsh environment. Visitors will also learn how to hone research questions, collect data, and analyze and visualize results. In fact, they will become citizen scientists.

Media Studios: Create music with the stroke of a brush or a wave of hands. Design jewellery that monitors the level of pollutants in the air. Make robots dance and clothing talk. Media Studios will encourage visitors to investigate the incredible potential of art juxtaposed with science.

Featuring a variety of media tools, Media Studios will be the place to discover what happens when the boundaries between music, fashion, art, technology and science start to blur. Whether it's a new game interface, a stop-motion animation or a video installation, each project created in Media Studios will be archived and made accessible to inspire future participants, who can then modify, build on or transform the material in perhaps unexpected ways. Technology in the Media Studios becomes a tool to enhance creativity and explore the juxtapositions that are the pathways of innovation.

Material World: We live in a "material world" – materials form our environment, our tools, even ourselves. And everyone is a materials scientist. Paper or plastic? Cotton or nylon? People are always making material choices, and experimenting with them. In Material World, participants will work with stuff that will stretch their ingenuity and creativity even further. Based on their explorations, they might produce a kinetic material symphonic sculpture out of simple kitchen utensils, devise a better snowboard or puck-proof new hockey equipment.

Material World will encourage visitors to look at the "stuff of life" in new ways, and let them explore how materials behave and how they might be used. They will be able to get their hands on exciting new materials, as well as create new uses for familiar ones. Some of the challenges could include experimenting with materials such as sports equipment and toys to improve their performance, dreaming up new materials with the properties to solve real-world problems, and working with artisans to explore the creative side of materials science. Surrounding participants in Material World will be inspiring solutions developed by materials scientists – from a truly recyclable plastic called baroplastic, to rechargeable polymer batteries that may one day power cars, to aerogel, the world's lightest solid material.

EXPLORATION PLAZA

The Exploration Plaza will dramatically transform the main entrance of the Science Centre and give visitors and neighbours alike an exciting taste of what lies ahead on their journey inside the building.

The outdoor experiences of the Plaza may give visitors the chance to explore a collection of sculptures that react to wind and rain, create music in a sound garden, become a sundial, or control water jets to choreograph a fountain.

GRAND CENTRAL

Earth, Air, Fire, Water…the four basic elements that form the foundations of science are the inspiration for Grand Central in the Science Centre's Procter and Gamble Great Hall. And Grand Central will be the inspirational starting point and end point of a Science Centre visit. The area will feature inspiring installation artworks that live at the nexus of art and science and that dominate a room of towering windows, an expansive floor space and a vista of the outdoors that contrasts a scene of primordial Canada immediate to a vibrant cityscape. Over the next year the Science Centre will develop collaborations with artists working in Canada and internationally to create the experiences of Grand Central, themed on the primeval elements of Earth, Air, Fire and Water.

KIDSPARK

KidSpark is a magnet for kids and their caregivers since it launched in November 2003. And in June 2004, KidSpark received the Best Exhibit award for 2003 by the Canadian Association of Science Centres.

Designed as a stimulating learn-through-play space for children eight and under, KidSpark is packed with more than 30 exciting experiences that offer much more than hands-on fun. Encompassing six themes: Play, Build, Flow, Sing, Shop and Move, KidSpark's open-ended, inquiry-based experiences are designed to foster creativity, problem-solving abilities and early innovation skills by focusing on the process of discovery and experimentation.

The space also features kid-size family washroom facilities, a place to park strollers and an enclosed Primary Workshop for weekday school programs. And to ensure that young visitors get the most from their KidSpark experience, senior students from Ryerson University's School of Early Childhood Education and Science Centre hosts work together to facilitate interaction among children, caregivers and materials, and bring focus to individual learning styles so that all find their spark of curiosity, inquiry and creativity.

In May 2004 the Science Centre announced that, in response to the tremendous popularity of KidSpark, it will more than double its size by early 2005. The expansion will also include new visitor amenities to meet the needs of families with young children.

YOUTH EXCHANGE

Located just above the Weston Family Innovation Centre, the Youth Exchange will encompass at least two state-of-the-art classroom labs, and a youth lounge. In this educational space, communities of interested youth will gather informally to mentor, discuss, debate and brainstorm programming strategies. Dedicated space to support these youth interns and volunteers will become the centre of program operations.

For more information, please contact:

> **Matt Akler, Media Relations Officer**
> **Phone**: (416) 696-3154
> **Fax**: (416) 696-3161
> **E-mail**: matt.akler@osc.on.ca

Agents of Change Backgrounder from Ontario Science Centre used with permission. www.ontariosciencecentre.ca

9.
Writing Features

Public relations writers often call feature stories evergreens, because they are always fresh. They are soft news contrasted to the hard news found in most straight releases. The timeliness element is rarely crucial. That's one of the reasons they're valuable in North American newsrooms, which may be why almost half of newspaper articles are features. They can be dropped into a page just about anytime there's an extra hole to fill. Features that can entertain and inform readers won't be trashed, unlike your news releases from yesterday that are date sensitive and no longer newsworthy. So it's beneficial for the PR practitioner to master both the art of creating ideas for feature stories as well as the skill of feature writing.

Sometimes you'll hear the phrase newsfeature. Is it a feature or a news story? Or both? Newsfeatures typically tap into a current news occurrence, but give it an informal, often human interest twist. A major snowstorm that sweeps across the Great Lakes in March is big news to the media. But a lot of other sidebars or newsfeatures can relate to the storm with a human element. Michigan ski resorts extend their seasons to become popular hangouts. Local grocery store clerks scurry to restock their depleted shelves. Stranded motorists sleep just outside Toronto in a manufacturing plant that provides cots and a warm supper. A Northeast Ohio food bank delivers meals using snowmobiles. You can see the possibilities if any of these organizations were your clients.

Another obvious difference between colorful features and straight news is the writing style. A formal news angle primarily is telling readers what happened. The facts are interpreted and delivered to the audience as they unfold. News releases generally follow the inverted pyramid style discussed earlier in this text. Factual items are selected for the story based on their newsworthiness, in a descending order of importance. They answer the basic questions of who, what, why, when, where and how. The end of the news release carries the most insignificant of details since the major news has been pushed to the top.

Casual features, on the other hand, usually try to let readers see what it was like to be on the scene. An old cliché heard in feature lectures is not to tell readers, but to show them. Don't say an energetic boss, for example. Let readers hear and see her pulling the tab on her third chilled can of Diet Dr Pepper before lunch.

Entertaining feature stories may be written on any subject at any time, unrelated to a recent news item. Although informal in style, they still need to follow proper grammar, punctuation and AP rules. Features have widespread appeal. Award-winning feature writer Tom Hallman described feature articles' popularity to his journalism colleagues:

> *"And they work because these stories have nothing to do with news, but with life itself. The best feature stories touch on universal themes in life, themes that remind us just how similar we are when it comes to hopes and dreams and fears. These stories help readers find meaning in life."* [1]

Although feature stories are popular among many audiences, the public relations writer must realize that almost all journalists love to put their own handprint on these rather informal creations. They even have competitions on both state and national levels for the best-written feature stories that have appeared in their newspapers. So the smart thing to do is give up your ego and let the professional reporter have fun with these valuable, but less-than-earth-shattering items for major external media.

Then why discuss feature writing for a whole chapter? For one thing, the reporter will still need assistance in researching, writing and, in most cases, even coming up with feature ideas about your organization or client that are geared for specific readers. Many practitioners will send regular beat reporters a personal pitch letter, describing a possible feature story concept. If it's appealing enough, the journalist may be enticed to tackle such an assignment. (Make sure you take turns spreading the gems around, so one medium doesn't feel slighted.) Since the writers and their employers are now investing time and resources on your suggestion, it stands a better chance of getting printed or aired. Being a skilled PR pro, you'll also be expected to quench the journalist's own thirst for unusual slants and profiles. Encourage and supply such materials. Anticipate questions and objections and be prepared to do a convincing (but not forceful) sales job with the reporter when necessary.

Second, you'll still be churning out plenty of feature articles yourself for various internal publications (newsletters, magazines, quarterlies), the company Web site and its up-to-date media kits. Your own submissions can also be sent to under-staffed, small-market television and radio stations in the region, all nondailies in the area, and those invaluable trade publications with their priceless editorial pages. Needless to say, there should always be an abundance of features to go around.

 ## Blueprint

Local Versus Cable TV

Pitch features to local stations.

If you're trying to decide where to pitch your next lifestyle piece — local or cable TV news — go local.

Even though you'd expect cable outlets with 24 hour-news holes to fill to be ripe for all kinds of features, they're not. That's because they devote most of their time to coverage of government and foreign affairs stories.

The Project for Excellence in Journalism reviewed local and cable news stories for a four-year period and found that while local TV focuses most on flashing red lights — the "if it bleeds, it leads" lineup — it's nonetheless more likely than CNN, FOX, or MSNBC to feature consumer, health, or other back-of-the-book pieces.

What do both local and cable story rundowns have in common? Very few science and technology stories.

How to Create Feature Ideas

"Ideas are to a writer what silver bullets were to the Lone Ranger," John Brady, former editor of *Writer's Digest*, once said. Freelance writers know they regularly have to depend on good ideas to put food on the table. Coming up with quality story proposals suitable for a targeted audience is essential for your client to get extended media coverage. You want good suggestions that will shed favorable light on your organization or its people, products and services. That's plenty of responsibility for the public relations staff. But it has to be done, so where do you start?

Ideas are everywhere. That may be a cliché, but it's true. Your company, client or organization provides products and services. It has management, employees, customers and competitors. It has a facility, a history and a location. If you as a PR writer are looking for newsfeatures, then look inward for suggestions. Make a habit of listening around the workplace: elevator, lunchroom, parking lot, wherever people congregate. Have you conducted any surveys lately among customers or employees? Such poll results frequently become fodder for features.

You'll also want to stay on top of current events, both locally and around the globe. If you're consciously looking for feature topics, you should read everything habitually. For starters, consider local and out-of-town newspapers (including the classifieds), industry publications and consumer magazines, both mainstream and offbeat. Have you ever read *Chip Chats* (wood carving), *Mavin* (multiracial issues), *Crappie* (sweepstakes), *Banana Magazine* (Asian-Canadian lifestyle), *Dirty Linen* (folk music), or *Along These Lines* (power consumption)? Just reading a few of these and other atypical titles should get your creative juices flowing. Don't forget to check out their display ads too.

See something interesting in a publication? Make a copy of it or just clip it out (when done legally) and file the item in a features folder. Remember, ideas cannot be copyrighted — only the words expressing those ideas. Creativity for feature writing develops more frequently for most of us from the file folder than the facility of the brain.

Perhaps a national trend or statistic you read about could be localized for your client and its media options. One of the reasons we suggest scanning smaller publications instead of the mainstream is that your ideas will be unique, rather than copying what millions of North Americans read last month. And smaller media — whether print or broadcast — employ smaller staffs. They are counting on assistance from reliable public relations writers. Your reading matter should also include billboards, junk mail, sundry bulletin boards at work and in the community, and all those pages of skipped-over material in the front or middle of telephone directories.

If your ideas folders are truly depleted, talk to sources. Although management may have some feature ideas, don't limit your search to those main characters. Talk to employees and volunteers. Look at events through the eyes and ears of bystanders, janitors and customers. Listening inside and outside the work environment is essential if you want good feature suggestions. Perhaps the barber, hairdresser, cashier or taxi driver can fill you in on what's happening in their world. Ask probing questions and pay attention to their answers.

Your job, of course, is to connect that information somehow with your product, service or company. You can always go online for some searches. Computer searches can be fast and thorough. Be careful of the time, however, since Web sites can occupy you for hours. Your client may have archives of news clippings, suggestion box submissions, newsletters and open house brochures to scrutinize. Maybe you'll discover an upcoming anniversary that no one recalled. Such milestones can be resurrected every 10 and 25 years for positive feature releases.

Ronald Levy, in *What's Your Big Idea?*, highlights 12 types of features that commonly make it into print with the help of astute public relations writers:

1. **Surveys** – if your company sells fishing gear, ask anglers questions you can use for feature stories in a variety of publications.

2. **Trends** – readers like to know what's "in" and what's going to be "in" soon.

3. **Then and Now** – new products seem superior when compared to the older models.

4. **Health Hints** – as the population gets older and lives longer, these should continue to be popular fodder.

5. **How It's Done** – this is the technical case history explained for the consumer slant.

6. **Gift-Giving Ideas** – these can pop up throughout the year for dozens of occasions.

7. **How to Buy** – tapping into the consumer movement will endear you to readers.

8. **Oddities** – offering unique or strange services and products can get you attention.

9. **Tips from the Top** – helping customers will always help you make a good impression.

10. **Money Matters** – many readers are involved with stocks, so financial news they can use is highly sought.

11. **Sights and Sounds** – destination pieces are popular any time of year.

12. **Weird and Wonderful** – there's always a catch-all category for great but unusual feature articles.[2]

The major hard news element normally developed in an informative straight news story may be supplanted in the informal feature by a focus directed on individuals. It may be about those at an event or even those behind the scenes of an event.

"People are interested in people," Jim Murray, legendary *Los Angeles Times* sports columnist, said. "They're not interested in things."

So who were the individuals instrumental in starting the company 50 years ago? And where are they today? Can you interview any of them? Or can you perhaps arrange for an appropriate journalist to meet them for a lengthy interview?

Personality profiles of interesting people make entertaining features. And they don't have to be about the top brass of a company. Employees overcoming disabilities or one who recently won an award are good topics. Let the characters carry the story with their action and thoughts as well as good quotes. Of course, knowing the publication and its readers are the keys for the writing process. You must make the feature vital reading to that audience. When finished reading it, they should care about your subject.

Whether you assist in research or write the piece, you must be thorough in your initial background search. Putting a reporter in touch with the employee you thought would make an excellent subject for a daily newspaper feature can backfire. What if the enterprising reporter discovers that the individual — who works in payroll — was fired and charged with embezzlement at a prior job 15 years earlier? Ask a lot of questions, even those tough, prying ones. A little embarrassment now is better than a newscast or front-page major fiasco next week.

How to Write Features

Beginning authors often assume that the feature is easy to write. After all, they reason, there's no meeting to cover, busy executive to interview or laborious report to study. They can just create some words off the top of their head, some would fathom, and *voila* — a feature story. Nothing could be further from the truth. Because you don't have an event that unfolds before you, you can't rely on the story to write itself. There's not always some inherent arrangement where you can place certain paragraphs in a logical, inverted-pyramid sequence. Those familiar with both writing tasks usually agree that the feature is much harder to develop and more time consuming than a straight news release.

Before you start hitting the keyboard, you need to think about some preliminary steps. One is to select your theme that you'll develop throughout the feature. Will it be emotional in intent or a straight newsfeature? Instructional or entertaining? What unifies your story? What will make readers care about your topic?

Travis Poling in the June 2002 *Quill* magazine, discusses this point:

> But what sets top-notch feature writing apart from the pack of promising prose is the narrative thread. There are two threads of a story — one for the reporting process and the other that makes it into print.
>
> When a reporter sees a glimmer of promise in a potential story, he or she grabs those obvious reporting threads and starts pulling to reveal details, secrets, motives, emotions. That is good reporting.
>
> The second thread is the narrative thread that weaves the whole story together from beginning to end. That is good writing....
>
> A strong, well-written piece can easily fall apart when the story skips around and abandons a strong narrative. Pull on the narrative thread. If it comes out in pieces, it is time to rethread the needle and start again.[3]

Study Other Writers

All serious students of writing must also be serious readers. You can't expect to flourish in a field that you do not enjoy and also aren't very familiar with. Read everything you can get your hands on.... Study what other writers are doing.

The Complete Idiot's Guide to Getting Published

Gathering and organizing material is also an essential step. Always conduct more research than you could possibly use for your feature story. Yes, you need to build your article on factual information. It's best to cover all the bases during your initial research instead of being sidetracked during the writing process to unearth some minor, time-consuming details that you could have and should have recorded the first time. The writing process will seem easier when your fact-gathering methods give you confidence that you sufficiently know your feature article subject matter.

A still-memorable sentence in an Oct. 23, 1995, *Sports Illustrated* feature indicates the writer did some calculating research. The piece was a profile by award-winning columnist Rick Reilly of NFL running back Craig "Ironhead" Heywood. "A reunion of Craig's sister and six brothers would be illegal in many elevators," Reilly wrote. Isn't that livelier than saying the eight of them weighed a combined 1,978 or so pounds?

Part of the research process, of course, includes targeting specific readers. As you must know by now, every news release and feature article should be slanted toward a particular publication's audience. That means you must study those coveted professional or trade magazines to understand their tone. The most common cited reason why editors reject manuscripts (from public relations writers and freelancers) is that the authors do not understand nor write for their particular readership. Therefore, try to mimic successful straight news releases by localizing your features as much as possible. Do your homework before writing, let alone submitting, any feature chronicles on behalf of your client or organization.

Likewise, even internal publications may be targeted to different audiences: employees, management, volunteers, stockholders. Each needs a different perspective on an issue, so try to slant your feature story toward a specific audience for best results.

"The best of these feature stories are built, not on fancy writing, but on strong, in-depth reporting," Hallman added in his *Quill* piece. "They require as much reporting as is needed to pull off a blockbuster investigative piece."

Unlike the straight news release that you send to the media, features rarely follow the inverted pyramid or similar structures. A feature release often saves key details for the middle or end of the article. The lead and the ending are by far the two most powerful pieces of the successful feature release. For example, features can sometimes conceal the punchline in the last sentence, rather than the first for a traditional news story.

Often the last paragraph hits the reader with a statement that ties in with the lead. The news release's standard summary lead is exchanged for such techniques as direct quotation, anecdotes or even dialogue. The lead is certainly the most important element in writing, however, whether it's for standard releases or features. In both cases, it has to capture the interest of the targeted audience as quickly as possible.

 **Blueprint**

Nut Graphs Tell Readers Precisely What Story Is About

Writers, especially feature writers, often begin their stories with a narrative paragraph or two. The explanatory paragraph following the lead is called the nut graph. This paragraph explains the significance of the story and gives its news peg.

An example of a nut graph (in this case, two paragraphs long for reasons of length) appears in paragraphs three and four below following two introductory paragraphs.

1 Lisa Tietgen fondly remembers riding her sled through the snowy St. Michael, Minn., farmland where she forged life-long friendships, and occasionally got a touch of frostbite.

2 Tietgen, who moved back to the Minneapolis suburb in early 2000 after more than 10 years living in New Jersey, owns the town's most prosperous real estate development firm. Now, she hopes to lend her expertise to help preserve the fond memories of her childhood while paving the way for development of this once remote countryside.

3 Appointed to the St. Michael Town Council Monday, Tietgen, 38, will help oversee a massive development project that includes adding a new downtown shopping area, hundreds of new homes and a massive business park.

4 St. Michael's population of 10,000 expects to swell to more than 40,000 within 10 years. The blossoming Minneapolis business community has spilled over to neighboring suburbs in the last 10 years creating an urban sprawl never before seen in the state. Tietgen said she hopes she can help preserve some of St. Michael's small-town flavor while carefully planning for economic growth.

The narrative found in the lead paragraphs sets the mood for the story and arouses reader interest. It then invites the news peg — the significance of the story — in the third and fourth paragraphs. Often referred to as the "so-what" paragraph, the nut graph draws readers into the story and paints a picture of the story elements.

The Power of Imagery

1. **Simile** – a comparison of dissimilar things using either like or as.

   Example: Good prayer is like a beautiful garden.

2. **Metaphor** – a comparison of dissimilar things without using like or as.

   Example: Good prayer is a garden.

3. **Personification** – giving human qualities to inanimate objects.

   Example: Our team is reaching for the stars.

4. **Exaggeration** (hyperbole) – overstating for dramatic impact.

   Example: Our team has moved mountains to win the championship.

Types of Feature Leads

A lead can be one sentence or it can be up to two or three paragraphs, as discussed earlier in chapter 5. Its task is not easy — to "hook" the reader into the remainder of the copy. A strong inviting lead has to entice your audience to jump into the feature head first. Those opening sentences have the responsibility to compel even casual readers to zero in on the topic as "must-read" material. Much of the success of the feature story rests in those crucial opening words. If the lead doesn't do its job, then the PR writer has failed to complete delivery of the message to an intended audience for the company or client.

The anecdote lead has both strengths and weaknesses. The strengths are that it humanizes a larger issue. We can see the flesh and blood results of a legislative action or a corporate board decision. Readers have an easier way to visualize the situation you're describing when they see its affect on one of their own. *The Wall Street Journal* does an excellent job of showing the impact of a national development upon a local individual with its frequent anecdotal examples.

Because anecdotes became such popular feature leads, critics said they started appearing too often. William E. Blundell, author of *The Art and Craft of Feature Writing*, cautioned staff about their overuse at a *Detroit Free Press* two-day workshop. He outlined three tests to determine if an anecdotal lead is right for a story. If it fails at any of the three, it should not be used.

The first is simplicity. If the anecdote requires explanation, it is too dense or complicated for a lead. Save it for later.

Next is theme relevance. The lead anecdote must illustrate the central point of the story. "But it's the best thing I've got," wails the writer within. Don't use it. It sends story and reader off in the wrong direction, and will make the reader feel misled.

Finally, to lead the story, the anecdote must have intrinsic interest. It must be good all by itself. "If you put the lead on an index card and took it out to Woodward Avenue and asked people to read it by itself, would their eyebrows go up? Even by a millimeter?" If not, Blundell says, don't lead with it.[4]

It's often possible to start a feature release using chronology. In fact, more than a few features effectively unravel in chronological sequence. As you know by now, that's rare for a straight news release. Readers are naturally curious, wanting to know what happened next. This is one of the few times when writing the feature may not be as labor-intensive as the straight news release.

A question lead is more applicable to features than straight news releases. Its inherent danger in both situations is to turn off readers. If they have no interest in your topic, based on the opening question, they will probably stop reading. "Did you ever wonder what happens to those recycled two-liter bottles?" A great feature about your client turning them into playground equipment may go unread if the audience never thought about it before, and thus, doesn't care to know now. Be careful, therefore, that your question doesn't lead to a possible "no" or "who cares?" response by the reader.

Quotations can be great tools for feature leads. They give your readers an immediate sense of being in on the action, of hearing sources' own words describe their feelings or plans. They make stories more personal and more conversational. As attention getters, full-sentence quotes are great ways to start paragraphs. Editors often are more hesitant about chopping such citations. However, three main problems stymie the service of direct quotes.

One is their overuse. Just because someone said it — and you took accurate notes — doesn't mean you have to write it. With a few exceptions, stories that are overstocked with quotes will probably lack understanding and background details. As a PR writer, your responsibility is to condense quotes to mine the nuggets within them. You are allowed to cut the CEO's five rambling sentences into two succinct ones that say it all. Additionally, another overuse problem is that too many quotations from too many characters can confuse your readers. Keep sources to a minimum when possible, and try to lump their comments in certain segments of the story, rather than spreading them throughout.

> Citations should be reserved for memorable statements, not mundane morsels of drivel.

The second drawback of direct quotations, related to the first, is quoting the wrong material. Citations should be reserved for memorable statements, not mundane morsels of drivel. "Our product will be on store shelves by Oct. 1" is hardly worth writing home about, let alone using as a lead. Paraphrasing and indirect quotes are better for much of your notes. Save the direct quotes for startling statements or things stated in a unique fashion.

And that brings us to our third reservation about direct quotation leads. It is typically arduous for individuals to derive with their own words a perfectly expressed, singular statement that can carry all the responsibilities of a good lead. Even excellent quotes don't always qualify as effective leads. They could be quite off target, giving readers the wrong impression about the main content of the ensuing feature release.

Humor and joke leads can engage readers or offend them. Redneck jokes, popularized by Jeff Foxworthy, are favorites of many and despised as sophomoric or politically incorrect by others. (Calling Atlanta his home, Foxworthy certainly understands his subject, his audience and his media.) Because defining funny is so subjective, it's often difficult to know how and when to use humor — and how much — in your feature stories. These articles should certainly be entertaining and memorable. Advertising copywriters have sadly discovered that customers may recall the humor in a commercial message but forget the product's name. Comedy is not easy to master and jokes can backfire. Never belittle your audience by making them the butt of the humor. Even classical humorist Mark Twain once said, "There are several kinds of stories, but only one difficult kind — the humorous."

A few other lead examples are metaphor, simile and analogy. A metaphor is merely stating a comparison between two unlike items or conditions. As Twain again put it, "Cauliflower is nothing but a cabbage with a college education." A simile makes the direct comparison, usually using *like* or *as*. "More than 250 customers lined up like penguins Friday, awaiting the Montreal Gap's grand opening." The analogy compares unusual concepts with common terms: "Basketball fans at Duke do a lot of jumping during home games. Latest estimates place them at 5.5 on the Richter scale."

Notes

[1] Tom Hallman. "Features Go Beyond Facts." *Quill*, July 2003, v. 91, n. 5

[2] Ronald Levy. "What's Your Big Idea?" *Public Relations Quarterly*, Fall 2002, v. 47, n. 3, p. 20.

[3] Travis E. Poling. "Good Features Use Narrative." *Quill*. June 2002, v. 90, n. 5, p. 36.

[4] Joe Grimm. "The Art and Craft of Feature Writing." *Detroit Free Press In-House Training Bulletin*, January 1999.

10.
Writing Persuasive Copy

Although you've been drilled about objectivity for those ubiquitous news releases, there are times when public relations practitioners need to provide persuasive messages to certain audiences. These convincing articles are useful to tell an organization's side of the story, to alert the public about some impending legislative action, or to convince a targeted public it needs to take some kind of action. Because it's not easy to get people to change their opinions or behavior, this is a challenging task. Historically, advocacy always has been an important role for public relations practitioners. The North American giants of modern public relations — Ivy Lee and Edward Bernays — both displayed genius in getting publics to adopt new behaviors and beliefs.

Yet some critics insist that the contemporary higher education system, with an emphasis on detached journalistic writing, has public relations students buying into a mindset that promoting and supporting a position is somehow unethical. "This instills in aspiring public relations counselors a higher regard for journalistic objectivity than for public relations advocacy."[1] Therefore, you need to be prepared that you might encounter resistance (even from yourself) when you create persuasive communication. Yet, it's a natural function for the practitioner to use advocacy in the right situation. The latest version of the PRSA Member Code of Ethics, in fact, lists advocacy first under its "Statement of Professional Values."

ADVOCACY
- We serve the public interest by acting as responsible advocates for those we represent.
- We provide a voice in the marketplace of ideas, facts and viewpoints to aid informed public debate.[2]

This whole textbook chapter discusses the somewhat rare occasion where subjective writing is expected and even encouraged, by management as well as media. This doesn't mean you get to throw out all the rules about objective news releases, since many of the same writing and research skills are needed to produce plausible arguments on behalf of your client. In fact, you have to thoroughly understand an issue to convincingly present not only your case, but a rebuttal against the opposite side.

Many of the writing tools we discuss in this chapter are among the most important for an organization or a company to use. (We will skip until chapter 13 brochures and other similarly produced controlled media that a company can also use as platforms for persuasive messages.)

Blueprint

Persuasion Theory in Public Relations

Public relations, by its nature, is considered to be persuasive. Much of what IABC and PRSA professionals attempt on a daily basis is influencing individuals or groups of people.

Earl Newsom's theory of persuasion rests on four principles:

1. **Identification** – Individuals will relate to an idea or opinion if they can see the connection with their own wants or hopes.

   This first point of identification is well summarized by radical demonstrator Saul Alinsky, who explained his simple theory of persuasion as: "People only understand things in terms of their own experiences...If you try to get your ideas across to others without paying attention to what they have to say to you, you can forget about the whole thing."

2. **Suggested Action** – People will adopt new concepts only if they are aligned with a proposed action, and the simpler the better.

3. **Familiarity and Trust** – People are reluctant to accept ideas from sources they don't trust.

   Thus a goal of PR practitioners is to build and enhance the confidence that the public places in their organizations or clients. This is a major thrust of proactive public relations, building credibility and goodwill among important publics.

4. **Clarity** – In order to be persuasive, the meaning of an idea in an event or message has to be clear.

   One of the often-heard complaints by journalists is the PR-produced jargon and doublespeak that clouds clear communication. Undoubtedly, that's one of the major reasons more than 90 percent of news releases are discarded by the media.

Pitch Letters

Before we tackle these major writing topics, we'll look at a small, but important tool in your PR writing toolbox. A short persuasive document that you may produce often is the pitch letter. This is a personally addressed business letter on company stationery to particular journalists to entice them to provide coverage of an event or to interview a client. Unlike a fact sheet or media advisory — that objectively gives an advance warning to the media about an upcoming occurrence — the pitch letter is meant to persuade. You spell out why it's crucial for the medium to provide information on this specific topic to its audiences. You try to politely convince the media gatekeepers that this is the "smart" thing to do as professionals.

For print, the letter goes to the beat reporter or editor who covers your organization. If you're not sure who that individual is, get the name from the publication and spell it correctly. Nothing upsets a journalist more than getting generic mail (business editor) unless it's mail with one's name misspelled. For most television stations the key contact is the assignment editor, whose job is to direct camera crews to specific locations at specific times.

It's always best if you have made personal contacts with these individuals before you need to send pitch letters. That can give you a foot in the door for making your persuasive appeal, one of many the media receive on a regular basis. If you have a reputation for suggesting solid news coverage, your future pitch letters should get noticed when they arrive. Make sure you provide specific details about the coverage you desire as well as its significance to the medium providing news to its community.

Position papers, op-ed pieces, guest editorials and advertorials provide an ideal platform to convey controlled messages to targeted publics. They might shape a client's future, determine how laws will affect its operation, and create favorable public opinion, especially following a crisis. Naturally, creating these documents and using them proactively is the optimum way of getting the most mileage from them.

TOOLBOX TIP

Points to Ponder in a Pitch Letter

- Include enough facts to support the full story you intend to write.

- Provide an angle of interest to the readers of the specific publication you have chosen.

- Offer the editor the possibility of alternative angles.

- Indicate your willingness to supply or aid the editor in securing quotes, interviews with credible sources, important statistics, arrangements for photographs and illustrations.

- Explain your credibility or authority to deliver the article and mention that you will call the editor for his/her decision.

(Fran Pelham, "The Triple Crown of Public Relations: Pitch Letter, News Release, Feature Article." *Public Relations Quarterly*, Spring 2000.)

Position Papers

Simply stated, position papers are persuasive documents written by a company's public relations team for a variety of audiences. They can be sent to the media, employees, legislators, investors, etc. Often called "white papers" in the corporate world, these are expanded editorials — often four pages long for PR purposes — that provide the organization's policies and position on a current or future situation. Somewhat similar to the much more objective backgrounder, the position paper gives writers the opportunity to conduct research, present the facts and then take a stand on what's the best option or course of action, and why.

Industry may go overboard at times with white papers, setting up a scenario as to why its product or service is necessary for other companies' survival. Nielsen Media Research produced a white paper in late November 2003 after that fall's prime-time television viewer studies showed a massive drop of the coveted male viewers in the 18 to 34 age group. Nielsen defended its survey methodologies despite criticism from ad agencies and TV networks. The white paper credited the growing popularity of DVDs, video games and personal video recorders as responsible for the decrease in the male TV audience.

> Position papers have sundry uses, which is why the public relations department has to be vigilant in seeking out possible topics on the horizon.

Unlike some white papers, however, you'll want to keep jargon and other technical language to a minimum. Other "inside" language should be avoided, such as acronyms. To win your argument, you need the readers to understand the situation as well as your credible solution. Talking over their heads will have the opposite effect. Their lack of understanding will be coupled with a sense of frustration. Chances are your report won't even be read to the finish if you annoy your audience with jargon.

Position papers have sundry uses, which is why the public relations department has to be vigilant in seeking out possible topics on the horizon. These can be local, regional or even international in scope. The media will often need position papers from your organization because of a timely news occurrence. Getting your company's reaction and perspective on that issue is a legitimate news function. So the PR staff needs to be prepared for media inquiries about such events when possible. However, do not send your position papers in a mass mailing to all regional media outlets. Editors and publishers like exclusives on their editorial pages. That's why syndicated columnists, by contract, cannot appear in competing newspapers in the same market. So parcel out your executive's essays so one medium doesn't feel slighted. A quick rewrite with a different lead will enable you to send the treatise on a hot topic to another publication if needed.

Once a potential issue has been identified, the PR staff alerts management with a draft outlining the organization's ties to the subject and implications for the future. After several drafts, a final version is formed. Whether intended for internal or external audiences, most white papers take a similar approach. A brief introduction and historical overview broaches the matter. As in the backgrounder, a position paper brings the readers thoroughly up to date on the topic. After informing, however, the latter document begins to persuade its audience. An organization's official stance on an issue must be effectively supported with convincing, objective documentation. As in typical newspaper editorials, opposing something is best supported if one can propose a better alternative solution.

Rather than ignoring the other side of the argument, successful position paper writers will acknowledge the opposite point of view. Then, with good, solid specifics — rather than stacking the deck — they will refute such merits with better solutions. Be careful, however, about exaggerations or overstating the facts. You need credibility with your audience if you want to persuade them. That involves research, so you need to be familiar with such techniques as Internet searches, clippings from publications, speeches, books and specialized sources. But be careful about overloading the document with too many statistics or numbing numbers. You may want to cite references, where interested readers can go for further information. Clear, logical arguments are most effective. Irrational and emotional pleas get less response, especially from the informed, educated audience that you're probably targeting.

Many papers will have a conclusive summary, knowing that busy readers often turn to that, and nothing else, to form an opinion about the document's merit. This is especially vital if the white paper gets lengthy, since some of them can reach 20 pages or more. Knowing that the length typically decreases readership and acceptance rates by the media, public relations staffs should strive for much shorter documents than technical writers from industry. One of the key things to keep in mind for brevity is to focus on only one main point in your position

Check Out More White Papers

To look at some other examples, do an Internet search of "white paper." Read some of them to see how similar they are. Others, of course, will be more specialized. Are some in your opinion too technical or too long? How much jargon is used? Which ones do you think are the most effective?

Blueprint

Persuasive Efforts Begin With Clear Audience Analysis

The most critical element to the success of any persuasive effort is having a clear sense of what you're trying to accomplish. Addressing the attitudes of the audience and moving the audience to action present the two most important goals of any persuasive communication.

Motivating your reader to take action offers the most difficult challenge for any writer. Writers face the challenge of overcoming situational forces that cause readers to say one thing but do another. For example, the writer may influence the reader to adopt a particular political position. However, if the reader gets opposition from friends concerning the political position, he or she may reject taking action for fear of scorn. Consequently, persuasive writing must anticipate objections and address concerns to help solidify the message in the reader's mind.

Public opinion is the sum of individuals' opinions on a subject that affects them. Writers must determine how differing opinions affect individuals before crafting a message. In doing so, writers must distinguish between opinions and attitudes.

An opinion is an expression of attitude. It may be expressed in writing, by speaking, by acting or by not acting. People who fail to express their opinions may do so because their attitudes are weak or because they don't believe that expressing them will do any good.

An attitude is a predisposition to think, speak or act in a given way about a specific subject. No one is born with an attitude; all attitudes are learned. Some attitudes are deeply rooted. When tied into other attitudes, beliefs and values, they may be hard to change.

Remember to first consider the four audience types:

1. **Active Audience**. Already actively participating in the issue.

2. **Latent Audience**. An existing audience that has yet to form an opinion.

continued on opposite page

paper. If research produces a bundle of material, consider writing other persuasive messages for different publications aimed at different audiences.

Producing position papers is not a difficult task. Some organizations might print them as single sheets, using letterhead for page one. Others run them off on both sides of 11 x 17 paper, so one fold will create the four pages, united in a convenient format. Those intended for internal audiences are usually not as elaborate as ones for external distribution. The latter are often printed on heavier stock with colorful graphics and covers. Position papers often appear as useful insertions

---

3. **Aware Audience.** An audience that knows that something is emerging but has limited facts to formulate an opinion.

4. **Passive Audience**. An audience that is indifferent on a subject and unaware of any impact it has on the members.

After first establishing the overarching persuasive goal, the writer must then decide the type and direction of the change. The following four persuasive aims help define the nature of the overall persuasive goal.

1. **Adoption**. Here the writer attempts to get the reader to adopt an idea or plan. Write the message clearly and without ambiguity. For example, if you're writing a persuasive message to get residents to approve a school bond referendum, use clean, crisp language. The message may read, "We urge every resident of Cumberland County to get out and vote YES on Nov. 8 to support school expansion in the district."

2. **Continuance**. Here the writer simply wants the audience to continue to behave as it did in the past. The example from above may read, "Residents of Cumberland County must continue their fervent support of Cumberland's schools and vote YES on Nov. 8 to support school expansion."

3. **Discontinuance**. Here the writer wants the audience to stop doing something. Continuing the example from above, "Residents of Cumberland County need to reverse the bad fortunes of recent bond referendums and support a plan to infuse much needed money into Cumberland's growing school system."

4. **Deterrence**. Here the writer's goal is avoidance. Simply, the writer wants to convince the audience not to do something. The final example from above, "Residents of Cumberland County have voted against the last two bond referendums to infuse needed funds into Cumberland's school system. This Nov. 8 let's reverse that trend and vote YES for school expansion."

---

in media kits or in special mailings to legislators or other targeted publics in order to generate timely support.

Don't think you have to wait until graduation to start writing position papers. Print yearbook sales have declined at many college campuses in North America. Should your school scrap this historic tradition and go with a video or CD-ROM version instead? Think about other controversial concerns on campus or in the community (such as year-round public schools) for other possibilities. The keys to remember for writing these persuasive documents are simple: research, inform and persuade.

Op-Ed Pieces/Guest Editorials

Op-ed contributions and guest editorials often stem from condensed white papers. In fact, those are fairly common methods to get more mileage and wider exposure from a well-drafted document. Op-eds and guest editorials are great opportunities to have an organization's viewpoint explained in great detail.

Furthermore, this public relations tool is rarely subject to any editing by the media gatekeeper. The four-page position paper, however, is probably way too long for a newspaper or magazine opinion article. It's wise to always check with the medium's guidelines regarding submissions for both op-ed pieces and guest editorials so they can be boiled down to the proper length and submitted before its deadline. These articles appear in a prominent position in the publication and usually get high readership.

Research at *The New York Times* revealed that its editorial section is second only to the front page for readership. Studies elsewhere show that editorial sections are consumed more by older, higher-income and higher-educated citizens than the average reader. Daily newspapers often rely on guest submissions to help fill the section, especially in weekend and holiday editions. We're familiar with one Tennessee newspaper that devotes one-third of its op-ed page to a local community leader's column each day during the latter half of December.

The op-ed page, which stands for opinion-editorial or opposite editorial, depending on whom you ask and where you're from, took shape across North America when newspapers decided to make their publications more open to community voices. The traditional editorial page still pronounced the institutional positions on a variety of topics, from local zoning proposals to international conflicts. But another key page in that section opened up to other viewpoints to allow a community dialogue to take place. In this way, publishers were attempting to show that the power of the press did not belong to only those who owned printing facilities. Credit for instituting the first op-ed page goes to Harrison Salisbury of *The New York Times* on Sept. 26, 1970. Some insist that *The Washington Post*, after being informed that its New York competition was about to launch such a page, actually beat *The Times* by inaugurating its own op-ed page a few days earlier. Many newspapers in big and small cities soon copied the leaders and adopted similar versions, with expanded letters to the editor, syndicated columnists, guest editorials and op-ed contributions.

An article in *Political Communication* pointed out the value of such a newspaper location for attracting readers:

> *The op-ed page is a hospitable environment to dissemi-nate an organized interest's message. The newspaper and the page lend their prestige, authority, and credibility to the organization's message. While the op-ed page may not offer the breadth or quantity of readership of some publica-tions or the audience of television and radio, it does offer quality of readership.*[4]

You as a public relations writer need to be proactive in seeking out opportunities for the placement of both guest editorials and op-ed pieces as promotion tools for your client or company. Some regional print media may ask for submissions occasionally, but why wait for that rare occurrence? Be alert to current events or future trends that could be developed into op-ed pieces. For maximum impact, enlighten and sway your audience without crass commercialism from the bylined author's organization.

TOOLBOX TIP

Tips on Writing Op-Ed Pieces from National Conference of Editorial Writers

➤ Put your main point on top. You have no more than 10 seconds to hook a reader. One of the most common mistakes is using too much wind-up before throwing the pitch.

➤ Make a single point — well. You cannot expect to solve all the world's problems in 800 words or less. Be as specific as possible.

➤ Avoid jargon. Simple language does not mean simple thinking. It means you are being considerate of readers who lack your expertise and are sitting half-awake at the breakfast table.

➤ Use the active voice. Don't write, "It is believed..." or "It is shown by studies...." Write instead, "I believe..." or "Studies show..."

➤ Tell the readers why they should care. Ask yourself, "So what? Who cares?" Explain why readers should care; appeal to their self-interest.

➤ Relax and have fun. Newspaper editors despair of weighty articles, called thumb suckers, and yearn for items filled with spirit, grace and humor. Readers seek to be entertained and learn something in the bargain.

➤ Avoid tedious rebuttals. In writing a response to an earlier piece that made your blood boil, mention the earlier piece and then argue your own case. A point-by-point rebuttal makes you look petty, and it's a safe bet many readers didn't see the first piece.

Advertorials

Advertorials are often called advocacy advertisements, but we'll clearly distinguish the two in this section. Advocacy advertising (see chapter 14) has been around for a long time. Typically the sponsoring organization attempts to run this paid form of commercial speech in the editorial section of the paper, if not on the actual op-ed page itself. Mobil Oil is often mentioned as one of the best examples of advocacy advertising. That's because the company started running its long series of commentary — often on controversial topics — in the op-ed section of *The New York Times*. The first such ad to appear there was on Oct. 19, 1970, when Mobil encouraged citizens to use public transportation. Even during a North American energy crisis, such a position was far from popular with the other oil companies. It was also during this period that the consumer movement was still going strong. Ralph Nader during the late-1960s had energized college students and others to join the crusade against big business. Thus, advocacy ads multiplied, especially on environmental and consumer issues, as corporations attempted to explain their actions.

However, Mobil (now ExxonMobil) was not the first to use advocacy advertisement to get across a viewpoint to key publics. In the 1930s, for example, labor unions went public via advocacy advertising with their concerns about better working conditions and higher wages. Many such ads at that time by industry were critical of government policies, especially those that hampered the free enterprise system. Even earlier than that, when modern public relations was evolving in the early 1900s, corporations fought back against the investigative reporting attacks of the muckrakers with paid print messages to supplement lobbying efforts.

Most advocacy ads today in both the United States and Canada appear in newspapers, although *Time* magazine and other news publications will run their share. Major metropolitan dailies and national newspapers — *USA Today*, *The Wall Street Journal* and *The New York Times* — receive the bulk of them. *The Times* often markets its bottom right corner space with a house ad when no advocacy spot appears on the page. It's not unusual for the hometown newspapers of the corporation and its manufacturing plants to also print advocacy ads. Their aim is to influence employees, taxpayers, opinion leaders and legislators. One of the advantages of papers over news magazines, other than cost, is the shorter lead time to make deadlines for urgent messages. Among common sponsors of such public lobbying efforts are trade associations, professional associations, environmental groups, health care industries and corporations.

Advertorials, on the other hand, lately have become synonymous with cleverly designed ads that resemble actual editorial copy. Similar to the electronic infomercials, they are written by more advertising copywriters than public relations practitioners. More commonly found in magazines, advertorials still crop up in papers, from national dailies such as *USA Today* to small-town nondailies. Most publications have established clearly defined policies on acceptance of any type of camouflaged ads. The problem is not with the writing of advertorials, but with the ethics when the publication does not plainly designate the piece as advertising. In many countries, such ads are required to be clearly identified with the words "advertising," "advertisement" or "special advertising supplement." On too many pages, when it does appear, such wording is in eight-point or smaller type.

> Readers are looking for solutions to their problems, and may not distinguish the source as a news item or an ad.

Despite such regulations, however, unmarked advertorials still appear in many newspapers. Often touting medical cures or revolutionary inventions, these ads will use testimonials and endorsements about the greatest thing since sliced bread. And naïve readers will buy into it literally, sending money to order the latest gadget, weight loss pill, golf ball or video.

The advertorial appears to have the credibility of news/editorial material married to the persuasiveness of an advertising message. These are blatant attacks by underhanded advertisers to make their purchased space resemble an actual news story, complete with headlines, bylines and news column widths. One online company providing the service will even make the font and spacing resemble a specific newspaper's style. And some unnamed magazines, in this day of value-added service, have offered ad clients a free advertorial for placing a paid ad elsewhere in the publication. Others are pushing multiple-page advertorial sections when the company refuses to purchase traditional advertising packages.

Readers are looking for solutions to their problems, and may not distinguish the source as a news item or an ad. The higher credibility normally afforded actual news copy will only confuse consumers as they make decisions that are far from objective. The deception from advertorials will hurt the company that pays for the ads as well as the publication that runs them.

In fact, their overuse by publications was featured in the magazine industry's trade publication *Folio*.

But media buyers are grumbling louder these days about how the glut of poorly designed special sections is weakening both magazine brands and the special-section format itself. Bad ones dilute editorial credibility, and even those with high production values raise questions about the line between church and state and the value of the magazine brand, buyers say. Finally, the buyers talk about overload: There are so many advertorials that they have lost their impact.[5]

Although many public relations practitioners are not involved in the practice of writing advertorials, their use by companies that employ PR professionals becomes a major image problem. Writing effective, plausible copy that deceives the public violates ethics codes from the profession.

Notes

[1] Ruth Edgett. "Toward an Ethical Framework for Advocacy in Public Relations." *Journal of Public Relations Research*, 2002, v. 14, pp. 1-26.

[2] *Public Relations Tactics: The Blue Book*. New York, NY: Public Relations Society of America, 2004.

[3] "Nielsen Report Defends Methods." *Advertising Age*. December 1, 2003. v. 74, n. 48, p. 16.

[4] Clyde Brown, Herbert Waltzer, Miriam Waltzer. "Daring to be Heard: Advertorials by Organized Interests on the Op-Ed Page of The New York Times, 1985-1998." *Political Communication*. January 2001. v. 18, n. 1.

[5] Sarah Gonser. "The Downside of the Advertorial Boom." *Folio*. November 1, 2003.

11.

Writing Effective Speeches

by
Douglas Perret Starr

Speeches are wonderful public relations tools. Unlike a news release that may or may not get noticed by the masses, a speech has the full, undivided attention of those in attendance. And, as you'll read in this chapter, it can also generate interest from many other key audiences. However much you personally dread giving a speech, writing one for someone else is often much more difficult. You have to reason and articulate as if you were in someone else's head. And, since an organization's executive is thrust into the limelight, that individual will be forced to give public speeches on a routine basis.

One of the key things to keep in mind when writing a speech is that the audience, unlike readers of a print document, cannot go back and double check items that are unclear. A speech, likewise, will not have boldface type or subheadings that help the reader sense the flow and direction of various topics. Speech writers always have to remember to write for the ear, not for the eye.

Successful ghostwriters of speeches demand high salaries, usually in six figures within a corporate setting. It's a valuable skill that you can take with you if you move from one employer to another. Writers need to understand their speakers and their audiences as much as their topics.

How to Analyze an Audience

Ghostwriting speeches is difficult at best and not always a lot of fun. But you can ease the process through an analysis of the speech audience. The more information that is known about the audience, the easier it is to ghostwrite a speech. It also helps your company spokesperson in the delivery.

Gathering information about the audience is fairly easy. All you need is a system.

Douglas Perret Starr, Ph.D., APR, Fellow PRSA, is a Professor of Agricultural Journalism at Texas A&M University in College Station, Texas.

As soon as possible after your speaker accepts an invitation to address an audience, and before you begin writing the speech, contact the group's program director and ask for the information you need. Be sure to have handy a list of questions.

A particular helpful list of questions is the "Audience Analysis Form" (see Blueprint). Once completed, it serves several purposes:

- The "Audience Analysis Form" provides a complete description of the audience in one place.
- Attached to the CEO's copy of the speech, it provides an invaluable summary of the entire speaking event that the executive may refer to before arrival at the speaking site.
- Filed with the corrected and last-edited copy of the delivered speech, it serves as a detailed description of the speaking event, an unparalleled reference for future speeches and speaking situations.

The reason for most of the items on the form is readily apparent, but some items need additional explanation.

Other Events on the Program

It's vital to know whether the group plans to conduct business or put on an entertainment program before your CEO speaks. If so, insist that your speaker go first for several reasons:

- Many speaking events include a cocktail party and a heavy meal. After a couple of hours of drinking and eating, the audience is groggy and sleepy, not very receptive to a delayed speech.
- Scheduling your executive before group activities allows for an early departure or time after the speech for an interview by reporters.
- Do not allow entertainment to be scheduled ahead of your spokesperson. A raffle or an exotic dancer before your speaker will result in a nonreceptive audience.
- If you cannot change such prespeech activities, your company spokesperson may wish to decline the speaking invitation.

Speech of Introduction

Know the name and title of the person who will introduce your CEO, so she can respond properly. You need to know this, too, so you can ascertain that the introducer has a copy of the speech of introduction. For maximum control, among other reasons, you need to write this introduction yourself.

News Media

Presence of reporters means that your CEO's message will be publicized. It may mean that the reporters will want to interview your executive after the speech, so you will need to brief your speaker in advance on major issues not covered in the speech.

Alcoholic Beverages

Alcohol and reporters are a dangerous combination, and your CEO needs a clear head around journalists. During the reception, you should provide your speaker with a nonalcoholic drink to hold.

Group Officers

Your CEO needs to know the names of the group's officers because he will be introduced to them, and he and the group's officers normally will be seated at the head table. It helps the memory to see the names in print beforehand.

Special Guests

Your CEO also needs to know the name and identification of such special guests as the mayor, national and state senators and representatives, other city, county, and state officials, and influential private citizens. In the preamble to the speech, your CEO may want to acknowledge their presence by name and title. It is politic and polite, and it enhances rapport with the group. (It's also good to get such formalities out of the way as early as possible so the speech itself can start with an effective attention-getting device.)

Attire

Although it's important for both men and women to be in the proper attire, it is especially important that you know and list the specific attire for women. A man can wear a suit about anywhere, but a woman executive's wardrobe is subject to critical eyes at all times.

Question-and-Answer Session

If a question-and-answer session is scheduled, your speaker needs notes on major issues not covered in the speech but sure to be addressed. Sometimes, you can arrange for a friendly member of the audience to ask a leading question, enabling your CEO to get her key points onto the floor for discussion.

Additional Information

Have available a small flashlight (with extra batteries) in case there is no light at the lectern for your CEO to see and read the speech.

Try to provide a copy of the program so your speaker will be able to relate quickly to the entire affair. If you cannot get a copy of the program beforehand, at least get a copy for the files.

Always bring along an extra copy of the latest version of the speech just in case your speaker left it in the car or someone at dinner spilled coffee all over it.

To help you ghostwrite the next speech, analyze your CEO's delivery and the audience's reaction. If you can't attend the speaking event, ask someone else to do it for you. You won't need much information. See the "Speech Evaluation Form." And be sure to file the form with the final corrected version of the delivered speech and the "Audience Analysis Form."

Speech of Introduction

It's the rule. Every speaker, even the president of the United States, must be introduced before beginning a speech. Of course, the president's speech of introduction is brief, only nine words:

"Ladies and gentlemen, the president of the United States."

That's because everybody knows the president, and because people attend a speaking situation to hear the president, not the introducer. But every other speaker, without exception, must be introduced in more detail, even though almost everyone in the audience knows the speaker's name, the topic and the reason for the speech.

Unfortunately, too often, the speech of introduction is left either (a) to someone who does not know the speaker or the

Blueprint

Audience Analysis Form

Organization
Name of group
Type of group (professional, political, religious, service, etc.)
Date of meeting   Time of meeting
Place of meeting (complete address, hotel room, city)
Group officers
        President
        Vice President
        Secretary
        Treasurer
        Other(s) (name and title)
Name and title of introducer
Special guests expected (name and title)
Time allotted for speech

Occasion
Purpose of meeting (regular, dedication, installation of officers, etc.)
Premeeting reception?   Yes   No
Will alcoholic beverages be served?   Yes   No
Does meeting include a meal?   Yes   No
Are spouses invited?   Yes   No
Attire: Men
           Women
Others on the program
What is before / after the speech?
What else is planned for the speaker?
                        Debate   Question–Answer Session
                        Panel Discussion   Other (what?)

Are news media invited?   Yes   No
Who are they? (names, news media)
Audience
Type of meeting room (auditorium, small dining room, large banquet hall, etc.)
Public address system available   Yes   No
Is there a light at the lectern?   Yes   No
Number of people expected
Range and average ages of audience
Major occupation(s) of audience
General educational level of audience
Anticipated knowledge of speech topic by audience
Attitude of audience toward speaker
Attitude of audience toward speech topic
Anything else?

Program
Copy of program attached?   Yes   Not Available

speech topic and, therefore, cannot provide a realistic introduction; or (b) to someone who knows the orator too well and laces the introduction with lengthy tales better left to private reminiscing. Either way, as far as the speech topic is concerned, such an introduction is at best an embarrassment and at worst a disaster.

The speech of introduction is not a biographical sketch of the speaker. It's an integral part of the speaking situation, serving two major purposes:

- It sets the stage for the speech, telling the audience what to expect from the presentation.
- It explains why the speaker is qualified to speak on that topic.

Therefore, if you're wise, you should insist on writing the speech of introduction as well as the main speech itself, crafting both into a meaningful whole. Then, you should contact the person designated to introduce your CEO and send a copy of your introduction with a request that it be used. More often than not, the introducer will be more than receptive to your doing such necessary work.

The Introduction

The speech of introduction should not intrude on the main speech, neither giving away details of the major address nor encroaching on the time allotted for your keynote speaker. To accomplish this, here are suggestions on writing such an introduction.

➤ It should be no more than 250 words (one double-spaced, typewritten page), no more than two minutes of delivery.

➤ It should mention the name and title of the main speaker frequently. It's no secret who is to speak. Nearly everyone in the room knows who is to speak and may have spoken with the individual, either during the reception or as the meeting began.

➤ It should include the topic of the speech, the reason the speaker was selected to address the group, why the topic is relevant to the group, and the orator's qualifications to speak on the topic.

➤ It should tie in to the theme of the speech, and serve as a lead-in, a teaser that will arouse the interest of the audience toward the speaker.

➤ It should not include the main speaker's life history. Date and place of birth, education, marriage and family, and employment generally are unimportant, as far as the speech is concerned. However, background — employment, education, etc. — that is relevant should be included. Briefly.

➤ If applicable, it should remind the audience of the person's latest achievements.

One other point: For a political speech, choose the introducer with care. The presenter should be someone who is held in high regard by the listening audience because people tend to favor friends of friends.

How to Ghostwrite a Speech

If you look for a good speech now, you undo me:
for what I have to say is of mine own making.
Second Part of King Henry IV, Act V, Epilogue – William Shakespeare

One of your major duties in public relations is speech ghostwriting, producing speeches for your chief executive officer or other key executives to deliver. You do most of the work; your speaker gets all of the credit. That is all right because the ghostwritten speech is a collaborative effort between you and your organization's speaker.

It's the speech ghostwriter's job to produce a speech that is not only accurate and factual but that reflects the thought processes and speech patterns of the CEO. The ghostwritten speech **must sound** as if the CEO wrote it.

The primary rule for success in speech ghostwriting is that only one person handle all of the speech writing for the CEO, one person with total access to the executive office with full and final responsibility for the preparation of the speech. That will help create a consistent voice on the podium.

Others on the PR staff or within the company may offer suggestions, but should not do any of the actual writing. If more than one person is involved in writing the speech, the difference in combined writing styles will lead to confusion on the part of the speaker at the time of delivery.

The key is writing so that the audience understands what the speaker is saying. As in writing for broadcast, writing a speech is writing for the ear, writing to be heard, not read, and to be understood at first listening.

To achieve understandability, follow these fundamentals of writing:

➤ Use specific terms.

➤ Use precise words (and look up words for both definition and usage).

➤ Use words and phrases appropriate to the topic, the occasion, and the audience.

➤ Write simply and in conversational style, in the active voice.

➤ Repeat key words and phrases.

Short, simple sentences are best. Pronouns — especially the pronoun you — draw listeners into the speech. Contractions lend an air of conversation and authority because people talk in contractions. Jargon or shoptalk is confusing unless it's appropriate for your audience or you explain it in simple terms. Numbers confuse listeners, so round off large numbers. Statistics should be used in simple terms. Try to bring a large figure into perspective for an audience: "That's $500 for every man, woman and child in Ontario." Quotations from the Bible traditionally tend to make people relax and agree with the speaker. Try to keep quotes short and blend them into the content of the speech. Synonyms may be confusing. Repeat key information and main ideas to reinforce your position.

When you're finally assembling the speech, remember that words exist in people, not in themselves. Words do not transmit meaning; they stir up meanings already present in people. Therefore, you must choose words that you think the audience will understand with a minimum of adverse emotional reaction. That may be difficult for you, so rely heavily upon your CEO's input.

Putting the Speech Together

As soon as you learn that your CEO has accepted a speaking situation, contact a representative of the group to learn what topic the group wants your speaker to address. Meet with your executive and explain the speaking situation and the speech requirements of the group and let your CEO make the final decision. Elected officials and politicians frequently have their own agenda for speech topics, and the group really does not care about the subject, only about having a particular speaker on the program.

On Brevity

A friend of my father's once told me: "Say what you have to say and when you come to a sentence with a grammatical ending, sit down."

Winston Churchill

As far as you're concerned, the topic of the speech is of little consequence, but you need to know it. Interview your CEO the same way a reporter interviews a news source. Ask detailed questions about the subject matter, writing full notes. You need to capture not only the idea of what your CEO wants to say, but also the exact words and phrases in which your CEO couched those thoughts. You may need a tape recorder for exactness.

In writing the speech, incorporate some of the exact words and phrases and sentences your CEO used during your interview so your ghostwritten speech sounds like your CEO wrote it. Regardless of who wrote the speech, however, once delivered, the speech belongs to the CEO.

Keep the speech simple, with preferably only one topic. And keep the speech short: no more than 2,500 words, or 10 double-spaced pages. Ten pages will take about 20 minutes to deliver, the typical length of modern speeches. Don't be alarmed in having to fill 10 pages. Plenty of help exists, from volumes of quotations to anecdotes to jokes. Just try a Google search under speechwriting to see the many resources from that site alone. Several subscription newsletters also provide assistance for the speechwriting profession.

Most speeches have three parts, of course. The beginning tells the audience the key point of the speech and the position your CEO is taking. The middle provides support for your speaker's position and includes adverse arguments that your CEO rejects logically. The end is a strong repetition and rein-forcement of the key point(s) of the speech and a request that the audience believe or act upon the key point(s).

Don't present a one-sided argument. People today are too well educated to accept biased arguments. They want to hear both sides, and they want to hear what makes the opposing position objectionable. So, presenting both sides of any issue and rejecting or ridiculing the opposing viewpoint gives opponents pause and gives supporters ammunition for their own arguments against opponents.

Write positively. Audiences tend to reject negative information. Avoid the use of *not* and *fail* and other negative words.

After you have written the speech, read it aloud, softly, and listen to the flow of language. Smooth out rough spots. Shorten breath-taking sentences. Repair awkward word combinations and time the finished product. Ask a knowledgeable person in your company to read the speech for accuracy.

Rewrite the speech as many times as is necessary. After you have produced the final version, give a copy to your CEO for final approval or additions and deletions. Then make any changes that are noted.

Prepare a final copy of the speech for your CEO, in large type and double spaced, and the Audience Analysis Form, and present both to your CEO. Prepare single-spaced copies for the news media, for other people as appropriate, and for your files.

Attend the speaking situation and complete the Speech Evaluation Form. Make sure you retrieve your speaker's copy of the speech for your files. Your executive may have made written notes and revisions on that copy, all highly useful for later speech-writing efforts.

Clip and file newspaper stories about the speech and speaking event, and send copies to your CEO. File all other related documents.

How to Get More Publicity from Speeches

Public relations professionals have two major routine tasks with regard to writing speeches for the chief executive officer and other company officials: to write the speech with its related introduction and to secure the widest publicity for the speech.

Of course, finding outlets for executive speeches is usually not a problem. If it is, you and your public relations colleagues need to make sure a speakers bureau is functioning at full speed within the organization. Its job is to find speaking engagements within the community by publicizing the types of speakers and topics available to groups needing a program. Regular employees with unusual hobbies and skills can be wonderful PR tools for your speakers bureau. Just recruit and train your stable of experts and promote them with a quality brochure throughout the area. Word-of-mouth and testimonials from satisfied audiences will help fill your speaking calendar.

Writing the speech involves hours, or even days, collecting information, conducting research, interviewing, reading, taking

Blueprint

Speech Evaluation Form

Speaker

Title of speech

Date of speech

Name of group

City, state

Evaluation of Speaker	(1 is least; 5 is best)				
Forcefulness of delivery	1	2	3	4	5
Impact of message	1	2	3	4	5
Facial expressions, animation	1	2	3	4	5
Gestures	1	2	3	4	5
Voice, tonal range	1	2	3	4	5
Enunciation	1	2	3	4	5
Visual contact with audience	1	2	3	4	5

Remarks

What specifically distracted you or diminished the maximum impact of the speech?

What specifically impressed you about the speech or the delivery?

What words or sentence construction did the speaker have difficulty pronouncing?

notes, and writing, rewriting and polishing the speech. In contrast, your CEO may deliver the speech in 20 minutes to a group groggy with the late hour and the aftermath of a heavy banquet. To make matters worse, the next morning, one local newspaper carries four inches of copy about the speech and the speaking event, and much of that story is unnecessary information, such as including the title of the speech and the theme of the convention.

That's not enough. Your speaker and the labor-intensive, speech-writing process demand far more than that. Every executive speech carries information wanted and needed by peers, by colleagues and competitors, by governmental and political leaders, by leaders in the business community, by employees, and often by the public.

Leaving the task of securing publicity to the one or two reporters who cover the speaking event is never enough. It's up to you to provide the appropriate publicity. To do that, you must understand that every speech has three audiences:

The primary audience — the smallest of the three — is the people listening to the speech as it is delivered.

The secondary audience — the largest of the three — is the people who read or hear about the speech through the news media — newspapers, news magazines, radio and television stations — and the Internet.

The tertiary audience — the most influential of the three — is the people who read about the speech in professional magazines and journals. This audience — leaders in the business, industrial, governmental, political and professional communities — needs to know what CEOs are saying publicly because of their leadership position in business, industry, government, politics and the professions.

The news media — print and broadcast — are hungry for well-written, timely, information-laden stories about the various communities: business, military, religion, medical, education, scientific, etc. News media do not have the staff to report on all of the news events they need to cover, so they depend upon public relations professionals to provide them with news items, including speech stories.

Professional magazines and journals are even hungrier for news about activities in their fields. Like the newspaper, but with smaller staffs, they must depend upon public relations professionals to serve as their reporters. Thus, publication of your CEO's speech is almost guaranteed by the professional magazines and journals that serve your organization's field. Your story may be rewritten or shortened by editors, but you will have publication among people of influence nationally.

And, of course, your own company magazine is a prime outlet for news about your executives' speaking engagements.

Here are some tips on how to reach those audiences and maximize exposure for your CEO's speeches. These suggestions are not difficult, and they are not guaranteed, but they do put the odds in your favor for several reasons.

➤ After your CEO has approved the final version of the speech, prepare a single-spaced copy for every news medium in your organization's geographic area and for your company Web page.

➤ At the speaking event, and before the speech is delivered, distribute copies to the reporters attending. The reporters will write their own stories, but you should be available for whatever help they need.

➤ Obviously, only a few reporters will attend the speaking event. Therefore, you must serve as the reporter for all the publications and broadcast stations that do not send reporters. After the speech is delivered, write the story, covering the speech and the speaking event as a reporter would, tersely, accurately and objectively. Include the name of the host organization and audience size, the frequency and length of applause, question-and-answer session, whatever.

➤ Write two versions of the story: one for print and one for broadcast. Keep them short, no more than 250 words for newspapers, 100 words for broadcast. And remember, broadcast news style differs from newspaper news style in that stories written for broadcast are written to appeal to the ear instead of to the eye.

➤ It's worth the effort to provide a broadcast version because broadcasters appreciate having their needs taken into consideration. Getting precious air time, in turn, makes your task seem worthwhile.

➤ E-mail a copy of the story and a copy of the speech to every news medium in your geographic area. And put a copy of your print and your broadcast story on your company Web page.

➤ Write a longer story about the speech and the speaking event, providing greater detail than your newspaper version. E-mail and snail mail a copy of that story to every professional magazine and journal in your organization's field of interest and to the publication of the organization to which your CEO spoke.

➤ If the speech is of more than parochial interest, that is, if it's of interest outside the profession, e-mail a copy of the delivered speech and the speaking situation — not of the story — to *Vital Speeches of the Day* (P.O. Box 1247, Mount Pleasant, SC 29465). That publication carries verbatim copies of speeches of general interest that have widespread effect. Be sure to include plenty of details about the speaking occasion.

After you have done all that, you need to know how successful your efforts were — how widespread your publicity was — and you need to tell your CEO. You may not be able to know how the broadcast media handled your CEO's speech, but you can know how it fared among the daily newspapers and professional magazines and journals. If your office doesn't subscribe to a clipping service, someone in the public relations department needs to thoroughly read and clip the papers and magazines.

Make copies of each clipping, with the name and date of each publication. Put the original in your file and send the copies, with an appropriate memorandum of explanation, to your supervisors to document their success (as well as your own).

How to Prepare and Deliver a Briefing

A briefing is just that, a short presentation designed to present a series of facts and ideas on a single issue. Sometimes, however, a briefing may encompass two related topics. At most, it is 10 minutes long: about 1,250 words, five double-spaced pages.

The briefing is presented best by the person who has the most knowledge about the topic because those attending the briefing need complete and accurate information, and they may ask questions after the presentation. Sometimes a public relations staff member is picked for the delivery since that individual has researched the subject and learned to deal with the challenges of the media.

Before the Briefing

Become thoroughly familiar with your topic; review your information with the presenter. You need to write as if you are the expert presenting the material. But be sure to minimize the jargon that most technical experts live with around the clock.

Determine the purpose of the briefing, what your organization hopes to achieve.

Analyze your audience. Know the education and background of all the members, including the job rank and duties (in general, of course, not in detail), and their knowledge of the particular subject matter.

Check the designated room for layout, arrangements, facilities and equipment. Ensure that you have plenty of room for the presenter as the focal point for the audience.

Make arrangements for whatever equipment is needed: computer, easel, slide projector, overhead projector, screen, chalkboard.

If you need a public address system, make certain that it works. In a small room, before a small audience, your presenter won't need one.

Preparing the Briefing

Organize your material in logical sequence. Type, double spaced, on one side of the page only.

State your main points right away. No guessing. Tell your audience members what you are going to brief them about. Then explain and describe. Your speaker is explaining, not trying to persuade — though that may be the result.

At the conclusion, summarize your main points.

Use simple words, simple sentences, active voice (subject, verb, object), oral language. After all, this is an oral presentation. Your designated expert is going to talk to your audience.

When writing the briefing, choose language that fits your audience. Don't talk up or down to them. Don't use words or terms they will not understand, unless you explain them.

Design simple visual aids (charts, graphs, multimedia, etc.) to explain and reinforce your main points. Use bold, vibrant, contrasting colors; few words; simple drawings; rounded-off numbers; and few details.

Remember, this is a briefing, not a detailed analysis. You should also have copies of a detailed analysis available for those who want it.

Rehearse, time and rewrite your expert's presentation to trim it to 10 minutes. You may have to repeat this step several times.

Delivering the Briefing

When your expert presenters stand before the audience, clutching your typed pages with sweaty fingers, they probably will have stage fright. It's natural. Even veteran professionals who stand before audiences have some degree of anxiety. Just remind them, they have everything going for them: They are the experts; your audience knows they are the experts; your audience is interested in their message; and your audience wants them to succeed.

Other tips to share with your briefing presenter are:

➤ Take a deep breath. Speak slowly and naturally. Lower the pitch of your voice. Enunciate your words so that every word is understood. Use plenty of pauses and plenty of facial expressions and gestures.

➤ This is a talk; audience members are your colleagues. Try to relax.

➤ Be sure to tell your audience members what you want them to do or to believe, what message you want them to carry away with them.

➤ When you present your main points, nod your head. This encourages agreement among the audience. If you can get your CEO to nod, too, that will help.

➤ Maintain eye contact with your listeners; let your eyes sweep the audience regularly. Don't concentrate upon just one or two listeners; it makes them nervous and makes everyone else feel left out.

➤ Above all, do not read your briefing. Children like to be read to; adults feel insulted. Speak from notes or from a full text, but use the full text as a guide. After all, you are the expert on this topic. You should know the information.

After the Briefing

Remind your audience that full information on the topic is available for those who want to get it from you later.

Call for questions from the audience. Have your experts respond as briefly as possible, one minute or so, at most, to each question.

Distribute to each member of the audience appropriate handouts, information that emphasizes and explains the main points in the briefing. This ensures that they will retain the information you researched and wrote for the briefing.

Notes

When using visual aids, don't leave them on the screen any longer than necessary. Otherwise, your audience will tend to read them and not listen to what your expert presenters are saying. As your speakers finish showing their visual aids, they should cover them or turn off the projection equipment.

People listen for facts rather than for ideas. Visual aids help them assimilate facts from which they will formulate ideas.

How to Handle a Hostile Interview

Interviews are considered hostile if reporters seek information or ask questions in a manner deemed harmful or unfavorable to the company. If your spokesperson is scheduled to face such a situation, use these suggestions:

➤ Have a PR staff member or an executive secretary present to take written notes and to tape-record the entire interview.

➤ Recognize that everything that is said could be published or aired. Don't say anything off the record. There's no guarantee such information won't be used anyway. Furthermore, forcing journalists into an unpopular off-the-record format will antagonize them even more.

➤ You need not answer any question directly. Challenge questionable statements and assumptions and dubious sources.

➤ Personalize answers and put them into language that people understand and relate to, rather than into company jargon. Speak to the camera, rather than to the reporter.

➤ Don't overreact to abrasive or unfair questions, but if necessary, let your indignation show, in moderation, of course.

➤ Do not speculate. If the reporter asks hypothetical questions, politely refuse to answer them.

➤ If the reporter makes a negative introduction to a question, interrupt immediately and say, "You're supposed to ask me questions please, not make a speech." Then restate the negative statement positively and respond to that.

➤ If the reporter asks a question that implies guilt regardless of the answer, qualify your answer, or refuse to directly answer such a question. However, avoid the "no comment" reply that's interpreted by the majority of the public as an admission of guilt.

➤ If the reporter asks a "yes-or-no" question, provide as much information as you deem necessary.

➤ If the reporter asks a loaded question, do not repeat adverse information, but do set the record straight. The reason the spokesperson should not repeat negative details is that

a partial quote could appear that contains only the damaging facts.

➤ If the reporter asks several questions at once, answer one you like and ignore the rest.

➤ If the reporter interrupts your answer with another question, either ignore the interruption or say that you will answer that question later. Continue with your initial answer. Insist upon your right to complete your answers.

➤ If the reporter predicates a question upon an unidentified authority, refuse to answer the question unless the authority is identified.

12.

Writing Memos, E-mails and Reports

by Suzanne Sparks FitzGerald

A Web page designed for college students tried to arouse a sense of activism in the students. Unfortunately, the Web page referred to famous activists like Ralph Nader whom the students didn't recognize.

An American T-shirt maker in Miami printed shirts for the Spanish market promoting a visit from the Pope. Instead of "I saw the Pope" (el Papa), the shirts read, "I saw the potato" (la papa).

The dean of a college sent e-mails to the chair**men** of the five departments. Three of the five were women.

The Dairy Association's success with the "Got Milk?" campaign prompted it to expand to Mexico. Unfortunately, the association unknowingly picked the following translation, "Are you lactating?"

These real-life examples illustrate what happens when you don't know your audience.

Know Your Audience

The first tip to effective writing is to know your audience. The more you know, the more you can tailor or customize your message for an individual or group.

First, think of the person or persons you write to most frequently. Visualize your supervisor or your key customer as you write. Try to obtain information such as age, education level, income and gender.

If you can uncover interests, opinions and values, you can persuade your readers more effectively. You need to know the reader's knowledge of your topic — is she an expert or does he know nothing about it?

Suzanne Sparks FitzGerald, Ph.D., APR, is chair of the PR/Advertising Department at Rowan University in Glassboro, N.J.

In the earlier example about T-shirts, if the writer knew the language of the readers, he could have avoided using the wrong translation. The Web page for college students to arouse activism ignored an important demographic, age. Students were too young to remember Ralph Nader, who made consumer activist headlines 40 years ago, even though he ran for president in November 2000 and 2004. The e-mail should have considered gender and referred to the chairs as chairpersons. The Dairy Council failed to address the Spanish market by not even translating the slogan correctly. You can see that if the writers of these pieces knew their audiences, they could have avoided serious blunders.

Readability

Whether it's a memo, report or e-mail, readability counts. Readers must be able to understand your message before they can act on it. Use short words. Lincoln used words of five or fewer letters for 70 percent of his Gettysburg Address. Keep your sentences to an average length of 17 words or less. Longer sentences discourage most readers. Make paragraphs no more than six lines long. Eye-appealing, tight writing invites the reader to continue.

Try the following hints for making your writing readable.

Feature clarity, economy and straightforwardness

Readability includes many facets, but most importantly clarity, economy and straightforwardness. *Clarity* is the opposite of ambiguity. If your writing is unclear, the reader can't be sure what you mean. In business or professional writing, you must ensure that the reader at least understands you. *Economy*, or using no more words than necessary, is one of the distinguishing marks of clear and forceful writing. And *straightforwardness* refers to the order in which you write, placing the subject close to the verb for easy understanding.

Clarity

If your message has more than one meaning, it is not clear. Don't use long words where short ones will do; it makes your writing dense and difficult to understand. Words ending in -ality, -ize, -ization, -ational and so on make sentences more complex than necessary. Use precision to make your writing clear. Make sure the words you choose have exactly the right (and only **one**) meaning. Use specific words. Don't say "organization" if you mean "The American Red Cross," unless the meaning is clear for your audience.

1. My educational background basically centers around a B.A. in business administration as an economics major.

2. I spent two quarters studying the stock market and three quarters of finance which will allow me to handle your financial accounts.

The first sentence confuses the reader — do you or don't you hold a degree? Don't use the term "centers around" as a center is a point. In the second example, what do the quarters mean? Five weeks? Ten weeks? If the information you offer is negative or not positive, omit it. Why say you've only studied the stock market for 20 weeks? Why not rephrase the unclear sentences like this:

1 I hold a B.A. in business administration with an economics emphasis.

2. I have finance experience as well as stock market expertise that will benefit your firm.

Economy

Business writers should use a 17-word rule when writing sentences. You want to vary the length of your sentences; however, when you use too many words, you may lose the reader. Sometimes you get to the end of a lengthy sentence and can't remember how it started. Elementary schools used to select primers about Dick and Jane and their dog, Spot. Not only were these sentences clear, but also economical, e.g., See Dick run. See Jane run. See Dick and Jane run after Spot. Not exciting, but effective!

If your message is delivered in long, arduous prose, no one may read it. Economy refers to the number of words in a sentence and the lack of redundant phrases or words. Active writing or verb writing reduces the number of words you use.

Straightforwardness

Straightforwardness refers to order and how close the subject is to the verb. Use S-V-O or subject-verb-object order with strong action verbs. If you write clearly, economically and in a straightforward manner, your audience will rate your reports high on readability.

Use the second person when you want to signal familiarity. Some of the best persuasive communication talks to the audience instead of about them. Use the third person when you want to signal objectivity. At times you want to avoid appearing personally involved.

Put your words in just the right order and use the right grammatical construction to make your point. For example, "We'll **only** write three major contracts this year," suggests we won't do anything else but these contracts. "We'll write **only** three major contracts this year," makes the meaning clearer. Also, try to keep your subject near the verb. Look at these next sentences to see what happens when you don't.

1. In response to your job opening notice concerning the public relations practitioner advertised in the Sunday, August 14, 2004 issue of *The Washington Post,* I am submitting my job application letter.

2. In response to the letter you wrote Dr. Busler, I am applying for the position of advertising assistant described in the aforementioned letter.

Not only do these sentences have an awkward order, but also they are unclear. Let's consider the following straightforward revisions:

1. I am submitting this application in response to your advertisement in *The Washington Post* for a public relations practitioner.

In the second example, who wrote the aforementioned letter is unclear. Try the following revision instead:

2. I am applying for the advertising assistant described in your letter to Dr. Busler.

Avoid the use of redundancy in your writing to ensure greater readability. When you use redundant phrases, you increase the sentence length and violate the 17-word rule. Research shows that if sentences contain up to eight words they have a "very easy readability" rating reaching 90 percent of the audience.

Blueprint

Caution

According to The Communication Workshop in Port Washington, N.Y., and the *Secretary's Letter,* we should avoid phrases and clichés like: To be perfectly honest; Needless to say; Enclosed herewith, please find; If you should have any further questions, please do not hesitate to call; For your perusal, review and consideration; We deem it advisable; It has come to my attention; The undersigned; Pursuant to your request; Transparent to the user; and Under separate cover.

Consider the Following Readability Tips:

- Use clarity — one meaning
- Use economy — 17 words as ideal average sentence length
- Practice straightforwardness — proper order
- Avoid clichés and jargon
- Avoid negative writing
- Avoid passive voice
- Avoid noun and adjective stacks
- Avoid italics and all caps
- Avoid the "me" attitude

Avoid Negative Writing

The quickest way to turn off a reader when writing is to use negative words. Research shows that it takes the mind longer to understand a negative statement than the same idea expressed in a positive way. Many times writers give unnecessary negative information like in this cover letter: "ICI Americas is eliminating much of its corporate staff, including me." Why not get the interview first before you deliver all the bad news? A cover letter is a persuasive document and the purpose is to persuade the reader to review the attached resume.

So instead of providing unnecessary negative information, omit it. When you must provide necessary negative information, do so in a positive way. Sometimes giving a reason for the negative information softens the message.

Avoid Passive Voice

According to William Zinsser in *Writing Well*, the difference between the active and passive voice is like life and death for a writer. In the active voice, the subject performs the action. "The president signed the proposal," versus "the proposal was signed by the president." To avoid the passive voice, don't use the verb "to be" or "to have." When you start a sentence with "there is" or "there are," you'll most likely write in the passive voice.

Avoid Noun and Adjective Stacks

Whenever you see two or three adjectives in front of a noun or several nouns in a row, you'll confuse the reader and use unnecessary words. Why say "the very pretty lady" when you

Blueprint

Write for the Web

According to Susan Perloff, writer for the *Philadelphia Business Journal*, you can make your documents more readable on the Web. Try the following tips:

1. Write short, declarative sentences (in other words, be concise).

2. Most people have a hard time paying attention to a computer screen so involve the reader by writing in the second person (use you).

3. Use the active voice.

4. Use the imperative (command) mood to suggest what the reader should do. (e.g., Send us an e-mail with any questions.)

5. Include bulleted lists of choices.

6. And conceptualize the hyper-links as you write. Remember that on the Web, you never see the whole thing at once.

Source: *Philadelphia Business Journal*, Oct. 1, 1997

could say "beautiful" or "stunning"? Why say "the very unattractive dog" when you could use "ugly"?

In this case, don't worry about withholding information from the reader. Readers don't need to know the machinery was rugged, militarized and field accessible. They only need to know that the machinery works in combat.

Avoid *italics* and all CAPS

Research shows that the use of italics and all capital letters makes it 20 percent harder for the reader to understand. Use italics for titles of literature, foreign words (e.g., *cul de sac*) or emphasis. Don't use it to "look pretty." You'll slow the reader down.

All caps have another problem. WHEN YOU WRITE IN ALL CAPS, IT'S LIKE SHOUTING AT THE READER AND HE DOESN'T LIKE IT! When you use acronyms and all caps, it can be quite confusing.

A memo from personnel read: BRING YOUR EARS DOWN TO HUMAN RESOURCES TO CORRECT THESE PROBLEMS. EARS was an acronym for Employee Action Requests; however, in a memo of all capital letters, we can't distinguish the meaning.

Fabrik Communications published an e-mail etiquette guide that suggests that messages written in all capital letters are hard to read and will be interpreted as shouting.

Structure Your Writing to Reach Your Reader

When constructing e-mail, memos, letters and reports, make sure you ask for what you need and explain why you need it. Many experts suggest ways to format internal and external communication. The following simple formats will help you write requests, informative letters, persuasive documents, and good news or bad news memos (and e-mail). In most cases, using these principles will serve you well and provide structure for your reader.

Try Subject Lines and Postscripts

Use subject lines and postscripts as additional inducements for the reader. A carefully crafted subject line reveals the topic of the e-mail, report, memo or letter and can motivate the recipient to skim the first paragraph. Similarly, most people read the postscript first. A postscript can be a helpful device, especially for persuasive documents. Consider using it to restate your most important point.

Traditional Letter Form

Let's start with the basic letter format. Since most managers today use their own computers, many also format their own correspondence. Let's use the following example (next page):

Use a *heading*, including your phone number and e-mail address, even if you're writing from home so that the reader can easily identify you or reach you, if necessary. This example centers the heading, but many designers like the clean look of flush left. Always use a date to identify the specific letter. The *inside address* fulfills two purposes; first, you can use the person's title, which most people like to see; and second, it routes the letter to the appropriate individual, even if someone else opens the mail.

Heading
Judy Lord
699 Knox Road
Ardmore, PA 19077
(610) 259-1241

December 5, 2005   *Date*

Mr. James Penrod   *Inside Address*
Vice President, Sales
ABC Computing
394 Vesper Road
Knoxville, TN 37966

Subject: QuarkXPress   *Subject line*

Dear Mr. Penrod: *Salutation*

I would like to order the most current edition of QuarkXPress. Would you please send me any appropriate documentation as well? I work at home as a consultant and prepare brochures and newsletters for my clients.

Body

As I need your product immediately, please send it quickly, perhaps by overnight mail. I have always used your software products and appreciate your service mentality. Thank you for handling this request quickly.

Sincerely yours,   *Closing and signature*

Judy Lord

ALD/jl.245   *Supplement line*
Attachments (2)   *Attachments*

P.S. I enjoyed your recent newsletter!   *Postscript*

The *subject line* clues the reader as to what you might cover in this letter. The *salutation* is also important. Always try to get a name. No one likes unsolicited letters or e-mail. If you absolutely cannot find a name, use Dear Student, Dear Customer, Dear Homeowner or something that identifies the type of person you're writing to. Only use Dear Sir/Madam or To Whom It May Concern as a last resort. Never use Gentlemen unless you know no woman may read the letter. After the salutation, use a colon (e.g., Dear Dean Jordan:).

Remember to use a short first paragraph to intrigue the reader and to indent each paragraph for reading ease, even though current usage is divided on the indent. Use one of the many good *closings* to end your letter: Cordially, Sincerely, Sincerely yours, Regards, Respectfully submitted, etc.

The *supplement line* usually benefits you, the writer, by indicating who formatted the final letter or where you can find this letter on a computer disk. If you plan to enclose a check or another document, indicate how many attachments you included (e.g., Attachment). The reader can look for the enclosed items.

Also, consider using a *postscript* to catch the reader's attention. If possible, put your main point emphasis again in the postscript for added impact.

The Memo or E-Mail Form

Most managers use memos for internal issues and letters for external communication. Sometimes the formality of the content suggests the use of a letter, memo or e-mail. In general, continue to use memos internally and letters externally.

In many organizations, e-mail has taken the place of memos because of its speed and ease of use. However, many employees misuse e-mail by sending private messages and by forgetting that others may judge their writing by viewing their sloppy e-mail messages.

E-Mail Etiquette

According to Marjorie Brody, president of Brody Communications Ltd., etiquette also applies to e-mail. She suggests seven tips:

1. Watch your words; be concise, eliminating follow-up phone calls.
2. Don't flame people or use antagonizing or critical comments.
3. Few people like "spam" or unsolicited e-mails.
4. Nothing is private — what will happen if the message is read by someone other than the intended recipient? Lawsuits have proven that e-mails can come back to haunt corporations.
5. Keep attachments to a minimum — most readers hate to download arduous documents.
6. Consider copying others in the office using the FYI or For Your Information designation.
7. Never assume anything — many users aren't familiar with the lingo and emoticons that you may know.

Minding Your Electronic Manners

According to Barbara Pachter, a communications trainer, sloppy e-mail illustrates bad business manners. She suggests eight guidelines:

1. Don't contribute to e-mail overload.
2. Keep your message short (one screen or 25 lines).
3. Use short paragraphs.
4. Use a subject line.
5. Don't use all capital letters.
6. Limit each message to one subject area or purpose.
7. Proofread each message.
8. Remember that e-mail is not private.

Basic Memo Format

Memos are common tools for internal communication within a company or organization. Most of them are short and informal, getting to the point much sooner than a formal letter.

Use a standard memo format with the following headings: TO, FROM, DATE and RE or SUBJECT. Use a colon after each capitalized heading and double space. Remember to initial (not sign at the bottom) the memo indicating that you've read it and that it contains what you want it to say. Keep in mind the etiquette tips for checking grammar, spelling and content before you write your initials next to the FROM name at the top of the memo.

Prior to the demise of the "carbon copy," the term "cc" was used at the end of a memo to indicate those who would receive carbon copies. Since carbon paper is extinct, most writers now use copy or just "c." Consider using a postscript in your e-mail or memo. It catches readers' attention causing them to look at the subject line. Thus, you can lure the reader into your memo in several ways.

Tips for Writing at Chip Speed

Our high-tech, high-speed business world demands to-the-point writing that gets its message across with no wasted words. According to Jack Gillespie, former editor of *Communication Briefings*, even when faxing, sending e-mails or surfing the Net, we still need good writing techniques like: simple sentences; short sentences (17-word average); "you" attitude

TOOLBOX TIP

A colon or a dash helps create a dramatic pause in a complete sentence.

Examples:

We must be clear on one key point: failure is not an option.

We must be clear on one key point — failure is not an option.

toward readers; active verbs; clarity; and short paragraphs with subheads to help your readers.

Now that we've reviewed the basic letter and e-mail format and how to write "at chip speed," let's look at five possible letter/memo structures.

Direct Request Letter or E-mail

When writing a direct request, the most important piece of information you should include is **why** you need the requested item or service and **how** you will use it. Your reader will usually welcome the direct request. The reader's attitude is **positive**; he wants to hear from you. Try this format:

Paragraph One   Request for information or services.

Paragraph Two   Show why you need the information and how you will use it.

Paragraph Three   State the specific action for the reader to take.

Paragraph Four   List reader benefits and use a goodwill ending.

If you write to a software company asking to purchase a program, the most important information you can give the company is why you need the software and how you'll use it.

1. Start by requesting the software package.
2. Explain that you'll use it for desktop publishing — then the company can send you appropriate literature and recommend other software programs.
3. Tell the reader exactly what you want her to do (i.e., send the package overnight).
4. Close with a benefit to the reader like, "I plan to purchase additional software in the near future."

Blueprint

When to copy someone

Copy a person's boss, particularly if your memo cites the person's achievements or accomplishments. When employees receive that kind of recognition, they tend to work harder. Also, many times managers copy employees on a "FYI" or For Your Information basis.

Now, let's look at an informative letter.

Informative Letter/Memo

Many times we write to provide information about upcoming meetings, policies or projects. Usually readers hold a neutral attitude toward informative letters, so the most important aspect of this letter is to capture their attention.

Ask dumb questions!
Never write something you do not understand. Ask dumb questions. It's better than making dumb mistakes.

TO:	All XYZ Employees
FROM:	Gail Roso, Human Resources Director
DATE:	September 12, 2005
SUBJECT:	Holiday Policy

Because our employee committee suggested a more flexible holiday policy, we have adopted several options. You may now choose either Columbus Day or Presidents Day as a paid holiday.

Previously, you had nine paid holidays; you now have a flexible additional day. If you have questions about the policy changes, call Johanna at 4265.

c: Board of Directors

P.S. Enjoy your extra holiday!

Paragraph One	Capture the attention of your audience.
Paragraph Two	Provide the necessary information.
Paragraph Three	Present any negative factors; show reasons for these factors.
Paragraph Four	List reader benefits.
Paragraph Five	Provide a goodwill ending.

Capture your reader's attention and then give the required information. If negative factors exist, embed them between other more positive paragraphs. For example, if an employer designates a room as a smoking lounge, a negative factor could be limited times that smokers could use the room. Never start or end with negatives! Always try to list benefits to the reader and a positive ending.

Sometimes we must not only inform, but also persuade our audience. Try the following format to persuade a resistant reader.

Persuasive Letter/Memo

(Reader may initially disagree with request)

Paragraph One	Catch the reader's interest; establish mutual goals or common ground.
Paragraph Two	Define the problem that will be solved if the request is approved.
Paragraph Three	Explain the solution, show how any negatives are outweighed by advantages of the solution.
Paragraph Four	List all reader benefits.
Paragraph Five	State the specific action you want the reader to take.

Even if the reader disagrees with you, try to establish mutual goals, agree on some point or establish common ground. Adult learners like to solve problems; give your readers a problem with multiple solutions. Most readers like choices; the multiple solutions allow readers the opportunity to select the option they prefer.

If you must list any negative information, make sure the advantages of the solution outweigh these negative factors. List any benefits that accrue to the reader as a result of her solution to the problem. And most importantly, state the specific action you want the reader to take. Many times readers feel persuaded by the message, but don't know what to do next.

And now for an easy-to-write letter — the good news format that the reader happily receives.

Good News Letter/Memo

(Reader's attitude — **positive**)

Paragraph One	Deliver the good news.
Paragraph Two	Provide any details.
Paragraph Three	Discuss any negative elements.
Paragraph Four	List the reader benefits and close with a goodwill ending.

Enjoy the opportunity to applaud a colleague or an employee by sending many good news memos. Research shows that employees perform better when they feel appreciated and recognized. In this memo, present the good news and any details of that news. Couch negative elements in between the good news and benefits. List reader benefits to reinforce the good news and close on a positive note.

Perhaps the most difficult letter to write, the negative news letter, is one the reader doesn't wish to receive.

Negative Message Letter/Memo

(Reader's attitude — **unfavorable**)

Paragraph One	Establish good will.
Paragraph Two	Present the negative message; **present reasons for the message**.
Paragraph Three	Explain positive aspects and re-establish good will.

This letter or memo most likely will inspire dread for you and your reader. Establish common ground or good will initially. Then give the negative message with the reasons, if possible. To close, explain any positive aspects and re-establish the good will of your reader.

Although no one desires to receive negative news, research shows that we prefer to know the reasons behind the bad news. And while most of us have received rejection letters, we feel less devastated when employers list the reasons for the rejection. Sometimes employers don't send letters at all or they send the "rejection form letter" which creates a poor relationship with the reader. As a writer, put yourself in the reader's place and you will write in an empathetic manner.

So, to design easy formats to guide your reader, consider using the aforementioned structures. Remember that having a purpose and identifying your audience won't work without an appropriate structure.

Writing Reports

Another common writing project for the public relations practitioner is reports. They range from simple, one-page articles about products or policies to lengthy, investigative documents with tables and charts. Many of the latter concern finances, feasibility or progress of a project, often issued monthly or quarterly.

Report writing is a treasured skill. Employees with solid experience in report writing are valuable staff members who are typically recognized and rewarded for their expertise. What we have covered previously in this text about quality writing applies as well to producing reports. Even if writing for a specialized audience, be careful of using too much jargon. Use enough specialized language so that your credibility is established with the readers, but simple English should be your goal.

The report's format itself is the major difference from many other writing examples. Organizational structure for the lengthy reports is fairly common, although not all documents use all the following elements. Their sole purpose is to ensure the report is well organized for ease of use.

Letter of Transmittal – Often clipped onto the entire packet, this letter or memo of transmittal (depending on the formality of the report) essentially says "here it is." It states that the report (requested by such a person or office) is now prepared to provide answers to the situation. The letter gives your report credibility by telling recipients why it is being sent to them. It usually includes a phrase from the authors about contacting them for additional information.

Cover Page – Heavy card stock is typically used, sometimes protected by a clear vinyl or plastic cover. The cover page simply presents (in a large font) the title of the report, often an explanatory subtitle, the parties for whom it's intended, the date and the authors.

Title Page – This is identical to the cover page, only it's produced on regular paper. The title page is part of the actual report, but it has no page number. Officially, it's considered page i.

Table of Contents – As the name implies, the contents page lists the various elements of the lengthy report and the page number where they begin. Do not list the title page.

Table of Charts and Graphs – Although often called other terms, this page likewise gives the page numbers for the various tables and illustrations used within the report. Some suggest that this insertion isn't necessary for documents with only two or three figures.

Executive Summary – We hate to tell you this, but for many reports this is the only page that is read by the busy CEO.

Therefore, you need to produce a one-page document as if the rest of the report didn't even exist. It has to summarize the content and persuade convincingly. A compelling synopsis may encourage additional reading of your report by the organization's leadership.

Abstract – This is an even briefer, concise statement about the report's contents. Ranging from a mere paragraph to one page, the abstract does not attempt to summarize any findings. It merely provides a short description concerning the report's contents.

Report – The report itself consists of three main parts: introduction, body and conclusion. A brief introduction should state clearly what is the purpose of the report. Repetition of who or what department authorized the document is often found here as well. It might also flesh out the table of contents so readers will better understand the document's organization. The lengthy body of the report delivers details that have been researched. Internal headlines and subheads will help readers follow the logic and sequence of the written project. The conclusion repeats key summary points and often suggests future action.

List of Works Cited – Publication details about sources used in the report can be listed here. Often used only for long, formal reports, the list should have complete publication details (including publisher and date) for those who want to consult such resources.

Appendix – This final section might include questionnaires, graphics, maps, or charts and tables that may have been too awkward to include in the body of the report. Items in the optional appendix are individually labeled Appendix A, Appendix B, etc.

Writing a Technical Report

Every real story you read has some sort of logic and point to it. Technical reports are no different. Most technical writers look at a technical report as a laundry list of information — something that the reader must labor through. However, writers should view technical reports more from a story-telling perspective and add some warmth and personality to the project. After all, real live people read technical documents and these documents relate to real live people and events.

Business professionals, like many casual readers, have limited attention spans. They want to get to the conclusion quickly. They generally concentrate their attention to the beginning and end of technical reports. And, they find facts and figures compelling. They also like subheads for easy reading. Before writing the technical report consider the following.

- **Technical reports** written by someone with a reputation for careful work have greater credibility.
- **Technical professionals** respond favorably to well-organized documents.
- **Warm**, conversational tone adds to the persuasive intent of a technical report.
- **Referencing authorities** adds to the credibility and acceptance of technical reports.
- **Technical writers** must focus on the needs of the intended audience.
- **Readers** tend to resist information presented in a "pushy" tone and tend to reject arguments one-by-one.

Finally, don't assume that because you wrote the document and understand the technical nature of the information that the intended audience fully understands the information and jargon. A well-written technical report begins with a clear outline that first considers the desired outcome. It then weighs all the possible reactions that the receiver will have toward the message. Simply, it anticipates objections. It then writes with an eye toward clarity, conciseness and consistency.

For Further Reading:

David Ingre. *Survivor's Guide to Technical Writing*. Mason, OH: South-Western, 2003.

Charles Marsh. *A Quick and Not Dirty Guide to Business Writing*. Scottsdale, AZ: Gorsuch Scarisbrick, Publishers, 1997.

13.
Producing Publications

T*he Writer's Toolbox* set out with one purpose. That purpose was to offer a comprehensive approach to writing with greater clarity, conciseness and consistency. However, one more important consideration must be addressed before disseminating the final work. That consideration is graphic style.

Good graphic design is a marriage of type style and visual elements working together to help communicate a message. Working in tandem with well-constructed prose, graphic design improves reader acceptance and understanding of a message. The marriage forms a bond between readability and legibility. Readability refers to the ease by which a reader understands the message. Legibility refers to the clarity of the physical aspects of the document.

Claudia Cuddy summarized the eternal debate between design and content best in her book *Communicating with QuarkXPress*. Cuddy wrote, "Without worthwhile content in a publication, great graphic design is wasted. The design might attract readers, but then they are disappointed in the message." On the other hand, she added, "Well-written, informative content can go unnoticed if the graphic design fails to attract the readers."

Incorporating powerful design elements into a document makes the message more attractive and powerful. Forceful design helps to communicate important messages. In essence, just as *The Writer's Toolbox* focuses on proper grammatical structure as the foundation of all good writing, a certain visual grammar exists that incorporates style and elegance with some fundamental rules.

While audiences may be unaware of the exact term or reason for a grammatical error when reading text, they still may recognize that an error exists. This logic holds true with visual grammar also. Consequently, writers must be aware of fundamental design elements to enhance message construction.

"Type can have character and personality," writes James Stovall. "It can speak to us in many ways, not just by what it represents in terms of words but also by its own shape and design."[1]

This chapter attempts to clarify some key elements of design that all writers should know. It also addresses two of the most common design projects for professional communicators — newsletters and brochures.

Type

Sophisticated desktop publishing systems offer novice designers the tools of professional graphic designers. Unfortunately, these powerful design elements are often overused and lead to serious design flaws that decrease, rather than increase, visual appeal. Therefore, it's important for professional communicators to understand the basics of layout and design. The first rung on the design ladder is *use of fonts*.

Fonts

Type can be categorized into many classes. However, for simplicity purposes, the most elementary classes are *serif*, *sans serif*, *script* and *novelty*. Various uses of these font classifications give publications certain personalities that help convey appropriate messages.

Serif fonts such as Times New Roman, Palatino and Bookman feature small finishing strokes or "feet" at the end of them. They tend to work best with body copy because they appear softer to the eye.

Sans serif fonts conversely work best with headlines because they appear bolder. The French word *sans* means "without." Their use conveys a forceful tone that attracts attention. Examples of sans serif fonts include Helvetica, Arial and Avant Garde.

Script fonts emulate cursive handwriting. Although beautiful, they create difficulty when reading large blocks of copy. They should be used sparingly for invitations or the occasional headline. Script fonts include Zapf Chancery and Brush Script. They create deciphering disasters when used in all capital letters.

Finally, novelty fonts such as Stencil and Stagecoach offer unique design elements for specialty publications. Like script fonts, they should be used sparingly.

In addition to font choice, other typographical elements include point size, type styles, kerning, leading and tracking. Each contributes to the communicability of a publication.

Points and Picas

Graphic artists use points and picas for measuring. Picas are used to measure the width of columns or photos. Six picas equal one inch. Points measure type and spacing between lines of text. One inch then equals 72 points high. The size of body copy depends on the particular look and feel that the writer is attempting to communicate. However, writers should make 12-point body copy the largest they use for most publications. Larger point sizes should be reserved for headlines, pull quotes or special design elements.

Type Styles

Type styles such as **bold**, *italic*, underline, outline, SMALL CAPS and **shadow** lend publications unique design features. Their use, however, should be limited to special occasions for added emphasis. Otherwise, long blocks of copy printed in novel type styles make a publication difficult to read and detract from its visual appeal.

Leading, Tracking and Kerning

Leading refers to the vertical space between lines of copy. The term's origin dates back to the time when printers used small strips of lead between lines of type to create white space. The general rule is to use slightly more leading for copy set in sans serif than copy set in serif. This helps with clarity and ease of eye movement.

Tracking refers to horizontal spacing between all letters in a selected text. Typical tracking ranges from 0 to -5 It differs from kerning in that kerning refers to the space between certain pairs of letters, such as fi, WA, Ty, to, ox. According to Cuddy, there are approximately 80 pairs of letters that require use of kerning. However, most fonts have the kerning automatically built into them in the computer program.

TOOLBOX TIP

Reverse Type

Reverse type, using white letters in a color box, should be used sparingly as well. In general, follow these tips:

- Use slightly larger font size.

- Use slightly more leading than usual.

- Don't use large blocks of type in reverse.

- Darken the box enough to create contrast.

Graphics Enhance Visual Appeal

Writers and designers need to understand how certain graphic elements enhance the visual appeal and acceptance of a publication. Good layout and design carefully balance items on a page to achieve a desired feel. That feel can be achieved either with a formal symmetrical purpose or an informal asymmetrical purpose. The designer uses graphic design to enhance the message. However, graphic elements done without a sense of balance and style can interject *noise* into the communication.

Noise is simply defined as anything that interferes with the communication. With respect to graphic layout and design, noise can be any element that detracts the reader's attention from the stated message. It could be something simple like a long block of text without any copy break or something more complex such as an unsuitable font or tracking that is either too tight or too loose.

Good design creates a balance that is pleasing to the reader and will distribute visual weight appropriately throughout a layout. Just as writers create outlines to plan for the order of their prose, designers create rough layouts to achieve harmony and rhythm in publications. In formulating outlines, designers must be aware of the graphic tools at their disposal to enhance message clarity and achieve message purpose. A list of graphic design elements is too lengthy to fit into a single chapter on design. However, having a sense of some core concepts will dramatically increase graphic sense and enhance the likelihood of success of many forms of written communication.

Page Elements

We'll first address the use of headlines, subheads and decks. *Headlines*, or *heads*, are important to any publication by summarizing the content of the stories they accompany. They should be informative and brief and written using short words. Above all, headlines must contribute to the article, not detract from it. Therefore, avoid cute or vague headlines. Those should be reserved for entertainment publications. Always use large type (often bold) to attract attention to the story. In general, headlines work best if done in sans serif fonts. However, some publications achieve success using a serif font. Seen occasionally, a sidesaddle headline sits to either the right or the left of the article.

Alignment Options

Designers have four choices of horizontal alignment: left, right, centered or justified.

This is flush left.

This is flush right.

This is centered.

And this is justified.

Summary Deck

Students protest boring textbooks

Students picketed the university bookstore Tuesday
to protest dull textbooks as professors held classes anyway.

Students say they have had enough. They have asked professors to consider finding more interesting textbooks. When 20 pages of straight text contain no subheads or copybreakers, students claim they fall asleep and can't get their reading done.

summary deck

Kicker

Letters to editor
Confidence in Public Schools at an All-time High

This one acts as a standing head that appears regularly in a publication.

Students Protest
Seniors Required to Take Exit Writing Sample

This one serves to give more information.

Hammer

Victory!

Toby Tennis demolishes every challenger

Sidesaddle Heads

Blood drive breaks record

An all-time record of 847 students donated blood at the annual blood drive sponsored by Rowan's junior class. As they stood in line on Tuesday in the 94° weather, many students shared emotional reasons for donating. Others said they did it for the free cookies and juice.

Another group of 15 sophomores from a fitness class stood with their professor. The professor thought it would be a good learning experience for them.

Junior students advertised the event, arranged for the bloodmobile setup and carried out the daily activities.

Figure 1. Various headlines styles.

Subheads are explanatory heads, set in smaller type than headline type (or italics), that appear under the headline. They should be used sparingly and only for clarity.

In addition, subheads act as transitional heads within an article. They help break up copy and give readers the sense that they can read sections independently from one another. Typically they should be reserved for longer articles to indicate a change in subject or direction. They should be used sparingly in newsletters but liberally in brochures.

A *summary deck* placed below the headline introduces the story. A *kicker* — a word or phrase placed above the headline — creates contrast and often is used as an introduction to the main head. A *hammer* is similar to a kicker except that it is larger and bolder than the headline.

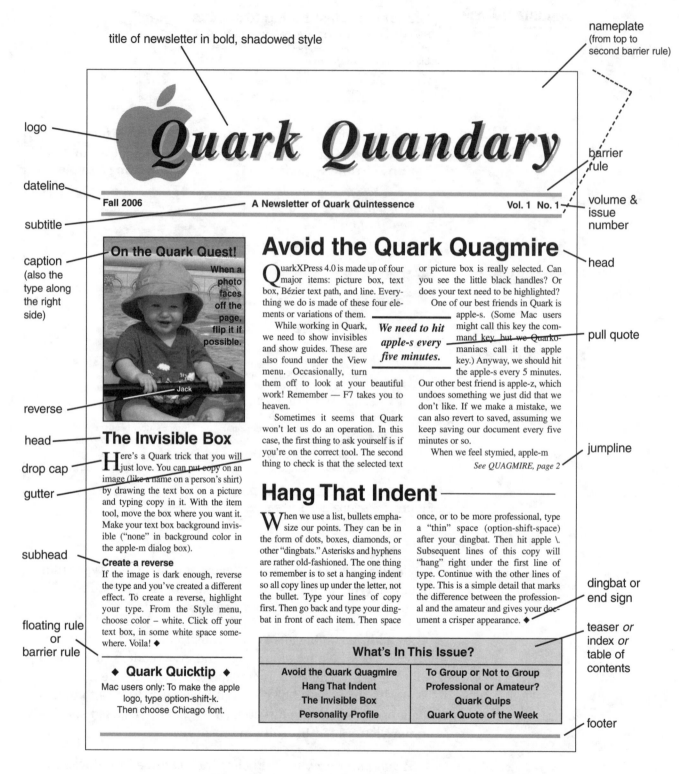

title of newsletter in bold, shadowed style

nameplate
(from top to
second barrier rule)

logo

dateline

subtitle

caption
(also the
type along
the right
side)

reverse

head

drop cap

gutter

subhead

floating rule
or
barrier rule

barrier
rule

volume &
issue
number

head

pull quote

jumpline

dingbat or
end sign

teaser *or*
index *or*
table of
contents

footer

Fall 2006   A Newsletter of Quark Quintessence   **Vol. 1 No. 1**

On the Quark Quest!

When a
photo
faces
off the
page,
flip it if
possible.

Jack

Avoid the Quark Quagmire

QuarkXPress 4.0 is made up of four major items: picture box, text box, Bézier text path, and line. Everything we do is made of these four elements or variations of them.

While working in Quark, we need to show invisibles and show guides. These are also found under the View menu. Occasionally, turn them off to look at your beautiful work! Remember — F7 takes you to heaven.

Sometimes it seems that Quark won't let us do an operation. In this case, the first thing to ask yourself is if you're on the correct tool. The second thing to check is that the selected text

We need to hit apple-s every five minutes.

or picture box is really selected. Can you see the little black handles? Or does your text need to be highlighted?

One of our best friends in Quark is apple-s. (Some Mac users might call this key the command key, but we Quarko-maniacs call it the apple key.) Anyway, we should hit the apple-s every 5 minutes. Our other best friend is apple-z, which undoes something we just did that we don't like. If we make a mistake, we can also revert to saved, assuming we keep saving our document every five minutes or so.

When we feel stymied, apple-m

See QUAGMIRE, page 2

The Invisible Box

Here's a Quark trick that you will just love. You can put copy on an image (like a name on a person's shirt) by drawing the text box on a picture and typing copy in it. With the item tool, move the box where you want it. Make your text box background invisible ("none" in background color in the apple-m dialog box).

Create a reverse
If the image is dark enough, reverse the type and you've created a different effect. To create a reverse, highlight your type. From the Style menu, choose color – white. Click off your text box, in some white space somewhere. Voila! ◆

◆ **Quark Quicktip** ◆

Mac users only: To make the apple logo, type option-shift-k. Then choose Chicago font.

Hang That Indent

When we use a list, bullets emphasize our points. They can be in the form of dots, boxes, diamonds, or other "dingbats." Asterisks and hyphens are rather old-fashioned. The one thing to remember is to set a hanging indent so all copy lines up under the letter, not the bullet. Type your lines of copy first. Then go back and type your dingbat in front of each item. Then space

once, or to be more professional, type a "thin" space (option-shift-space) after your dingbat. Then hit apple \. Subsequent lines of this copy will "hang" right under the first line of type. Continue with the other lines of type. This is a simple detail that marks the difference between the professional and the amateur and gives your document a crisper appearance. ◆

What's In This Issue?	
Avoid the Quark Quagmire	To Group or Not to Group
Hang That Indent	Professional or Amateur?
The Invisible Box	Quark Quips
Personality Profile	Quark Quote of the Week

Figure 2. Anatomy of a newsletter, page 1

(From *Communicating with QuarkXPress* by Claudia Cuddy. Copyright 2003 by Claudia Cuddy.
Reprinted by permission of Kendall/Hunt Publishing Company.)

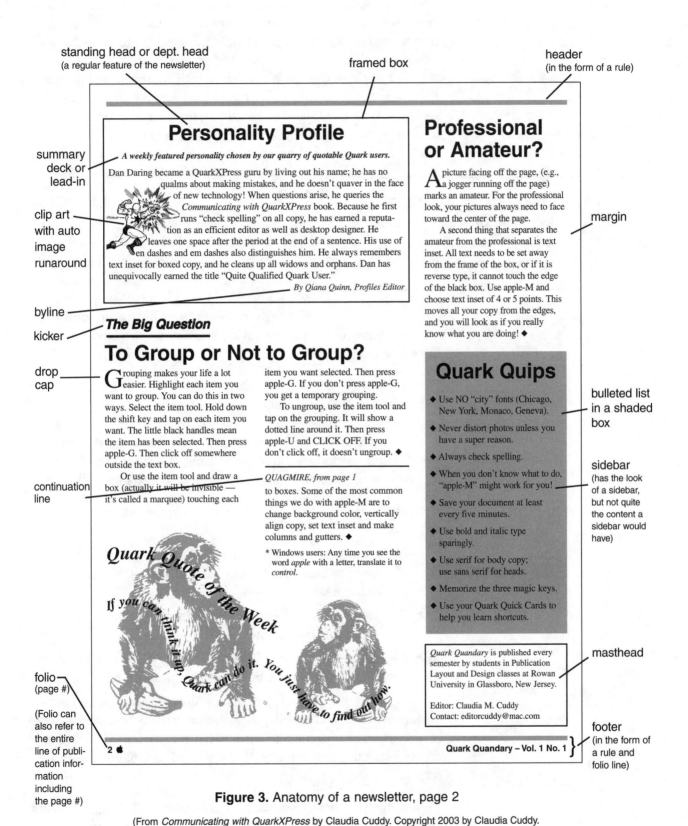

standing head or dept. head
(a regular feature of the newsletter)

framed box

header
(in the form of a rule)

summary
deck or
lead-in

clip art
with auto
image
runaround

byline

kicker

drop
cap

continuation
line

folio
(page #)

(Folio can
also refer to
the entire
line of publi-
cation infor-
mation
including
the page #)

margin

bulleted list
in a shaded
box

sidebar
(has the look
of a sidebar,
but not quite
the content a
sidebar would
have)

masthead

footer
(in the form of
a rule and
folio line)

Personality Profile

A weekly featured personality chosen by our quarry of quotable Quark users.

Dan Daring became a QuarkXPress guru by living out his name; he has no qualms about making mistakes, and he doesn't quaver in the face of new technology! When questions arise, he queries the *Communicating with QuarkXPress* book. Because he first runs "check spelling" on all copy, he has earned a reputation as an efficient editor as well as desktop designer. He leaves one space after the period at the end of a sentence. His use of en dashes and em dashes also distinguishes him. He always remembers text inset for boxed copy, and he cleans up all widows and orphans. Dan has unequivocally earned the title "Quite Qualified Quark User."

By Qiana Quinn, Profiles Editor

The Big Question

To Group or Not to Group?

Grouping makes your life a lot easier. Highlight each item you want to group. You can do this in two ways. Select the item tool. Hold down the shift key and tap on each item you want. The little black handles mean the item has been selected. Then press apple-G. Then click off somewhere outside the text box.

Or use the item tool and draw a box (actually it will be invisible — it's called a marquee) touching each

item you want selected. Then press apple-G. If you don't press apple-G, you get a temporary grouping.

To ungroup, use the item tool and tap on the grouping. It will show a dotted line around it. Then press apple-U and CLICK OFF. If you don't click off, it doesn't ungroup. ◆

QUAGMIRE, from page 1

to boxes. Some of the most common things we do with apple-M are to change background color, vertically align copy, set text inset and make columns and gutters. ◆

* Windows users: Any time you see the word *apple* with a letter, translate it to *control*.

Quark Quote of the Week

If you can think it up, Quark can do it. You just have to find out how.

Professional or Amateur?

A picture facing off the page, (e.g., a jogger running off the page) marks an amateur. For the professional look, your pictures always need to face toward the center of the page.

A second thing that separates the amateur from the professional is text inset. All text needs to be set away from the frame of the box, or if it is reverse type, it cannot touch the edge of the black box. Use apple-M and choose text inset of 4 or 5 points. This moves all your copy from the edges, and you will look as if you really know what you are doing! ◆

Quark Quips

◆ Use NO "city" fonts (Chicago, New York, Monaco, Geneva).

◆ Never distort photos unless you have a super reason.

◆ Always check spelling.

◆ When you don't know what to do, "apple-M" might work for you!

◆ Save your document at least every five minutes.

◆ Use bold and italic type sparingly.

◆ Use serif for body copy; use sans serif for heads.

◆ Memorize the three magic keys.

◆ Use your Quark Quick Cards to help you learn shortcuts.

Quark Quandary is published every semester by students in Publication Layout and Design classes at Rowan University in Glassboro, New Jersey.

Editor: Claudia M. Cuddy
Contact: editorcuddy@mac.com

2

Quark Quandary – Vol. 1 No. 1

Figure 3. Anatomy of a newsletter, page 2

(From *Communicating with QuarkXPress* by Claudia Cuddy. Copyright 2003 by Claudia Cuddy. Reprinted by permission of Kendall/Hunt Publishing Company.)

As we read in chapter 6, *sidebars* complement a major story and offer an attractive way to introduce parallel information. In newsletter design, sidebars help interject a humanistic touch and align related stories and ideas. In annual reports they help bridge the gap that exists with communicating raw numbers. For example, in many annual reports accounting statements and tables are the story. However, these raw numbers often confuse readers. By using a carefully placed sidebar, written by someone who can interpret the data, the publication increases its readability.

A pull quote inserted into copy is the way to break up a gray page. It is a sentence or a phrase drawn out of the text and set in bold type.

Pull quotes — sentences or phrases drawn out of the text and set in bold type — offer two design advantages. First, they help accentuate an important idea or quote. Second, they help break up long blocks of copy. Pull quotes (also referred to as blurbs or sandwiches) sometimes use large quotation marks and are boxed or have lines above and below.

Another copy breaker that has become a favorite graphic device for many writers is the *bullet*. Bullets — bold dots, boxes, arrows or check marks — that introduce an ordered list, offer an attractive design feature and a wonderful tool for writing efficiency. The following list contains some key rules for effectively using bullets.

➤ Hang copy in a bulleted list so all copy lines up under itself.

➤ Maintain parallel structure by using the same part of speech to begin each item (all infinitives, all gerunds, all participles).

➤ Use icons such as Wingding and Zapf Dingbats sparingly and maintain consistency.

➤ Avoid excessively long lists of bulleted items (six or seven items in a row should be about the maximum).

Finally, photos, clipart, frames, borders, drop caps and other graphic devices add certain panache to written documents. The combination of graphic elements helps the writer and designer create and carry out a particular look and feel. They enhance readability through increased legibility.

Perhaps the most important of all layout and design projects for professional communicators are the newsletter, the brochure and the annual report.

Newsletters

TOOLBOX TIP

Newsletter Consistency

Repetition is a major factor in the unity of those pages. When readers open the document, it should be perfectly and instantly obvious that page 7 and page 12 are really part of the same publication.[2]

PR and business writers use a variety of methods to reach various audiences. One of the most popular of these communication tools is the newsletter.

Newsletters cater to both internal and external audiences. In fact, their varied uses enable writing practitioners to tailor creative, informative messages to selected audiences. Modeled after newspapers and news magazines, newsletters provide information to a variety of readers through an inexpensive, yet powerful, medium.

The appropriate design and content of a newsletter depends on the audience targeted and the tone and style of the information needed to be communicated. Publications generally have two primary purposes:

1. They help present special information to selected audiences.
2. They reinforce organizational attitudes and opinions.

Newsletters generally contribute to an organization's overall communication package. In fact, their specialized use contributes to the overall organizational effectiveness and establishes another credible source for dissemination of relevant information.

However, simply knowing how to use computer hardware and software does not qualify someone to design and produce effective publications. This new technology is merely a tool that relies on sound understanding of graphic layout and design coupled with clear and precise writing.

One of the most basic, yet often overlooked, elements to producing first-rate newsletters is to understand what constitutes a newsletter. To qualify for newsletter status, a publication must first meet the criteria of serialization.

Serialization involves the regular production and distribution of a publication. Organizations catalog newsletters by printing volume and issue numbers on each issue. This enables readers to keep track of the publication and gives a sense of permanence to the publication. Such durability adds credibility to the messages being communicated and the communication vehicle as a whole.

Public relations professionals have at their disposal various formats to produce effective newsletters. Of course, before deciding on a format, practitioners must first carefully analyze the audience and then select the design that best complements the messages being conveyed.

Some design types to consider include:

> **Newspapers**. Usually produced in four-column or five-column newsprint, newspaper design provides an inexpensive way to communicate "hard" news items.

> **Magazines**. This style emphasizes more of a creative feel for your publication and generally capitalizes on the use of color photography and high quality coated paper stock. The style also works best with feature story copy.

> **Minimags**. This half-size magazine style format (5½" by 8½") is generally used more for promotion purposes. Its simple design invites readers to sample the publication.

> **Maganews** and **Magapapers**. These hybrid formats are unique for their generous use of white space and emphasis on graphic design. They provide a unique forum for conveying company information through a creative vehicle.

Key Design Issues

Proper production of newsletters begins with a thorough understanding of four basic elements of composition:

1. Body type (text)
2. Display type (headlines, titles, kickers, hanging indents, etc.)
3. Art (photos, drawings, graphic elements)
4. White space (air or space that gives a publication a sense of freedom)

Newsletter editors must also pay attention to:

• **Nameplate**. The name of the publication. The nameplate may also include a logo along with the volume and issue number of the publication.

• **Masthead**. Block of text identifying the publication, including staff, address, copyright information and so on. Generally found on the second page of the publication.

Publications such as *Communication Briefings*, an award-winning monthly newsletter, stress a style known as modular design. Essentially, modular design combines a variety of geometric shapes to produce a publication that is easy to read and invites readers to spend time with the publication.

Despite a desire to produce super creative publications using a variety of graphic elements, an editor must remember these sound layout and design practices:

> **Emphasize white space.** Publications that are too heavy in copy and graphics are considered to have a "gray" look. This diminishes reader appeal.

> **Avoid butting heads.** Publication designers must be careful not to place headlines directly next to each other in the publication. This causes confusion on the reader's part and often results in decreased readership.

> **Vary shapes.** Consider the design of a publication like a mix of geometric shapes. Each different shape complements each other yet maintains its own unique quality.

> **Focus on writing.** Even the most creative and unique design can't make up for a poorly written newsletter. The design of the publication must work in combination with the clean, crisp and concise writing. This provides an effective communication vehicle.

Brochures

Unlike newsletters, which have serial publications, brochures are generally published only once and distributed to special publics for a single purpose. University interns often get their introduction to publications through newsletters and brochures.

Brochures differ from fliers and leaflets because they are more lavish in design and generally convey more detailed information.

Designers must begin by writing copy using active voice verbs and with an emphasis on short sentences and short paragraphs. Bulleted lists also add clarity to a brochure and help communicate information quickly. The use of subheads also adds to the clarity and visual appeal of a brochure.

Carefully planned folds can add design creativity and functionality to a brochure. Special tear-off panels can be used for mail-in promotions or as coupons for consumer goods. They provide an attractive and cost-effective design element.

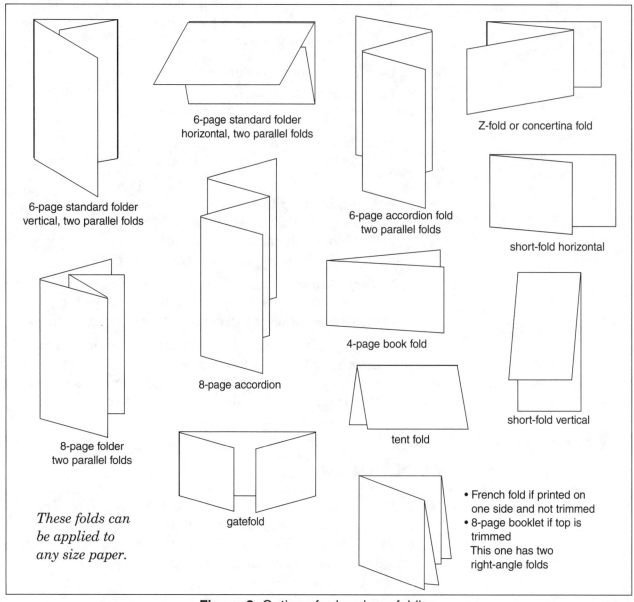

6-page standard folder horizontal, two parallel folds

Z-fold or concertina fold

6-page standard folder vertical, two parallel folds

6-page accordion fold two parallel folds

short-fold horizontal

8-page accordion

4-page book fold

short-fold vertical

8-page folder two parallel folds

tent fold

These folds can be applied to any size paper.

gatefold

• French fold if printed on one side and not trimmed
• 8-page booklet if top is trimmed
This one has two right-angle folds

Figure 2. Options for brochure folding

(From *Communicating with QuarkXPress* by Claudia Cuddy. Copyright 2003 by Claudia Cuddy. Reprinted by permission of Kendall/Hunt Publishing Company.)

Brochures can also include a mailing panel. Use of a mailing panel eliminates the need for sending the brochure in an envelope. The decision to design the brochure as a self-mailer or one that requires an envelope must be made after considering a number of factors such as budget for the project and the message tone the designer wishes to convey.

Finally, brochure designers must be bold enough to take chances with their design but also fundamentally skilled to follow the rules of good writing and the principles of effective design.

Annual Reports

The annual report ranks at the top of the corporate communication pyramid. Surveys rank it as the single most important document. Company annual reports afford professional communicators with perhaps their greatest challenge. On one level they contain information required by the Securities and Exchange Commission for reporting financial information for publicly traded companies. At another level they serve as a valuable marketing tool for organizations to attract potential stock investors. They typically are provided to members of the media to help them do a thorough job of covering businesses and nonprofit organizations.

While all reports contain information the SEC requires, most annual reports also contain optional elements. The mandatory elements include:

➤ **Auditors' Report**. Summary of the findings of an independent firm of certified public accountants to show whether the financial statements are complete, reasonable and prepared consistent with generally accepted accounting principles (GAAP) at a set time.

➤ **Management Discussion**. A series of short, detailed reports that analyze the company's performance.

➤ **Financial Statements and Notes**. Provide raw numbers pertaining to the company's financial performance and recent financial history. The SEC requires three statements — statement of earnings, statement of financial position and statement of cash flow.

➤ **Selected Financial Data**. Summarizes the company's financial condition and performance over five years or longer.

In addition to the mandatory elements, an annual report may contain a host of optional elements. Some optional elements include financial highlights, letter to stockholders, management report, names and titles of key personnel and product information.

The bulk of an annual report's financial information takes the form of tables and charts. However, the optional information that appears in most annual reports prepared for major corporations includes lavishly designed information printed on glossy paper stock. Most annual reports over the past 10 years have become more reader friendly, looking more like magazine spreads with color photos, generous white space and stunning graphics. They are the most expensive documents regularly created by public relations writers. Fortune 500 companies typically use their own staffs to coordinate the colossal effort with outside consultants.

Well-designed and well-written annual reports should stand alone as respectable, hard-working publications. Their primary purpose is to recruit stockholders. However, they also present an interesting picture of the company, painting broad strokes about the culture and serving as a valuable image-building tool. Many organizations that are not required to file annual reports, such as nonprofits, still produce them for all the public relations benefits they create.

Notes

[1]James Glen Stovall. *Infographics: A Journalist's Guide*. Needham Heights, MA: Allyn and Bacon, 1997.

[2]Robin Williams. *The Non-Designer's Design Book*. Berkeley, CA: Peachpit Press, 1994.

For Further Reading

Claudia Cuddy. *Communicating with QuarkXPress: Integrating Principles of Design and Techniques of Layout*. Dubuque, IA: Kendall/Hunt, 2003.

14.

Using Advertising for Public Relations

by Suzanne Sparks FitzGerald

Public relations practitioners often choose between public relations and advertising options. According to Public Communications/West, a marketing communications firm, no communication plan is complete until it embraces elements of both public relations and advertising.

Many people lack the knowledge of the difference between public relations and advertising. Public relations is usually thought of as unpaid and "earned," while advertising is "paid-for" publicity. Public relations gives up control of the MAC triad (the message, audience and channel) to garner third-party credibility from a media outlet. A major strength of advertising is that it allows you to control all three aspects of the MAC triad. But, because advertising is considered paid-for space or air, it lacks third-party credibility, which is public relations' major strength.

When asked, "What is the difference between public relations and advertising?" these experts said…

"I view advertising as part of public relations — just one of the many tools those in public relations use to reach their audiences."
Jack Gillespie, former editor, *Communication Briefings*

"Advertising is what you pay for; PR is what you pray for."
John Elsasser, editor in chief, *PR Tactics*

"Simply stated, advertising is space or time purchased with the message controlled by the advertiser. Public relations delivers messages through various techniques and the media control what the intended target audience actually hears and sees."
Rene Henry, director, Office of External Affairs, EPA

Suzanne Sparks FitzGerald, Ph.D., APR, is chair of the PR/Advertising Department at Rowan University in Glassboro, N.J.

Public Relations Versus Advertising

Public relations and advertising are closely related, and integrated marketing practitioners use techniques from both to produce comprehensive communication programs. In smaller organizations, the same people may be called upon to produce both. Public relations and advertising differ in several important ways, however, including: the level of control of the message, audience and channel; the credibility factor; and the way they use the media.

Control – If PR practitioners need to have total control of the message content, audience, channel or timeframe, they should choose advertising. If achieving credibility through a third-party endorsement (or implied endorsement) overshadows the need for control, a public relations technique should be used.

Credibility – The credibility of public relations generally outweighs that of advertising in that it offers another person or organization recommending or conveying information for you rather than an identified sponsor. Consumers have grown suspicious of invalid advertising claims. Public relations practitioners cannot control the way that gatekeepers use the information they provide, but they can develop media relationships that produce more accurate coverage.

Media Use – By paying for time or space, advertisers maintain control over their message's content and timing, audience, and channel while guaranteeing access to the media. Public relations practitioners, on the other hand, use media gatekeepers to carry their messages. Public relations pros must trust these "gatekeepers" (editors or producers who control the flow of information by deciding how much of a story, if any, they'll use) to maintain the intended meaning of a story.

As a PR writer, you should decide how to best deal with media gatekeepers. If you need absolute control, such as in a crisis or when dealing with a controversial issue, use predominantly advertising. If third-party credibility is more important, use primarily public relations.

Public Relations Advertising

When most people think of advertising, usually a brand commercial comes to mind. However, because public relations practitioners often deal with issues like advocacy, image, persuasion and public information, they tend to use certain types of advertising more frequently. When public relations writers use paid-for media, the message is usually to feature an image, advocate a position, or evoke a behavior other than buying. The following section briefly discusses common types of public relations advertising.

Advocacy/issue – Advocacy advertising seeks to change public opinion concerning an issue or an organization. Sometimes referred to as issue advertising, it adopts a position on a particular issue or advocates a particular cause, rather than promoting the organization itself.

You can use advocacy advertising in several ways:

1. To counteract public hostility toward corporate activities. For example, you might write an advocacy ad featuring the benefits of a new nuclear energy facility or to allay the fears of its opponents.

2. To communicate views on issues that affect an organization's business. For instance, you might use an advocacy ad to address the regional power shortages and your position on the reliability of your industry.

3. To promote the organization's philosophy. For example, public relations practitioners for domestic violence shelters could use advocacy ads to state the philosophy of the shelter and what it can provide for battered women and children.

4. To make a social statement. Your organization might advocate only heterosexual marriage and its benefits as a social statement.

House – An organization prepares an ad for use in its own publication or a publication over which it exerts control. No money changes hands. For example, a television station may run a house ad announcing its new fall programming. Because the public relations function usually controls in-house promotions and publications, this type of advertising often falls under public relations advertising.

Cooperative – This type of advertising allows a manufacturer to share costs with a retailer, saving money because local advertising rates are less expensive than national rates. For example, Famous Footwear features Rockport sneakers in a co-op ad.

Often two national advertisers join together. For example, in

Promotional Writing

Promotional writing is a style of writing. The Latin roots of *promote* mean to move forward. Therefore, in promotional writing you're often trying to move an idea forward — to a point at which the audience accepts it.

The PennStater magazine, the Penn State Alumni Association and MasterCard ran a cooperative ad featuring the Nittany Lion and Penn State Alumni Association logo on a MasterCard as a selling point.

Cooperative advertising also allows two organizations to "tie in" with one another. In one example, Midas Muffler ran a co-op campaign with the Better Hearing Institute to promote good hearing. Midas benefited from positive public opinion and the Better Hearing Institute from lower advertising costs.

Cause-related Marketing or **Sponsorship** – Sponsorship offers an alternative to advertising in traditional media by allowing an organization to sponsor an event or programming. Sponsorship tends to reach a wide audience and can create brand or corporate name awareness. For example, Virginia Slims cigarettes used to sponsor women's tennis — now Advanta (an insurance company) is seen as a better fit for a sport. Federal Express sponsors one of the college bowl football games.

Television sponsorship can have a powerful impact on viewers because of the control the advertiser exerts on not only the placement of commercials, but even on the content of the program. Many playing fields have product logos superimposed on them, either actually or merely for TV viewers. Thus, the product name is viewed during the activity, not just during commercial breaks. Often several advertisers sponsor a sporting event together.

Cause-related marketing comprises sponsorship, product placement and percentage of profits as techniques. Sponsorship is the most common, although **product placement** on television programming has become a phenomenon in the last few years. A famous "Friends" episode was based on a Pottery Barn catalog.

Actor Paul Newman offers consumers the opportunity to preserve the rain forests by donating a **percentage of profits** from sales of his food products to conservationists.

Many companies that make controversial products like cigarettes use cause-related marketing to create a more positive image for their organization.

Institutional or Image – Corporate or institutional advertising concerns the image of an organization and thus focuses on public opinion formation or change. Commercials using the

Blueprint

Top Ad Mistakes to Avoid

According to Roy H. Williams on Entrepreneur.com, you should avoid these advertising blunders:

1. **Instant gratification** – Ads that attract urgency might be forgotten immediately once an offer expires. Good ads establish the advertiser's identity in the mind of the consumer.

2. **Over-reaching the budget** – You must have enough repetition to establish retention. Certain options may allow you to reach more people, but not with enough frequency.

3. **Assume the client knows best** – Business owners are not objective. "It's hard to read the label when you're in the bottle."

4. **Unsubstantiated claims** – Don't claim to have what the customer wants and fail to offer evidence.

5. **Improper use of passive media** – Use intrusive rather than non-intrusive media such as radio and TV to patiently and consistently reach relational customers.

6. **Create ads instead of campaigns** – Don't believe a single ad can tell the whole story. The most effective and memorable ads are those most like a rhinoceros. They make one point, powerfully.

7. **Using mostly late-week schedules** – Don't compete with everyone else for customers; garner their attention alone on Sunday, Monday or Tuesday.

8. **Great production without great copy** – Slick, clever, funny and different are poor substitutes for informative, believable, memorable and persuasive.

U.S. Army's "Be all that you can be" slogan featured the benefits you can derive from a career in the Army. Beginning in 2004, the recruiting advertising campaign uses "An Army of One." The newer slogan emphasizes personal growth and individual opportunity. For years, General Electric used the "We bring good things to life" campaign to enhance its image. Hallmark uses the image-building slogan, "When you care enough to send the very best."

According to Fraser Seitel, practitioner and author, corporate ads should strengthen the bottom line, be persuasive and appeal to what the public wants. Institutional ads should improve consumer, community and employee relations.

A survey by the Association of National Advertisers showed that the major purpose of institutional advertising was to build recognition.

Public Service Announcements – Public service announcements provide the means to disseminate public information. These PSAs require no fee to air or print. Many times agencies will produce PSAs on a *pro bono* (for the public good) basis, eliminating all charges for a nonprofit organization.

Bergh and Katz in *Advertising Principles* note that some highly successful PSA campaigns include: American Red Cross for blood donation; Federal Voting Assistance Program for getting out the vote; National Institute on Drug Abuse for drug abuse and AIDS prevention; and the U.S. Department of Transportation for drunk-driving prevention.

If a practitioner doesn't find a specific agency to produce an ad or an ad campaign, the Advertising Council, a private nonprofit organization, conducts public service advertising campaigns in the public interest. The council receives approximately 400 requests from private organizations and government agencies annually requesting campaign support.

Writing Public Relations Advertising

Often in developing a campaign, an advertiser will design a plan. This evaluation of the circumstances surrounding the campaign helps advertisers to focus the messages in a targeted way. A situation analysis should include the advertising problem or challenge, a profile of the target audience, an analysis of the issue, a look at the competition, and a Strengths–Weaknesses–Opportunities–Threats (SWOT) analysis.

After the situation analysis is complete, advertisers formulate a creative plan. Creative people often develop a list of features and benefits to help stimulate creative thinking. When addressing a passive audience, **benefits** draw in those who may have only a minimal interest. Conversely, if you face an active audience, this audience wants **features** to help it discriminate among the options.

As a PR writer, you may not have the time to formulate a full-fledged advertising campaign. It's important, no matter what the time/cost constraints, to develop a **creative** (or copy) **platform** — a document (or brief statement) that outlines the message strategy decisions behind an individual ad. With your copy platform in place, you're ready to write.

Basic Ad Components

When designing an ad, practitioners should keep in mind the following tips: keep the message simple, speak directly to your publics or audiences, and know the target market for your message.

Print ads – The following elements of a print ad will help you develop your creative approach. The **headline** should grab the reader's attention early and entice the reader into the body copy. According to advertisers, the headline, which usually appears in large type, has four seconds to catch the reader's attention. Common types of headlines include: (1) benefit, (2) news/informative, (3) provocative, (4) question and (5) command.

Sometimes advertisers use an overline or an underline to entice the reader to get into the body copy of the ad. In a Taster's Choice ad the overline read, "The dilemma," while the headline stated, "Andrew or Michael?" The underline read, "It's your choice!" This old but popular print campaign refers to a soap-opera-like campaign where a woman who drinks Taster's Choice must pick between her estranged husband and her next-door neighbor.

The **overline** draws the reader into the headline and the **underline** draws the reader into the body copy. Advertisers use both direct and indirect headlines — the previous example was indirect. A **direct headline** is straightforward and informative, but may not lure the audience into the body copy. An **indirect headline** should compel the audience to read on, but provides less information than the direct head.

The **copy** or main textblock should be written for the target audience — at its level. It should build on the headline, promise, reward or benefit. The copy should heighten the reader's interest and desire and offer proof in the form of facts and testimony. Perhaps most importantly, the copy should encourage the reader to take action.

The **illustration** or artwork (or photo) should relate closely to the headline and copy, attract the reader's attention, and appeal to the reader's emotions. Many creative directors recommend the use of two-thirds artwork to one-third copy for effectiveness.

The **logo** should convey the image of the sponsoring organization and should always include contact information. Often a slogan or tagline accompanies the logo. These devices are used for memorability. To differentiate, a **slogan** is repeated from ad to ad. A **tagline** wraps up the idea at the end of a particular ad.

According to Sandra Moriarty in her text *Creative Advertising*, practitioners can use this checklist to write effective copy.

➤ Use pictures and words together to create impact.

➤ Write to someone you know who represents the target audience.

➤ Make it conversational!

➤ Use short, succinct statements.

➤ Use short paragraphs to maintain reader interest.

➤ Personalize the copy by using the word "you."

➤ Avoid the word "we."

➤ Try not to sound preachy or pushy.

Research shows that the use of white space directs the eye of the reader, provides separation from adjoining messages and relieves a cluttered feeling that could make the ad difficult to read.

In summary, the creative plan often makes or breaks the success of the advertising campaign. The strength of the creative effort affects the results of the persuasion. When a campaign causes behavioral change, most practitioners would consider it a success. Now, let's write some advertisements!

Types of Persuasion

The Greek philosopher Aristotle identified three types of persuasion.

1. Appeals to the intellect.

2. Appeals to the emotion.

3. Appeals to a sense of ethics.

Writing Advocacy Ads

Advocacy ads should persuade the target audience to behave or to think in a certain way. They most often advocate the position of the organization on an issue. Let's say you're writing an ad for a national Greek organization advocating how to avoid date rape.

1. You should develop a copy platform or a series of ideas for the ad or ad campaign and then test it on a small number of your target population.

2. Using that research, you should design some direct and indirect headlines and see which work best.

3. Consider the use of an overline or underline to draw readers into the body copy.

4. Never make the first paragraph of body copy long — you'll lose your readers.

5. Write the ad in a nonpreachy, conversational style.

6. Consider telling a story of a date rape to catch the attention of your readers.

7. Don't give the end of the story until you've made your point or advocated your position.

8. Close with an action for the reader to take as well as the end of the story.

9. Give appropriate contact information.

10. Make sure the sponsoring organization's logo is clear and readable.

11. Look over the ad for white space — do you have enough?

12. Is your visual compelling?

In any type of persuasion, you deal with inert audience members. Convincing them to agree with you is easy compared to causing them to act. Don't expect miracles, but target your audience to receive maximum effect.

Writing House Ads

A danger in writing house ads is to assume that in-house audiences know as much as you do about your product, service or organization. Many house ads fail because audience members do not have the comprehensive overview of key managers or PR staff.

Because your audience knows you more than they know an "outside advertiser," in-house ads must have a strong creative appeal to attract attention. Audiences may have a vested interest in owning or joining a related product/organization, for example, the alumni association of their university. Always write in a conversational tone and avoid "pushy" language.

Writing Cooperative Ads

The writing in this instance is complicated by having to serve two organizations. In a *Philadelphia Magazine* ad, Nordstrom's and Sergio Ferragamo teamed up to produce a simple visual of a pair of men's dress shoes with the headline of Sergio Ferragamo and the Nordstrom's logo on the bottom of the photo. Several messages seemed evident — Nordstrom's sells quality men's shoes; Sergio Ferragamo makes top-quality men's shoes.

To write a cooperative ad, as any other ad, develop a copy platform; test your idea; design your headline and visual; and write the body copy. In this case, make sure each logo is displayed as well as contact information.

Writing Cause-Related Marketing Ads

For product placement, you don't have to write an ad, but rather determine where the use of a product placement would work most effectively. As mentioned in the sidebar, many organizations are integrating their advertising with programming to make it more invasive and persuasive.

For sponsorship advertising, one important consideration takes place well before writing the ad — what kind of organization do you want to sponsor/support? If you jump on the bandwagon like many post-Sept. 11 organizations did and force your organization to look patriotic — your efforts may get lost amid all of the other similar campaigns. If, on the other hand, your organization can determine what values the target audience holds, you can appeal to those values. For example, many organizations whose primary audience is women choose to sponsor breast cancer research or treatment.

When writing sponsorship ads, adhere closely to the truth — beware even hyperbole or exaggeration. If you don't have a particularly positive image and wish to ally yourself with a cause or an organization with a more beneficial image, you don't want to exaggerate your claims. Avoid even the appearance of misleading your audience. So, to write sponsorship ads, do your homework. Find out more than demographics of your target audience. Appeal to deep-seated emotions. In a thesis conducted by Rowan University graduate student Ralph DeSimone, he noted that women seem more affected by cause-related marketing than do men. If you have an audience of primarily women, this is good news.

Writing Institutional Ads

As mentioned earlier, a major purpose of institutional advertising is to build recognition. Most organizations need to enhance or maintain an image. First, a caution — don't take on a client with a poor identity. You can't change the identity with communication, but you can help change an image. In other words, make sure the organization does what it says it does and stands behind its ideas, products or services.

Institutional ads are "big picture" ads — without detailing product or service features — conveying an image or a perception of the organization. Many nonprofits can shape their identity through institutional advertising. For example, many believe the American Red Cross does one thing — collect blood. If you ever have the American Red Cross as a client, consider stressing the emergency aid the organization offers worldwide and its first-responder status.

So, to write institutional advertising, get a sense of what the organization offers to its publics. In the case of General Electric with its theme of "We bring good things to life," notice how general and overarching the headline. The organization doesn't want you to think about missiles or washers and dryers, it wants you to think of the public good served by GE. Develop an overall theme for the organization.

A CIGNA company that offered worker's compensation insurance needed an institutional ad. It chose a Stradivarius violin being restored and the headline, "The art of restoration." The association between a fine instrument and its restoration, and workers and their rehabilitation, was stressed.

Consider an analogy like the CIGNA advertisement used. Research is key here — you must understand enough about the organization to equate it to a commonly understood example. Then use the principles we've discussed to complete your headline, body copy, logo and tagline.

Writing Public Service Announcements (PSAs)

Public service announcements often lead to awards for the sponsoring agencies because nonpaying clients allow agencies creative freedom without the restrictions of budget approvals and many corporate lawyers. One of the most successful campaigns of all time, Smokey Bear and prevention of forest fires, has saved lives and property by educating people on fire prevention. The furry spokesbear celebrated his 60th anniversary in August 2004. Likewise, the seat belt dummies have increased seat belt usage and thus have saved lives as well.

When creating PSAs, an organization has three choices: (1) design and produce the announcement in-house; (2) find an advertising agency to produce it on a pro bono basis; or (3) write a script (for electronic media) and allow the media outlet to produce it. For example, the on-air talent reads the script. Always prepare a variety of formats (10-second, 20-second, 30-second spots). The different formats will allow the media outlet the flexibility to use the spot at its convenience. Also,

Blueprint

New Advertising Options

According to *The Wall Street Journal*, New York City is now offering a 20-year contract to outdoor advertisers to include new bus-stop shelters, public toilets, newsstands, trash cans and information kiosks. Referred to as "**street-furniture advertising**," these ads may gain the city as much as $300 million over the 20 years. The winning bidder will install, operate and maintain at least 3,300 bus shelters, 20 public toilets, 330 newsstands as well as trash cans and information kiosks.

Product placements we remember from the NCAA Final Four telecasts in 2004 — Chevrolet for an in-program placement on a "scholarship program."

Cingular Wireless for the in-program placement of the "Greatest Championship Game" poll.

"**Product integrations**" we remember from *The Swan*, a reality program — Jenny Craig showed contestants visiting weight-loss centers to receive diet plans. Jaguar's announcer names a car as part of the prize.

Situ-mercials or situational commercials are designed to play off the shows consumers are watching. Geico, an insurance company, has successfully run a situmercial on what looks like a scene from a crime drama on court shows and dramas like *Law and Order: SVU*. **The Army blended real life with TV** when it created situational ads to play off the popular miniseries on WW II — *Band of Brothers*. The Army ads blend scenes from the miniseries with interviews with soldiers who have served in Iraq or Afghanistan. According to a Starcom Entertainment senior vice president, we're going to see more advertisers getting closer to content with their advertising.

Magazine ads go for the spine — *Modern Bride*, in an effort to move beyond the traditional magazine ad page, is running an ad for Target on the cover's spine. According to the *Wall Street Journal*, finding new ways to please advertisers has become a fact of life for magazine publishers. BMW's Mini Division bought the **margins** around news stories in several titles creating what it termed "**corner ads**." The copy read: Nothing corners like a Mini.

National regulators in China have banned "offensive" product ads such as feminine hygiene pads, hemorrhoid medication and athlete's foot ointment during meal times. Chinese viewers complained that the commercials were too graphic and too frequent during dinner.

Financial services firms appeal to women on the Academy Awards, considered the women's Superbowl. According to Neilsen Media Research, two-thirds of Oscar viewers in 2003 were women, who are now recognized as key financial decision makers.

New Bingo TV channel lets players win prizes during a live two-hour broadcast. Rather than airing 30-second spots, the hosts deliver ad pitches about the prizes for which viewers compete.

Internet advertising features webisodes starring Jerry Seinfeld and Superman. American Express has unveiled this four-minute webisode to find new customers and engage them longer. According to Interpublic Group's Universal McCann, up to 18 percent of consumer media time is spent on the Web. American Express has taken the best from traditional advertising (celebrities, cartoon icons and humor) and adapted it for the Web.

Advertisers hitch a ride on mission to Mars — advertisers linked their products with space exploration. Spirit Airlines ran a newspaper ad that read, "Spirit to Mars? Sure, but our fares are $1.2 million less." When the rovers went to Mars in 2004, Volkswagen's Audi ran an ad stating, "Mars rover still stuck. Quattro all-wheel drive. You never know when you'll need it."

Madison Avenue wants a piece of the videogame industry — according to agency giant Young and Rubicam, families rarely gather together in front of the electronic hearth. *The Wall Street Journal* notes that you can't market to the 18- to 24-year-old age group today without using gaming in the media mix. Advertising agencies are opening gaming divisions to preserve their status as middlemen.

remember to send a script with an audio or videotape to make it easier for the broadcaster. Public service announcements should be for the good of the public and you should write them accordingly.

Summary

As a PR practitioner, you'll face the decision of whether to use public relations, advertising or some combination in the IMC collection. Because various types of advertising are closely related to public relations, you may be called upon to write the script or even the print ad yourself. If you have the luxury of collaborating with an agency creative team, you should now know the basics of constructing an ad from a copy platform through the contact information. Writing advertising copy is somewhat different from public relations writing. As a practitioner, you'll enjoy the flexibility of a different genre.

For Further Reading

Sandra Moriarty. *Creative Advertising*. Englewood Cliffs, NJ: Prentice-Hall, 1991.

Bruce G. Vanden Bergh and Helen Katz. *Advertising Principles: Choice, Challenge, Change*. Lincolnwood, IL: NTC Publishing Group, 1999.

15.
Writing and the Law
More than just knowing the First Amendment

A scene that plays out all too often in corporate litigation today involves the mining of company e-mails and other internal communication for the purpose of serving as "Exhibit A" in a lawsuit against the company. With alarming frequency, these poorly crafted internal documents serve as the genesis in framing a case against a company. So the business writer in the 21st century needs to worry as much about internal memos as news releases sent to the media.

In fact, damaging internal communication can be mined from a host of sources in a company, even a CEO's hard drive, such as one used by Microsoft chief Bill Gates who found out the hard way that electronic communication leaves a long and lingering aftertaste. During the government's antitrust case against the computer software giant, prosecutors confronted Gates with copies of e-mails he had previously written that seemed to contradict what he said in sworn testimony. Time and time again, Gates found that e-mail messages written years earlier contradicted his spoken testimony. This destroyed Gates' credibility in the eyes of the judge.

The dramatic growth of computer technology has redefined the way that business operates in today's information economy. However, the increased use of computer technology has also placed a daunting burden on corporations to control the production and dissemination of information. From the perspective of a plaintiff's attorney, it places a great advantage in the hands of the client who can capitalize on an embarrassing mistake or inadvertent communication produced by someone within the corporation.

Of course, today's corporations must develop mechanisms to control a literal warehouse full of information generated by a workforce that lists as its primary duties the production and dissemination of information. What becomes paramount is the need to properly educate and train today's information worker concerning the potential disasters associated with poorly constructed prose rather than developing innovative strategies for coping with the aftermath of a lawsuit. Put in different terms, the best defensive strategy for a corporation may be to teach employees effective writing skills and to identify the potential landmines that exist on the information battlefield.

First Amendment Basics

The First Amendment to the United States Constitution reads, "Congress shall make no law...abridging the freedom of speech, or of the press...." Of course, we all know that Congress has passed numerous laws abridging free speech.

The First Amendment means that government may not tell you to shut up just because it doesn't like the content of your message. It may, however, put reasonable restrictions on the time, place and manner of your speech, and it can also balance your rights of free speech against other important rights.

According to constitutional law scholar Erwin Chemerinsky, the Supreme Court of the United States frequently has declared that the very core of the First Amendment is that the government cannot regulate speech based on its content. Perhaps the most central feature of First Amendment law is the distinction between restrictions based on the content of expression and restrictions not based on content.[1]

When the court is determining the constitutionality of a restriction not based on content, it uses some form of balancing test. Content-based restrictions, by contrast, are judged by a more strict categorical approach. If a content-based measure does not fall within one of several relatively narrow categories — such as obscenity, fighting words, defamation, commercial speech or incitement — there's a nearly conclusive presumption against its constitutionality.

Business at one time was treated as second-class citizens where the First Amendment was concerned. Finally, in 1976 the United States Supreme Court held that commercial speech can be just as worthy of protection by the First Amendment as noncommercial speech. This happened in the landmark case Virginia State Board of Pharmacy v. Virginia Citizens Consumer Council. The court said that even speech that does no more than propose a commercial transaction is protected by the First Amendment.

The Supreme Court also ruled that free speech cannot be restricted merely because the speaker is a corporation rather than a natural person; nor is the corporation's right of free speech limited to matters that affect the company's business. In First National Bank of Boston v. Bellotti (1980), the court struck down a law forbidding spending for corporate advocacy.

In 1980 the Supreme Court announced a four-part test to help lower courts and the business world determine what commercial speech would be protected:

1. Does the commercial speech concern lawful activity?
2. Is the government interest in restricting the speech a truly important interest?

   *If **yes** to these two then the court asks,*

3. Does the proposed governmental regulation directly advance the interest asserted?
4. Is the regulation more extensive than necessary to serve that interest?

With respect to the fundamental requirement in financial reporting is that information, when released, not be false or misleading. Three especially important requirements for financial communications involve:

1. **Timely Disclosure** – It means that all material information, that which a reasonable investor might consider important in making an investment decision, must be disclosed publicly on a timely basis, so that all investors have equal access to the information.
2. **Insider Trading** – Anyone who comes into contact with "material" inside information before public release is considered an insider.
3. **Quiet Registration Period** – This refers to that period of time after a new securities offering has been filed with the SEC and before the registration becomes effective. During that time, a company may not use any written communication to sell the securities except a preliminary prospectus.

   Red-Herring Prospectus – Distributed during prefiling and waiting period, it describes the offering but indicates that it is not for sale.

Defamation – Libel and Slander

Defamatory language is language tending to adversely affect one's reputation. Defamation is divided into two areas — libel and slander, although many courts today lump the charges into a generic defamation suit. Simply, libel is written defamation and slander is spoken defamation. But even that isn't ironclad. Defamatory statements made in a broadcast, for example, usually fall under libel. Courts assume that the offensive language stems from a written script, even though spoken.

The type of fault that individuals must prove depends on their status. For example, public figures, or those people who thrust themselves into the public spotlight, relinquish some of their privacy rights. Therefore, under the ruling in *New York Times* v. Sullivan (1964), such an individual must prove actual malice.

Conversely, the Supreme Court ruled in Gertz v. Welch (1974) that a private person need only show negligence regarding the falsity if the statement involves a matter of public concern. Where a defendant is negligent, only "actual injury" damages are recoverable. However, where malice is found, damages may be presumed, and punitive damage (punishment) is allowed.

Five elements must be present for libel to be actionable:

1. Defamation – any inflammatory statement, even innuendo.
2. Publication – to a third party.
3. Identification – but not necessarily by name.
4. Damage – physical or financial, not just emotional.
5. Fault – failure to exercise reasonable care.

Furthermore, four libel defenses are:

1. Privilege – Fair and accurate reporting of government proceedings, for example, is a privilege, even if the report quotes accurately one official calling another "a crook."
2. Truth – This is always your best defense.
3. Fair Comment – The right to criticize matters of public interest is used regularly by film and theater critics, for instance.
4. Retraction – A quick correction is more of a method of mitigating damages than serving as a pure defense.

Related to defamation, one of the fastest-growing areas of concern in the 1990s was the so-called right of privacy, or the right not to be thrust into the limelight. Again, both internal and external communications can cause problems for the PR writer.

Four major types of invasion of privacy exist. Each of these can subject you to a lawsuit and potential liability:

1. *Intrusion into solitude* – Prying into someone's private affairs.

2. *False Light* – A classic example is using a picture of someone to illustrate a story that talks about wrongdoing. Juxtaposing the picture with the story can imply that the person in the picture is one of the wrongdoers. Assuming, of course, that the individual is not a wrongdoer, that would be placing that person in a false light.

3. *Public Disclosure of Private Information* – Giving publicity concerning the private life or personal matters of an individual.

4. *Appropriation of One's Name or Likeness* – A typical example is using one's picture without permission for publicity or commercial gain.

Copyright

The next major area of concern is copyright. Copyright affects items that a company deals with all the time — writings, pictures, graphics materials and audio visual works. Keep in mind that facts and ideas cannot be copyrighted, only the way that information happens to be expressed. Public relations writers need to be concerned with two issues: (1) using other people's copyrighted material, and (2) preventing others from using your material.

The exception to the first is called fair use. It says you may reproduce copyrighted material in certain circumstances, depending on: (1) the purpose of the use, commercial vs. noncommercial; (2) the nature of the copyrighted work; (3) how much you copy; (4) the effect your copying may have on the potential market for the copyrighted material. It's primarily protection for reviewers, researchers and educators to access protected works. When you're not sure about using copyrighted material, always use caution and seek legal advice. Many companies mistakenly think it's OK to print Dilbert or Peanuts cartoons, for example, in employee newsletters. Permission must be sought — usually at a price — for such reproduction and use.

Who owns work produced by a freelancer? The copyright statute by itself seems to say that the employer owns it. The Supreme Court ruled in 1989 that in the case of independently produced work the freelancer owns the copyright, unless there is an express agreement to the contrary. A "work for hire" contract usually spells out such ownership issues. If your agency or company hires freelancers, check the language provisions on the contract concerning copyright to make sure the ownership issue is clear.

Trademark protection gives you exclusive use of a particular word, name, symbol or slogan to identify your company's products. "Kleenex," "Xerox" and "Coke" are all examples of protected trademarks.

Companies that sell services rather than products can have something analogous to a trademark, called a service mark. American Airlines slogan, "Something Special in the Air" is an example of a service mark.

What Constitutes a Bad Document

When employees exercise poor written communication in their daily activities, they weaken the organization's effectiveness. However, in the hands of a plaintiff's attorney, poorly written documents become more than simply a blight on the organization's effectiveness and competency. They become material for framing a lawsuit. While one poorly constructed document may not seem incriminating on the surface, in the hands of a skilled attorney it could be made to seem incriminating. An attorney assembles a case in an attempt to create a reasonable assumption of a defendant's guilt or wrongdoing. Tangible proof, obtained from the recesses of computer hard drives, certainly goes a long way in coloring the perception of guilt.

The risk posed to an organization by a poorly written document rises in proportion to the nature of its business. Heavily regulated businesses such as pharmaceutical companies, investment firms and high-tech industries run higher risks of being subjected to litigation as a result of poorly worded documents landing on an attorney's desk.

Modern business, therefore, is at a crossroads where two important trends meet. At one point modern business reaps the benefits of instant communication. However, intersecting this technological road is modern litigation. Here, savvy lawyers can analyze and assemble pieces of a puzzle to frame a case against the organization. Most alarming is that the organization itself supplies the pieces to the legal puzzle through its own internal documents.

Several issues complicate today's businesses as they attempt to navigate in the information economy. These factors include:

1. Regulating the content and quality of internal communication — especially e-mail — without violating privacy rights of the individual employee and without creating an atmosphere where employees feel that they are being watched constantly.

2. Developing cost-effective safeguards that maximize the ease and speed of modern business practices while implementing safeguards that protect the organization from potentially ruinous situations.

3. Hiring and training employees who are both skilled in their area and proficient in constructing clear and concise written communication.

4. Educating employees about the strategic mindset needed for written communication, and minimizing the risk of legal exposure by respecting the power of instant communication.

Like its predecessor the telephone, e-mail has become an indispensable business tool. The lightning speed of the medium, coupled with its relative low cost, provides a tremendous business asset to modern organizations. It also creates a significant liability to companies that fail to use and manage it properly. What then constitutes so-called bad documents? Essentially they are any poorly written communication that unwittingly undermines the organization's integrity and credibility. For a plaintiff's attorney, they are a treasure trove of information. For a defense attorney, they are a nightmare.

A bad document can be an internal memorandum, a letter or report, or even an innocent e-mail message. What these forms of written communication all have in common is the potential that the author created a smoking gun by writing without first thinking. In today's highly litigious society, lawyers who can unearth enough evidence are in an excellent position to settle the case before it even gets to a jury. In recent years, electronic records have played a much more prominent role in corporate litigation.

Steve Davidson, chairman of the intellectual property and information technology law department at the Minneapolis-based law firm of Leonard, Street and Deinard, says three important changes have altered the legal landscape. First, more companies and more attorneys are aware of the existence of electronic evidence. Second, the courts now recognize how important this kind of evidence can be. Third, the sheer volume of electronic records — all of it evidence or potential evidence — is increasing every minute of every day.[2]

Standing for a Lawsuit

The fundamental principle of standing is that the moving party has demonstrated sufficient evidence to warrant redress by the judicial system. The lawyer's job, therefore, begins with framing the complaint and piecing together sufficient evidence to show that the court system could provide redress. What remains open to judicial interpretation is what the court considers sufficient evidence to hear the case.

Of course, a civil or criminal claim must be substantiated with more than just hearsay evidence or circumstantial evidence. Therefore, framing a case involves gathering enough evidence to warrant its presentation to a jury.

In doing so, lawyers have turned to information technology specialists to mine the recesses of company hard drives to piece together components of a case. This mining, the equivalent of unearthing pieces and putting them in place like a high-tech jigsaw puzzle, can create enough self-doubt in the minds of judges to satisfy the standing doctrine. Once satisfied, and the case now on the court's docket, the defense must make serious business decisions. In much of modern corporate litigation, an otherwise defensible case can be rendered untenable by the existence of poorly written internal documents.

Corporate defense attorneys recognize that the stakes are high. They must weigh the high cost of litigation against factors such as company reputation, uneasiness in the investment community, and the potential that other plaintiffs may sense blood in the water and institute lawsuits of their own. Often the decision comes down to a company making quick settlement of a case that would seem defensible. In much of today's corporate litigation, the decision to settle may come down to the content of internal company documents, mined from the company's own information system, that give the perception of impropriety. These poorly structured business documents often catch people at their worst, such as writing with a sarcastic tone, expressing an opinion without having all the facts, or venting frustration. When framed properly, these unwittingly constructed messages create enough of an illusion about wrongdoing to warrant the organization to seek a settlement.

Case Studies in Controversies: The pen is mightier than the sword

Written communication has the potential to derail an organization. When opinions, comments and other organizational ideas are committed to writing they create documents that may be vulnerable to multiple interpretations and have potentially hazardous legal ramifications. Of course, the stakes have risen exponentially with the rapid rise of the information economy. Advancements in technology that provide greater flexibility for workers also increase worker productivity. However, the quest for increased productivity potentially heightens an organization's vulnerability and risk of lawsuit.

The notion of work being conducted largely online and the increasing demand for traditional communication skills have created an unprecedented demand for workers with broad skills and an ability to accomplish work from remote locations. In addition, the globalization of business has resulted in a demand to hire professionals who possess a range of skills including advanced computing, planning and problem solving. However, effectively incorporating these skills and maximizing worker potential requires successful businesses to demand heightened written communication skills that advance organizational output and also diminish the likelihood that poorly constructed prose will create a legal nightmare. The old adage that the pen is mightier than the sword rings true today. The stakes are high, and poorly worded documents and inappropriate communication represent costly problems.

Legal experts attempt to protect the integrity of the organization by revising e-mail policies and creating a laundry list of writing pros and cons. Technology experts address the problem from a software perspective by designing applications that block objectionable language and limit the use of company e-mail. While these methods are helpful, they fail to fully provide all the necessary support for winning the war against bad documents. This can be illustrated in a number of recent cases.

Perhaps the most celebrated of all bad document cases involves software giant Microsoft. During the government's antitrust case against Microsoft, prosecutors forced the company to hand over an estimated 30 million documents — mostly e-mails. These documents were carefully assembled to frame a case against Microsoft for antitrust violations. The long and protracted case was made more damaging by the company's own internal documents.

Upjohn Company, manufacturer of the sleeping aid Halcion, faced its own challenge when the Food and Drug Administration investigated the safety of the drug. The most sensational case involving suspected Halcion side-effects is that of a 58-year-old Utah woman who claimed that she shot and killed her 83-year-old mother after ingesting the sleeping aid. The company settled the case after more than 8,000 pages of company documents were seized, casting a cloud of doubt over the drug's safety.

Cerner Corp.'s CEO Neil Patterson learned a valuable lesson in using company e-mail to vent anger. Patterson sent an angry e-mail message to his Missouri employees questioning their commitment to work. Unfortunately, his spirited message was passed throughout the company and eventually worked itself into the mainstream investment community via the World Wide Web. Jittery investors, fearing internal problems at Cerner, started trading company stock in large volume. The result — a 22 percent drop in the value of company stock in a three-day trading period.

Finally, when Crown Life Insurance Co. faced a request for written documents related to a 1993 lawsuit, the company provided only hard-copy materials — in spite of the fact that an electronic database contained the most relevant evidence. When a witness confirmed the existence of the database, Crown claimed it was not included in the request because it did not meet the definition of a written document. Neither the trial judge nor the appeals court agreed with Crown's distinction. The courts ruled that Crown should have known that the law does not draw a distinction between print and electronic documents, no matter how the defendant phrased its request.

Bad Documents, Risks and Uncertainty

Frank H. Knight writes in his classic book *Risk, Uncertainty and Profit* that risk and uncertainty differ in an important respect: for risks a probability can be calculated, but for uncertainty this isn't possible. Much strategic action of firms is directed at reducing risk and uncertainty to manageable levels. In today's information economy, reducing risk goes beyond products, working conditions and consumer safety. Companies today must reduce the risk associated with the fallout from ever-increasing production and dissemination of information. From a practical standpoint, litigation provides too much uncertainty, but preventive measures such as formal policies and writing training can reduce the risk.

Companies must weigh the daunting possibility that even if the facts appear to be in their favor the presence of the smoking gun created by vague, erroneous or misguided internal communications may destroy their credibility in the eyes of jurors.

Policies are fine — but no substitute for writing efficiency

As a traditional defensive strategy against the potential damage from poorly written internal documents, companies have revised e-mail policies. Generally, internal legal counsel drafts these policy revisions. While these guidelines detail the purpose and appropriateness of company e-mail policies, they do little in terms of outlining efficient ways of constructing internal documents. The all-important writing process is still left to chance, which increases uncertainty and exposes organizations to greater risk.

One possible reason for the reluctance of organizations to address this writing dilemma is that writing behavior is a difficult area to address. Writing habits are hard to break and employees from varied academic and professional backgrounds bring to the process their own set of beliefs and styles. Therefore, stipulating policy merely satisfies the need for organizational compliance officers to meet the minimum safety precautions.

What still must be addressed is the more difficult task of improving writing efficiency to meet the demands of the workforce in the information economy. Before addressing the writing process, it is important to look at the process of corporate litigation and determine what actually a plaintiff's attorney looks for in framing a case.

E-Discovery and E-Evidence

Corporations of all sizes today construct and disseminate massive amounts of information that never see the light of paper until a dispute arises and the computerized data is requested during the discovery period. This dynamic growth in electronic communication has bogged down traditional management tools for control of information processing and dissemination. While paper records remain the primary source of information in a legal proceeding, the use of electronic files is rapidly becoming a dominant type of discovery material.

The assumption that hitting the delete button destroys all records of a document creates countless and costly problems for individuals and companies. Firms routinely spend millions of dollars on storage and backup devices intended to prevent even the smallest possibility of lost or damaged data. But for many companies, collecting too much information — or even worse, keeping the incorrect kind of information — can become a costly error.

American Home Products Corp., manufacturers of the diet drug fen-phen, was forced to settle a class action suit with some 365,000 individuals after a critical bit of information was discovered on a company backup tape. Even individuals such as Oliver North are not immune to electronic discovery searches. During the investigation of the Iran-Contra affair from the 1980s, prosecutors found critical documents on an e-mail backup tape. E-mail systems, backup tapes and other data sources play a growing role in litigation.

Plaintiff attorneys recognize that each time workers use their computers they expose the organization to litigation by creating a discoverable document. These documents, if not carefully crafted, can become "Exhibit A" in a courtroom. Therefore, as a pretrial device, electronic files have become a wealth of information for lawyers as they attempt to obtain standing and piece together the nuances of cases.

At the center of managing the discovery process rests the notion that the organization is an intricate roadmap of information. Therefore, the business unit and the legal department must put in place the architecture necessary to reduce litigation uncertainty and establish standards and procedures for information processing, dissemination and retention. A clearly defined and intricate information roadmap will help reduce the risk of uncertainty of potential litigation and get all the units working in sync. After establishing the procedural process, the organization must then address the more complicated training aspects with respect to the writing process. This will further reduce the risk of uncertainty of poorly written prose becoming a legal liability for an organization.

Training as a Defensive Writing Strategy

Reducing the risk of damaging internal messages crippling an organization's economic stability constitutes a three-tiered process. First, as detailed above, an organization must develop a comprehensive company e-mail policy that management closely monitors and one that is adhered to closely by employees. This policy must include systematic electronic monitoring of internal messages.

Also, the organization can better plan for uncertainty and prepare itself to deal with sparks before they become fires. In essence, monitoring creates a pre-discovery system that lessens the potential for costly litigation and promotes a defensive posture. The second component to reduce uncertainty is the implementation of a thorough corporate training program that provides employees with the necessary writing skills to better accomplish their activities efficiently and without peril. Finally, employees must be aware of the legal process and how internal legal counsel can provide a safe haven for dealing with sensitive message construction and dissemination.

The problem of poor writing creeping itself into the courtroom predates the information age. In fact, countless court cases have been settled out of court because an old-fashioned memo, letter, report or handwritten note was brought to the attention of a plaintiff's attorney. However, the widespread use of e-mail and the increasing dependence of information as a commodity have accentuated the problem.

Four reasons — three new and one old — explain the widespread problem of poor writing creating litigious situations for companies. E-mail fosters a hurried writing environment where employees seem to pay less attention to writing formalities and become more reckless with their word choices. Second, the sheer volume of information crafted and distributed daily increases the likelihood that mistakes will occur. Third, e-mail has a much longer shelf life. Once the writer hits the send button the message could be stored in a number of places includ-

Behavioral Objectives

Well-written behavioral objectives specify what the trainee will be able to accomplish after successfully completing the training program. They also serve as a benchmark to evaluate the success of the training program.

ing individual hard drives, backup tapes and even hard copies in files. Finally, the fourth reason behind the problem is that writing has traditionally been taught as a form of self-expression. Writers who fail to develop a message construction strategy increase the likelihood that their message will be off target and fraught with errors.

Among the most common writing maladies afflicting the writing process are using inflammatory language, spreading rumors, speculating on issues without factual grounds, expressing opinions outside of the employee's field of expertise, and scribbling notes in the margins.

1. **Inflammatory Language**. Inflammatory language often implies fault without first gathering all the facts. This type of writing often occurs when an employee exhibits the hero syndrome. Here the employee broadcasts that he or she has unearthed a major organizational problem without having proof to substantiate this assertion. Unsubstantiated assertions such as these provide fodder for a legal proceeding.

2. **Spreading Rumors**. Passing a rumor in writing often creates havoc in an organization because it must defend itself against information that is often completely without merit. It often requires great efforts to disprove what was in essence false information and casts a shadow of doubt over the organization's credibility.

3. **Speculating on Issues Without Factual Grounds**. Employees speculate when they communicate what they think they know rather than what they actually know. When statements are made without first getting valid details, the information can cast a cloud of uncertainty over the organization and create a need for substantial follow-up information to rectify the damage.

4. **Expressing Opinions Outside the Field of Expertise**. A plaintiff's attorney can weave a web of uncertainty and doubt about an organization's guilt when written information is attributed to someone in the organization who does not have the expertise in that particular area. For example, marketing personnel in the pharmaceutical industry can carry on an e-mail discussion about the appropriate dosage of a drug. A defense attorney could present this information to a jury with the implication that in this organization dosage requirements of drugs are made by marketing professionals rather than medical professionals. Often these company insiders are commenting on areas outside of their field of expertise but their words — or written messages —

loom as factual information when framed by a plaintiff's attorney. Defense attorneys must weigh the overall consequences of a particular case and the damage that it can do to the company's reputation in general before information gets presented to a jury.

5. **Scribbling Notes in the Margins**. Handwritten notes in the margins of printed internal documents often catch employees at their most unguarded moments. These notes, often penned without thought to clarity and appropriateness, have been deemed admissible in court.

Furthermore, poor writing skills can distort meaning and damage credibility. While writing mishaps and errors afflict credibility, they also, in severe cases, alter meaning. For example, improper word use can be construed to mean something completely different than the writer intended it to communicate. This lack of clarity through ambiguous and error-filled writing requires subsequent communications to get the message across. From a business standpoint, poor writing skills prove wasteful and inefficient. From a legal standpoint, they give rise to litigation.

On the plus side, advancements in technology that provide greater flexibility for workers may also increase productivity. The speed at which business processes and disseminates information continues to increase and revolutionize how corporations conduct business. Computers enable us to process and disseminate information at greater speeds. In an information economy, this is akin to automation in an industrial setting. Workers can produce more at faster rates but it gives rise to increased chances of error. That is a potential Achilles' heel for corporate legal counsel.

Consequently, the increased potential for liability from bad documents has caused organizational training specialists to rethink traditional modes of training and emphasize development of core skills such as writing. To reduce the risk of uncertainty, corporations must develop a strategic mindset that emphasizes writing only when necessary and one that reinforces the simple rule that business writing must contain nothing but factual information. If the message contains speculation or expresses doubt about a sensitive issue then other modes of communication, such as face-to-face meetings, would be more appropriate before committing anything to writing.

Recognizing that e-mail has a long shelf life helps employees rethink their purpose in committing information to writing.

E-mail subpoenaed

According to *Public Relations Tactics* (October 2004), 21 percent of employers have had employee e-mail and instate messages subpoenaed in a lawsuit or regulatory investigation. The 2004 survey was done by the American Management Association and the ePolicy Institute.

However, it is important that employees also be empowered to contribute to the organizational success without fear that their words will be used against them.

In accomplishing this task, writers should master some simple tips on effective writing. First and foremost, writers must emphasize the systematic purpose to writing and how to first outline and structure the purpose of the message, the desired result from the communication, and the elements that the message should contain. Unfortunately, this process contradicts much of the ingrained writing beliefs established in primary and secondary education.

For most people, writing was taught as an exercise in creative expression rather than a systematic process. In short, most people dive into the writing process without first determining the intended purpose of the writing and the steps necessary to reach the goal. This often results in vague and unclear messages that fail to properly communicate the intended message. These unclear messages may also lend themselves to multiple interpretations. Litigation often begins here.

The following chart details some areas of in-house training that will help writers to avoid errors and possible legal consequences.

Writer's Checklist With Respect to E-Mails

Area of Emphasis	Anticipated Outcome/Benefit
Legal Pitfalls = You should be familiar with the following: 1. The attorney-client privilege; who may use it. 2. The work product doctrine and when to use it. 3. How to lose protection under the attorney-client privilege. 4. How to safeguard against documents becoming admissible evidence.	Learning the proper way to label and distribute sensitive internal documents.
Spotting Writing Issues = Learn to avoid using strong language, passing rumors, speculating on sensitive information, and commenting outside of the writer's particular field of expertise.	Knowing this would help unearth messages that may circulate internally and appear harmless but ones that plaintiff attorneys look for in framing a case.
Tips on Effective Writing = Keep a list of tips on effective writing handy. This will help serve as a quick reference when doing any writing assignment.	This handy list will be an invaluable tool that will take the guesswork out of written communication.
Proofreading = Learning how to effectively proofread your own work will help you gain a watchful eye against grammatical errors, misuse of words, and other writing issues that help create bad documents.	Most writing errors result from simple language errors that could be easily corrected with better proofreading.

Notes

[1] Erwin Chemerinsky. *Constitutional Law: Principles and Policies*. New York, NY: Aspen Law & Business, 1997.

[2] Matthew McKenzie. "Caution: Data disposal can be hazardous to your health." *Storage*; 2002, vol. 1, no. 3.

For Further Reading

Donald M. Gillmor, Jerome A. Barron, Todd F. Simon. *Mass Communication Law: Cases and Comment*. Belmont, CA: Wadsworth, 1998.

Karla K. Gower. *Legal and Ethical Restraints on Public Relations*. Prospects Heights, IL: Waveland Press, 2003.

Don R. Pember and Clay Calvert. *Mass Media Law*. New York, NY: McGraw-Hill, 2005.

Index

Toolbox Tips

(In order of appearance)

Blueprints

(In order of appearance)